THE
STUDENT
EQEDGE

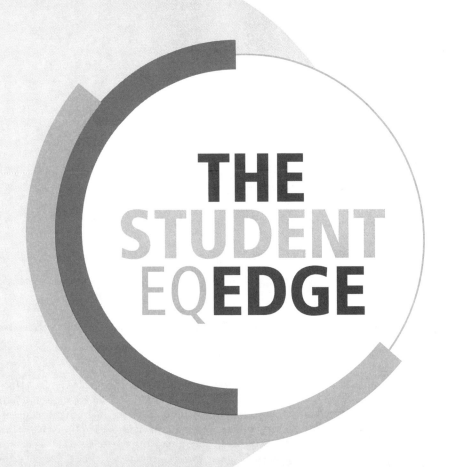

THE STUDENT EQ EDGE

FACILITATION AND ACTIVITY GUIDE

Korrel Kanoy • Steven J. Stein • Howard E. Book

JOSSEY-BASS
A Wiley Imprint
www.josseybass.com

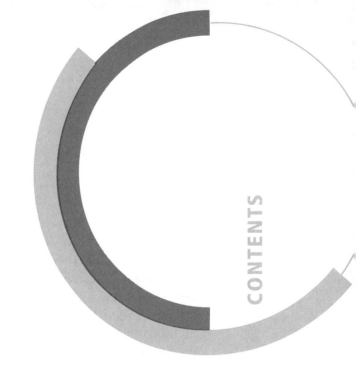

CONTENTS

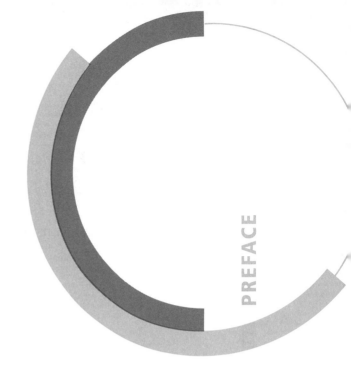

We know that educators take their business seriously and toil diligently and willingly to challenge and support students' mastery of content and skills such as writing and critical thinking. But there's more—a lot more! How are we helping students find their passion and learn to set goals that are both challenging and realistic? Where are students learning the assertiveness needed to stand up to unethical business practices in their careers or a domineering college roommate? And what about teamwork skills? They can't learn those merely by working in groups, any more than a person can become a talented pianist by sitting in a room with world-renowned pianists. In fact, many ineffective teamwork skills get further solidified: "A" students take over the project, and students who've learned they can slack off because the "A's" will take over become even more disengaged.

Are we teaching students how to persist when faced with obstacles, how to make effective decisions, or how to curb destructive impulses? The list goes on. You may be thinking that all of these things are the purview of the family. They are. But in today's economy and—for better or worse—era of accountability, educational institutions are being asked more and more frequently about "outcomes" such as students being admitted to the best colleges, performing well in college, getting jobs after college graduation, and getting into graduate programs. There is abundant research to support that higher emotional intelligence (EI) is related to such outcomes. (See Chapter 1 of this guide and Chapters 19–23 of *The Student EQ Edge: Emotional Intelligence and Your Academic and Personal Success.*) Teaching emotional intelligence can occur within existing classes (for example, senior capstone courses and internship support courses), leadership courses as a stand-alone course, during training for campus leaders, and in first-year experience classes, just to name a few options.

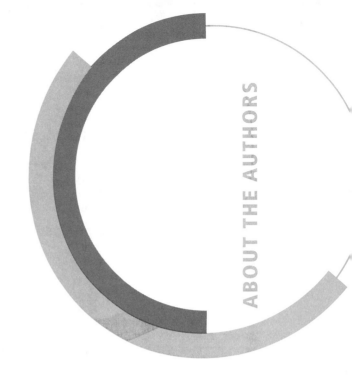

Korrel Kanoy, Ph.D., is a developmental psychologist and served as a professor of psychology at William Peace University (formerly Peace College) for over 30 years, where she was recognized with the McCormick Distinguished Teaching Award and the Excellence in Campus Leadership Award. She has taught college-level courses in emotional intelligence since 1998. Korrel designed a comprehensive approach to infusing emotional intelligence into first-year experience courses, disciplinary senior capstone courses, and college and university service offices. She has worked with over 200 college students to help them develop emotional intelligence skills and has worked with schools to use EI as one component in selecting and developing faculty. She has published a children's book, *Annie's Lost Hat,* which includes a parents' section related to emotional intelligence. She is a coauthor of *Building Leadership Skills in Adolescent Girls.*

 Steven J. Stein, Ph.D., is a psychologist and CEO of Multi-Health Systems (MHS), a leading international test publishing company. He has authored several books on emotional intelligence, including the original *The EQ Edge: Emotional Intelligence and Your Success* (coauthored with Dr. Howard Book), *Make Your Workplace Great: The Seven Keys to an Emotionally Intelligent Organization, and Emotional Intelligence for Dummies.* He has given presentations on emotional intelligence to audiences throughout the United States, Canada, Mexico, Europe, Asia, and Africa. As well, he has appeared on hundreds of TV, radio, online, and print media productions.

For over a dozen years, **Dr. Howard E. Book**'s area of expertise has been benchmarking and enhancing the emotional intelligence of individuals and groups, as well as developing training programs to enhance the strength of this ability. Dr. Book has also written, lectured, and offered workshops on the importance of emotional intelligence and success in the real world internationally. He is a member of the Consortium for Research in Emotional Intelligence in Organizations, part-time faculty at the INSEAD School of Business in France and Singapore, and a former board member of the International Society for the Psychoanalytic Study of Organizations, and with Dr. Steven Stein he coauthored the book *The EQ Edge: Emotional Intelligence and Your Success*. Dr. Book holds the rank of associate professor, Department of Psychiatry, Faculty of Medicine at the University of Toronto.

Chapter 1

Introduction to the Facilitation and Activity Guide

You made a wise choice when you decided to help students learn about and develop their emotional intelligence (EI). Research summarized in *The Student EQ Edge: Emotional Intelligence and Your Academic and Personal Success* shows how important EI is in predicting success in college and across a wide variety of professional careers. Unlike IQ, EI can be learned and improved at any age. Rarely, however, do secondary schools, colleges, or universities teach this topic to students. You chose to do so, and your students will benefit.

EMOTIONAL INTELLIGENCE DEFINED AND RESEARCH OVERVIEW

Emotional intelligence is "a set of emotional and social skills that influence the way we perceive and express ourselves, develop and maintain social relationships, cope with challenges, and use emotional information in an effective and meaningful way" (Stein & Book, 2011, p. 13). Research with college students demonstrates that EI can predict academic success. Consider the following examples:

Schulman (1995) found that the EI skill of optimism was a better predictor of first-year students' college GPA than their SAT score.

Schutte and Malouff (2002) found that incorporating emotional skills content into a college transition course enhances student retention. First-year students who received emotional awareness and development strategies in their course not only demonstrated growth in EI between pre- and post-measures, but were also more likely to persist to the next academic term than a cohort of students who did not receive the emotional intelligence content.

Mann and Kanoy (2010) found that first-year college GPA could be predicted by the following EI scales: optimism, independence (negative predictor), self-regard, impulse control, and problem solving. The students with the highest GPAs (3.35 and higher) scored higher on EI than the middle third of students (2.50–3.34) for assertiveness, stress tolerance, and problem solving; mid-performing students scored higher on social responsibility and impulse control than low-performing students.

Sparkman (2009) studied 783 college students over a five-year period and found relationships between EI and college outcomes.

- Social responsibility, followed by impulse control and empathy, were the three strongest positive predictors of college graduation.
- Self-actualization, social responsibility, and happiness were positive predictors of cumulative GPA, but very high independence and interpersonal relationship skills were negative predictors of cumulative GPA. Students who will not ask for help when they need it (high independence) tend not to do as well as those who seek help from Learning Centers, Career Centers, or Counseling Centers. And if a student is too skilled at interpersonal relationships, it's likely that person spends more time

Figure 1.1. Emotional Intelligence Defined

SELF-PERCEPTION

Self-Regard is respecting oneself while understanding and accepting one's strength and weaknesses. Self-Regard is often associated with feelings of inner strength and self-confidence.

Self-Actualization is the willingness to persistently try to improve oneself and engage in the pursuit of personally relevant and meaningful objectives that lead to a rich and enjoyable life.

Emotional Self-Awareness includes recognizing and understanding one's own emotions. This includes the ability to differentiate between subtleties in one's own emotions while understanding the cause of these emotions and the impact they have on the thoughts and actions of oneself and others.

STRESS MANAGEMENT

Flexibility is adapting emotions, thoughts and behaviors to unfamiliar, unpredictable, and dynamic circumstances or ideas.

Stress tolerance involves coping with stressful or difficult situations and believing that one can manage or influence situations in a positive manner.

Optimism is an indicator of one's positive attitude and outlook on life. It involves remaining hopeful and resilient, despite occasional setbacks.

SELF-EXPRESSION

Emotional Expression is openly expressing one's feelings verbally and non-verbally.

Assertiveness involves communicating feelings, beliefs and thoughts openly, and defending personal rights and values in a socially acceptable, non-offensive, and non-destructive manner.

Independence is the ability to be self directed and free from emotional dependency on others. Decision-making. Planning and daily tasks are completed autonomously.

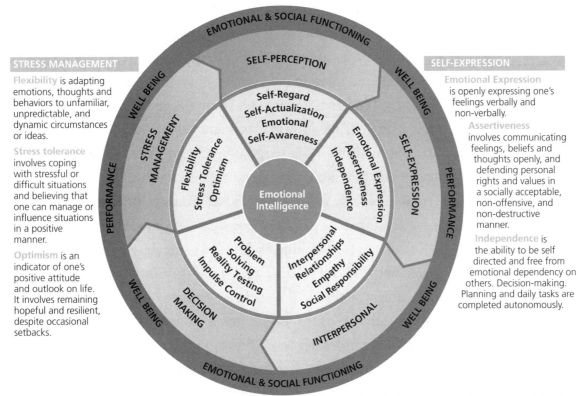

DECISION MAKING

Problem Solving is the ability to find solutions to problems in situations where emotions are involved. Problem solving includes the ability to understand how emotions impact decision making.

Reality Testing is the capacity to remain objective by seeing things as they really are. This capacity involves recognizing when emotions or personal bias can cause one to be less objective.

Impulse Control is the ability to resist or delay an impulse, drive or temptation to act and involves avoiding rash behaviors and decision making.

INTERPERSONAL

Interpersonal Relationships refers to the skill of developing and maintaining mutually satisfying relationships that are characterized by trust and compassion.

Empathy is recognizing , understanding and appreciating how other people feel. Empathy involves being able to articulate your understanding of another's perspective and behaving in a way that respects other' feelings.

Social Responsibility is willingly contributing to society, to one's social groups, and generally to the welfare of others. Social Responsibility involves acting responsibly, having social consciousness, and showing concern for the greater community.

doing just that—interacting with others—which leaves less time for study.

Figure 1.1 shows the five realms and 16 scales of emotional intelligence as measured by the EQ-i 2.0. Consult *The Student*

EQ Edge: Emotional Intelligence and Your Academic and Personal Success for additional information about each scale.

PLANNING YOUR CLASSES

One of the authors, Korrel, has been a college professor for over 30 years, and during that time she has learned there is no one style or formula of teaching that works best at all times and with all classes. Passion about what you teach and actively engaging students are key ingredients. Throughout this guide, you'll find exercises, tips, and ideas to help you engage students in their learning. Rarely will the plan dictate that something must be done in small groups or must be done in class rather than assigned for homework. Sometimes it can work just as well to have a class of 20 to 25 discuss a topic rather than dividing into four or five small groups. This is especially true if you need to monitor the discussion for accuracy, focus, or progress. For those of you who prefer a more detailed plan for teaching each topic, each chapter will contain suggested activities for leading a 50- to 60-minute class or a three- to four-hour workshop. (These three- to four-hour workshops can be broken into two or three different segments for a class that meets two or three times per week.) Additionally, Appendix A contains a suggested course syllabus that can be used for a semester-long class or adapted to accommodate a two- to three-day student workshop.

STUDENT REFLECTION

Reflection is one of the most effective tools to encourage student cognitive and social-emotional growth; thus each activity in this book will contain reflection questions for students. Reflection—unlike reasoning, which requires a systematic process that is evidence based—allows students to engage in mental inquiry meant to help develop self-discovery rather than help them arrive at a correct answer. The more reflection they do, the better! Thus this *Facilitation and Activity Guide* provides two different opportunities for reflection.

- Reflection questions are included on the student worksheets. Ask students to submit written responses or to think about their responses prior to class discussion, or include the questions during the in-class debrief.
- In-class debrief questions should be discussed in class after the worksheet or activity has been completed. Debriefs are designed to solidify learning and insights related to an activity.

Because reflection promotes cognitive growth, it's a key part of student learning. And it's possible to grade worksheets and the reflection questions for quality. Appendix B provides an example grading rubric for a reflection exercise.

STUDENT EMOTIONAL INTELLIGENCE ASSESSMENT

Students can complete the EQi 2.0, a reliable and valid measure of emotional intelligence that provides scores for overall emotional intelligence, five realms (self-perception, self-expression, interpersonal, decision making, and stress management), and the 16 scales outlined in each chapter of this book. For more information about how to give the EQi 2.0 to your students, go to *ei.mhs.com*. Free assessments of emotional intelligence are also available but are not guaranteed to be reliable or valid and most likely will not align with the chapters outlined in the *Facilitation and Activity Guide* or the *Student Workbook*.

FACILITATING CLASS DISCUSSIONS

For the first couple of days, while you're building rapport, choose activities and discussions that are fairly safe but highly engaging. Also, have the group develop guidelines, or you can suggest three to five like the following suggestions. Either way, make sure everyone in the class agrees to some version of these guidelines:

- Personal information that is shared does not get repeated outside of class.

- Use conventions of good interaction, including not interrupting others, not dominating the conversation, and not judging others' comments.
- Everyone must participate some of the time and listen all of the time.

To make sure everyone gets to participate, encourage the students to be brief. Succinct comments help the conversation flow better. Introverted students are encouraged by the idea that they don't have to talk for long, and extroverts who have some self-awareness appreciate the help in self-monitoring. And everybody appreciates not having one or two people who drone on and on!

Finally, give small groups questions to discuss and then have them "report out" to the larger group. There are two reasons for doing this. First, if there are inaccuracies in content (for example, maybe they don't understand the definition of *self-regard*), those can be corrected. Second, if they have to report out, they usually take the assignment more seriously.

AGREE-DISAGREE ACTIVITIES

When discussing controversial issues or trying to get students to take a position on an issue, using an agree-disagree activity usually works well. Here's how it works. On the far right side of the board, write the word "agree" and on the opposite side, write the word "disagree." (Or just point to each side of the room if you don't have a white board to write on.) Then pose your question and have students get up and move to the side of the room that best represents their opinion. Standing in the middle of the room is highly discouraged! Ask students from each side to explain why they chose to agree or disagree with the statement you read. For example, near the end of your course, after students have learned a lot about emotional intelligence, you might pose the following question: "Emotional intelligence learning should be required of all students at this school."

ORGANIZATION OF THIS GUIDE

This guide and the activities within it are organized so you can find what you want and pick and choose the activities that work best for your class.

Chapters follow the same order and numbering as found in *The Student EQ Edge: Emotional Intelligence and Your Academic and Personal Success* and in *The Student EQ Edge: Student Workbook.*

Although some of you will prefer the "pick and choose" approach when selecting activities for your class, each chapter outlines a comprehensive plan for a 60-minute class and one for a half-day workshop. You will find these suggestions in the "Planning Your Class" section.

If you only have a few hours within an existing course to discuss emotional intelligence, it's probably best to pick two or three scales that are highly relevant to that class (for example, emotional self-awareness, empathy, and interpersonal relationships in an Interpersonal Communication course) and focus on building those skills.

Each chapter contains these elements:

- Student Learning Outcomes
- Suggested Reading, Movies, and TV Shows—students love watching movie or TV clips; these clips are very effective for demonstrating EI concepts, and watching others demonstrate effective or ineffective EI makes the concepts come alive.
- A list of activities by name, with a brief description.
- A step-by-step guide for preparing to lead the activity, facilitating it, and debriefing it, and the expected time each will take.
- A copy of the worksheet found in *The Student EQ Edge: Student Workbook.*

● MATERIALS

For almost every class period you will need access to the following:

- White board or flip chart
- Markers
- TV with DVD or VCR player
- Internet connection (if you want to access TV clips through www.hulu.com or YouTube clips)

Also, we highly recommend you have a copy of *The Student EQ Edge: Emotional Intelligence and Your Academic and Personal Success*.

Finding TV Shows That Demonstrate EI

Go to www.hulu.com to find the most recent six episodes of most TV shows or http://www.free-tv-video-online.me/ to find episodes of former TV shows. If you join Hulu for a small monthly fee, you can access all episodes of a particular show. One way to find great clips is to assign homework for the students to find clips that illustrate certain EI characteristics. You can have students volunteer to show their clips to the class and access them through Hulu or free-tv-video-online.

Movies

Appendix C contains an extensive list of movies, plot summaries, and the EI characteristics that the main characters possess or lack. Each chapter in this facilitator's guide will include two or three featured movies where specific scenes are identified that illustrate the EI characteristic. Characters often display multiple EI characteristics; thus featured movies are listed for multiple scales, allowing students to see more of the movie (something they *always* ask to do!) and focusing your preparation time on just a few movies. The featured movies are listed here by EI composite area. If you need an extra activity for one of the chapters, just assign one of the movies listed and have students write an analysis of EI that was (or was not!) displayed.

- Self-Perception Composite: *Odd Girl Out, Patch Adams, The Rookie*
- Self-Expression Composite: *Erin Brockovich, Odd Girl Out, The Blind Side*
- Interpersonal Relations: *Erin Brockovich, One Fine Day, Patch Adams*
- Decision Making: *Catch Me If You Can, Odd Girl Out, What About Bob?*
- Stress Tolerance: *Catch Me If You Can, The Pursuit of Happyness, What About Bob?*
- Happiness and Well-Being: *Patch Adams, The Pursuit of Happyness*

YouTube Clips

It's inevitable that some clips will not be active when you teach the course. Replace the removed clip with a movie segment or do a search by key word for other appropriate clips.

A NOTE ABOUT LANGUAGE

Educational systems across North America and Europe use different language to describe levels of education. In this guide, the terms *college* and *university* are used interchangeably to indicate education beyond the secondary or high school level.

Chapter 2

Case Studies of Emotionally Intelligent (and Not Emotionally Intelligent!) Behavior

I t's always easier to recognize the flaws in someone else's behavior than those in our own. The case studies give students a way to see how emotional intelligence innervates everyday behaviors. And they'll see how enhanced EI can help them achieve better grades, perform better on a sports team, get along better with peers or a roommate, and handle the stress of a student's life. The table gives you an overview of the case studies and indicates which EI dimensions are most relevant to the case. It's okay to assign case studies that demonstrate EI skills *before* you cover that chapter; students will recognize the effective or ineffective behavior, even though they may not label it using emotional intelligence terms. This gives you the opportunity to foreshadow what they will learn as they go through the course.

Summary List of Case Studies

Case Study # and Name	Most Relevant EI Skills	Brief Summary
1. Why Can't I Make an A?	Emotional Self-Awareness, Self-Regard, Stress Tolerance, Happiness	A student makes a B but her friends make an A on the same paper, which ruins the rest of her day.
2. Twenty Years to Graduate	Emotional Self-Awareness, Self-Regard, Self-Actualization, Stress Tolerance, Problem Solving, Empathy	A woman returns to college after a 12-year break to complete her degree and faces her doubts about whether she can succeed.
3. But I'm Good!	Self-Regard, Reality Testing, Problem Solving, Impulse Control	A high school soccer star finds the transition to university soccer challenging and frustrating.
4. Starting College	Self-Actualization, Independence, Impulse Control, Reality Testing, Happiness	Two roommates begin their university careers; one handles the transition better than the other one.
5. Shared Responsibilities	Assertiveness, Emotional Expression, Social Responsibility, Problem Solving	Two resident assistants (RAs) are supposed to share the responsibility to complete reports and paperwork, but one RA has been doing all of the reports and now wants to share the task.
6. A Costly Decision	Reality Testing, Problem Solving, Assertiveness	A university student does not ask enough questions about a financial aid situation and ends up keeping a class he should have dropped; he makes an F in the class.
7. First Job Jitters	Self-Regard, Independence, Impulse Control, Self-Actualization, Social Responsibility, Stress Tolerance, and more!	A new university graduate takes her first job in an accounting firm during tax season; her work performance is good, but things go badly because she lacks key emotional intelligence skills.
8. No Way	Flexibility, Independence, Emotional Self-Awareness	A college senior faces her fears and agrees to travel internationally with other students and her professor—and the experience transforms her.
9. Twins?	Stress Tolerance, Optimism, Independence, Interpersonal Relationship, Happiness	Twin sisters who have recently moved to the United States from Mexico respond very differently to a social invitation.

Directions for all case studies:

1. Have students read the case study and answer the reflection questions.
2. Discuss the reflection questions until the group comes to an accurate understanding of what EI skills (or lack thereof) the main character(s) displayed and what EI skills would have benefited the main characters.

CASE STUDY #1: WHY CAN'T I MAKE AN A?

Briana just found out she made a B on a paper and her two friends made A's. She understands the professor's comments and knows that her writing is improving and needs to improve more, but she still can't shake the negative feelings she's having. When her friends ask what grade she got, she doesn't want to discuss it with them. And she doesn't like hearing how happy they are about their A grades. Later, in math class, she begins thinking about the paper and misses an important formula explanation. She's too embarrassed to ask the faculty member to repeat the information. After classes that day, another friend approaches her and asks if she wants to go to shopping. Briana declines the invitation and instead goes to her room, puts on her headphones, and listens to her favorite music. Later that evening she attempts her math homework, but she struggles to work problems using the formula covered in class earlier that day. After a few minutes, she closes her book and goes to bed. She's restless, though, and it takes her a long time to go to sleep.

Reflection Questions

1. Citing information from the case study, identify what emotional intelligence skills are most relevant to this case study.
2. What values or hot buttons may have been activated when Briana found out she made a B on her paper? Do you think these same values or hot buttons would have been triggered if her friends had also made Bs?

3. How does Briana's emotional reaction affect her behaviors throughout the rest of the day? Is her behavior more or less productive the rest of the day? Explain your response.

CASE STUDY #2: 15 YEARS TO GRADUATE

Jane was a 32-year-old woman with three kids ages 10, 9, and 5. She had dropped out of college at age 20 to marry her long-time boyfriend; since having her children she had worked part-time in administrative assistant positions. She was bored with these positions and wanted a bigger challenge and more money. Her husband, Mark, was a college graduate and worked as an accountant. He supported her decision and was eager to take on a larger role at home.

Jane enrolled in a nearby institution that offered degree-completion programs for adult learners. The week before classes began, Jane told her husband she didn't want to go back to school after all. When he gently probed for what had changed her mind, she replied, "What was I thinking? When will I have time to study? I've forgotten the math I learned, and I haven't written a paper in 12 years. What if I don't do well?"

After a lengthy conversation, Jane decided to give it a try. She could always drop out if her fears were realized.

The first month was very challenging. Jane frequently felt nervous, especially when she had to take a test or turn in an assignment. She came home every night exhausted and thinking about quitting. She couldn't find time to study as much as she thought she needed to. But she told herself that this was a big transition and she should give it some time.

Soon she developed a routine of studying while the kids were doing their homework, and she stayed on campus between her classes to study instead of racing home to do laundry. She and Mark developed a chore list for each kid so that everyone took on more responsibility at home. Studying with her kids while they did homework relieved some of her guilt because she could stop what she was doing to provide help if they needed it.

Two years later, Jane graduated with a degree in psychology. She was accepted to a master's program in counseling, and her goal was to open a business to work with adults who are making a mid-life transition.

Reflection Questions

1. Describe how Jane's self-perception changed from the time she entered to the time she graduated.
2. What EI skill(s) did her husband demonstrate?
3. What were Jane's biggest challenges, and how did she use EI to help overcome them?

CASE STUDY #3: BUT I'M GOOD!

Roberto is an average student but a very good athlete. His sisters both make all A's in their classes while he makes mostly C's and B's. But that's okay with Roberto because he excels at soccer. He starred on his high school team in his small hometown and earned a scholarship to play on a college team.

The first day of college practice did not go well. Roberto was surprised by how fast and strong everyone was. He got beaten badly on several plays, and the coach called him aside to give him pointers about his positioning and footwork. He vaguely remembered his high school coach saying some of the same things, but he hadn't paid attention then because he was playing so well.

Roberto didn't make the changes the coach suggested because what he had always done had worked great so far and this new coach didn't know him very well. Over the next several weeks, the coach kept emphasizing the same points to him and not offering him any encouragement or praise. Roberto began to get frustrated, but he kept his frustrations to himself. The coach just needed more time to understand his style of play.

During the first game of the season, Roberto started the game. But after he got caught out of position and the other team scored a goal, the coach took him out. Roberto sat on the bench and fumed. Everybody made mistakes—why did he get benched when others did not?

The same pattern continued for several weeks. During the fifth game of the season, Roberto played only the last couple of minutes, after his team had a 4–0 lead. Later that night, when talking to his parents, he told them he was thinking about quitting the team. He heard himself say, "I just don't think I'm good enough to play at the college level."

Reflection Questions

1. Citing information from the case study, identify which emotional intelligence skills are most relevant to this case study.
2. Was Roberto aware of his soccer weaknesses? What about his EI weaknesses? Explain.
3. Do you agree with Roberto's thoughts about quitting the team? Explain your answer.

CASE STUDY #4: STARTING COLLEGE

Jerome and Chris are first-year college students and roommates, and it's the first time either has lived away from home. Jerome has declared a major in premed; he signed up for a heavy academic load this semester and has two science classes with labs. He spends lots of time in the library, and at the end of the first semester he has a 3.5 GPA. Jerome likes to go out on the weekends and have fun and often attends sports events or parties. He has lots of friends and is adjusting well to college. He sometimes gets bored when reading or studying, but if he does, he takes a short break to play video games.

Chris came to the university without a major and remains "undeclared" at the beginning of second semester. He doesn't see a need to rush to declare a major, so he did not take a class in Career Exploration that his faculty advisor recommended. Chris made good grades in high school but is finding it harder to attend college classes without his parents around to make sure that he gets up on time. He's asked Jerome to make sure he gets up in the morning and goes to class, but occasionally he goes back to sleep after Jerome wakes him up. Chris tends to study right before a test by staying up all night. He goes out a lot during the week and plays every intramural sport offered. Chris made a 2.2 GPA first semester. He's surprised he did not do better because he was such a good student in high school.

Reflection Questions

1. Citing information from the case study, identify what emotional intelligence skills are most relevant to this case study.
2. Which student are you more similar to right now? What is your motivation for academic work? If you don't see yourself as similar to either of these students, where do you see yourself on the continuum from not knowing what you want to study to being absolutely sure what you want to study? Explain.
3. Many college students do not declare a major during their first year of college. In that case, what could students do to ensure that they stay on track and motivated?

CASE STUDY #5: SHARED RESPONSIBILITIES

Keandra was a resident assistant (RA) in a college dorm. The other RA, Ian, had been relying on Keandra to file all of the reports and paperwork instead of the two of them taking turns as they agreed to do at the beginning of the year. The reports have deadlines, and if they are not turned in on time, the RAs could be fired.

Keandra went up to Ian's room one afternoon and brought up the paperwork issue. Here's their conversation.

Keandra: "There's been a lot of paperwork lately. You need to do your part of it."
Ian: "I'm not very good at paperwork."

Keandra: "Maybe so, but you took the job knowing that was part of what you had to do."

Ian: "Well, I have a heavier course load than you do. Can't you just keep doing it this semester?"

Keandra: "I have a heavy load too. We both get paid the same amount, and I'm doing a lot more of the work than you are."

Ian (in irritated tone): "I don't have time for this discussion." Ian walks out of the room.

Reflection Questions

1. What emotional intelligence dimensions are relevant to this interaction? Cite examples from the scenario to support your opinion.
2. What should Keandra do next? What EI skills can she draw on to help her resolve this issue?
3. Compare how you typically handle a situation in which someone is trying to take advantage of you to how Keandra handled this situation.

CASE STUDY #6: A COSTLY DECISION

James was a junior in college with a 3.3 GPA who was taking 12 credit hours for the semester. He missed the first several classes of a one-credit hour course. He emailed the financial aid office to ask whether he would be considered a full-time student if he audited the class instead of taking it for a grade. They responded that audits don't count toward total hours, so he would be considered a part-time student with just 11 credit hours if he audited the class. James then assumed that if he dropped the class he would lose his financial aid and have to pay for his classes. James knew he could not pay his tuition, so he decided to stay in the class, but he never attended again and did not complete any of the assignments. Nor did he contact the professor.

One day the professor saw James on campus and offered to help him complete the coursework through an independent study. James was on his way to look at the latest iPad when he ran into the professor, so he thanked the professor and asked if he could come by the professor's office the next day.

The next day James had to work on a major term paper. He was so tired the following day from pulling an all-nighter that he went to sleep as soon as he turned his paper in. One week later he remembered the professor's offer, but he was sure the professor wouldn't still let him do an independent study. James never went to talk with the professor, and ultimately he earned an F in the course, which hurt his overall GPA.

The Reality (facts about financial aid at James's school)

- At James's institution, students are allowed a one-time exception to go below 12 credit hours during one semester and not lose any current or future financial aid. James has never used this exception.
- James was given the information about the one-time exception for going below 12 hours when he received financial aid, but he did not consult this information when the situation occurred.
- An Independent Study option would have been available through the first six weeks of the following semester with the professor's agreement.

Reflection Questions

1. What questions should James have asked the financial aid office that he did not ask?
2. What difference would these questions have made in this situation?
3. What emotional intelligence challenges does James face?

CASE STUDY #7: FIRST JOB JITTERS

Stacey completed her college degree in December and was hired by a major accounting firm to help them with their caseload during tax season. January involved lots of meetings with clients and getting to know her colleagues. Up to this point, Stacey loved her job.

In February the workload picked up, and Stacey was given several tax returns to complete that she thought were very difficult. She checked in frequently with a senior partner about whether she was doing things correctly. He always praised the quality of her work. One day the senior partner remarked that she was a better accountant than she gave herself credit for. Still, she sought his advice a lot.

At the beginning of March, she noticed that the partner was keeping his door closed more often now, and she was scared to interrupt him. So she asked one of the other new hires to look over her work. As the caseload built, Stacey got farther and farther behind. She carefully checked and rechecked every return before submitting it because she knew it would look bad if she made errors. She stopped doing yoga and going for weekend runs and used that time to catch up on work. Even though she was spending more time at work, it was taking her longer and longer to get each tax return done. One day, after Stacey complained to an administrative assistant (AA) that she had not known how hard tax season would be, the AA told her to "get a grip." Stacey fled to her office in tears.

By March 25, Stacey didn't see how she could make it through another three weeks. When she woke up that morning, she decided to quit her job. She called the office and told the senior partner she was resigning. He asked her to reconsider, citing the fact that her work was quite good and that she had 30 returns she needed to complete in the next three weeks. There was no way anyone else in the firm could take on more work, he said, and they were counting on her.

Stacey held firm and said no. She felt really bad about it at first, but as the day went on she felt better. She went to her yoga class, then went shopping and spent $400 on new clothes she would need for interviewing with other companies.

Reflection Questions

1. What EI characteristics are evident in this case study? Cite examples from the case to support your choices.

2. Which one or two EI areas were most problematic for Stacey in this case study?

3. Do you agree with Stacey's decision to quit? Why or why not?

CASE STUDY #8: NO WAY

After child development class one day, Professor Tripp said, "Chloe, I think you should consider going on this international study trip this summer with me. You'll get to visit five different countries, learn about other cultures, and earn three credit hours."

Chloe responded, "No way."

The professor inquired why not, and Chloe remarked that she couldn't stand to travel because she liked things "just so" and travel disrupted that.

The professor replied, "Well, you told me at the beginning of this child development class you want to have kids one day. You can't always control what happens next when you have kids."

Chloe looked stunned. She had been learning about children's development but had not yet connected that to how she would have to adapt her life. So she decided to go on the trip.

The first few days of the trip, usually the most exciting for students, were horrible for Chloe. She hated the fact that each day brought a different schedule; she didn't eat well because the food was different; and she clung close to the professors whenever the group had to take the Tube, the London subway system. She refused invitations from other students unless one of the professors was going with the group. The thought of accidentally getting separated from the group was a constant concern for her.

As the days passed and nothing horrible happened, Chloe began to relax a little. By the end of the first week she was experimenting with new foods, going off with other students to explore the city during free time, and beginning to have a good time. By the end of the second week, Chloe had emerged as a group leader. She planned evening outings for the students (sans the professors!) and was always among the first to master the public transportation system of a new city. The transformation was incredible.

Her reflection paper at the end of the travel experience concluded with a simple but telling self-assessment: "I always feared change because I liked my life the way it was; I had no idea that change could be so exciting and freeing. Also, I had no idea how much I would benefit in other ways. I feel more confident in myself and more equipped to handle things that may happen to me as an adult."

Reflection Questions

1. What were Chloe's biggest challenges in terms of emotional intelligence?
2. What areas of emotional intelligence were the most positively affected by Chloe's willingness to take this trip? Explain how she improved in each area.

CASE STUDY #9: TWINS?

Maria and Lupe are fraternal twins. They grew up together in Mexico and moved to the United States when they were fourteen. They started high school that fall after living in the United States for only a month. Although they both had studied English in school, speaking it every day and writing papers in English was very difficult. They confronted other challenges, such as forming new friendships at their high school and finding interests they could pursue.

One day in the school cafeteria, they were approached by a popular girl named Emma, who invited them to go to the Friday night football game with them. Maria eagerly accepted for both of them.

After Emma left, Lupe told Maria how upset she was that Maria had agreed for them to go to the game. She wondered what they would talk about, how they would fit in with Emma's group of friends, and whether they would be made fun of because of their noticeable accents. Maria, on the other hand, expressed excitement about going. She tried to convince Lupe that this was a great opportunity to make new friends, to get involved at their new school, and to do something on Friday night other than stay home.

As Friday night approached, Maria's excitement grew, but so did Lupe's anxiety. Lupe could hardly pay attention in any of her classes that Friday as she thought about all the things that might happen that night. She worried about what to wear, how they would find Emma and her friends in the crowd of people at the game, and what she could talk about. She ate little of her lunch, and by the time school was over, she told Maria she didn't want to go that night.

Maria couldn't believe what Lupe was saying. This was their big chance to make some new friends! She had gone online to find pictures of previous football games, and she knew what to wear. She had also texted Emma and found a place to meet at the game. Yes, she was nervous, but she knew she would find things to talk about once she got to the game. She finally talked Lupe into going.

As their parents drove them to the game, Maria's excitement grew. She chatted with her mom while Lupe sat quietly, thinking of the many things that could go wrong and how embarrassed she would be. When her parents stopped the car to let the girls out, Lupe turned to Maria and blurted out, "I'm not going."

Maria was stunned. She tried to talk Lupe into changing her mind, but Lupe wouldn't budge. Maria finally turned to her parents and asked, "Can I go alone?" Her parents agreed if she would text them after connecting with Emma.

Maria got out of the car, made her way through the crowd, and finally saw Emma and her friends near the entrance. She was still nervous but glad she had come.

After a night filled with watching an exciting game and talking with Emma and her friends about music, clothes, and everything happening at school, Maria felt terrific. By the end of the night, she couldn't wait to see everyone again at school on Monday.

1. What emotional intelligence areas are most evident in the Twins case study?

2. Emotional intelligence involves, among other things, managing our emotions and effectively managing our relationships with others. How are those evident in this scenario?

3. Lupe obviously felt strong anxiety, and most people cannot just tell themselves to calm down or to quit worrying. What can you do in such a situation to help yourself?

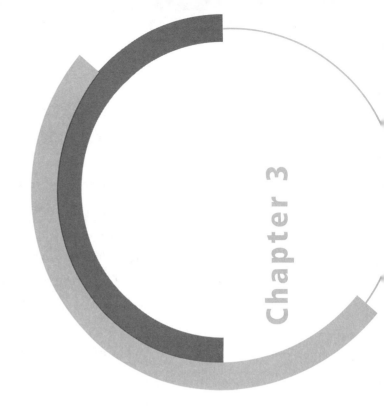

Chapter 3

Emotional Self-Awareness

What is emotional self-awareness? It involves (1) understanding what emotion you are experiencing, (2) being aware of your emotion in the moment (not minutes or hours later), (3) knowing what triggers different emotions in you, and (4) understanding the impact of your emotions on others. It's quite possible that someone is good at one of these components and not skilled in the others. The activities in *The Student EQ Edge: Student Workbook* are designed to tap each of these different elements.

Students today enjoy finding out about themselves through surveys, reflection exercises, and the like, so many of the tools needed to enhance emotional self-awareness work well in the classroom. Be prepared for some students to share their self-insights with the group—even insights or experiences you may consider very personal. Thanking the student for being authentic and courageous recognizes the risk taken and often leads to a vibrant discussion.

Emotional self-awareness provides one of the basic building blocks of emotional intelligence. For example, imagine a student who is not assertive. To overcome concerns about speaking up, the student first needs to understand what causes the concern.

Was the student raised in a family with authoritarian parents who believed that children should not speak up and thus the student fears doing so?

Does the student lack confidence in his or her opinion and thus worries about embarrassment? As you can see, without emotional self-awareness, development of assertiveness may be more challenging.

Can someone have too much self-awareness? Although well-developed self-awareness is very beneficial, students who have very high self-awareness may experience intense reactions to circumstances that others would respond to more mildly. If the student is also high in emotional expression, the intensity of the felt and expressed emotions can sometimes overwhelm other people or leave the individual feeling a bit drained. Having said that, if we lack emotional self-awareness, we are captive to our emotions (and the behaviors they produce) without clear knowledge of the cause or the intensity.

STUDENT LEARNING OUTCOMES

In the course of completing the activities in the workbook, students will:

- Become more aware of their emotions, preferably as they are happening
- Understand how values can cause emotions
- Understand how our performance and behaviors are affected when certain emotions get triggered
- Understand how our emotions affect others and their emotions affect us
- Describe how to change thoughts so as to change emotional reactions

SUGGESTED READINGS, MOVIES, AND TELEVISION SHOWS

The Student EQ Edge: Emotional Intelligence and Your Academic and Personal Success, Chapter 3.

Movies

- *Odd Girl Out*—at 70 minutes (Stacey in the hospital and her mom talking with her) the mother finally becomes aware of the reason for her emotions surrounding the bullying.
- *Patch Adams*—Scene 2, "Look Beyond"—Patch recognizes the cause for his feelings of despair and, equally, what will make him happy.
- *The Rookie*—Scene 5, "Speed Limit 35"—Jim becomes aware of his desire to pitch again and deals with unresolved feelings related to his first attempt to play baseball.

Television Shows

- Reality TV shows designed to create stress (for example, *The Amazing Race*, *Survivor*, *The Bachelor*, and *Top Chef*) provide great material. Focus on parts of episodes in which participants become angry, anxious, or frustrated and what then happens with their behavior and their partner's; pay attention to whether the person knows what triggered the emotion and how the emotion impacted the person's behavior.
- *Modern Family*—Episode 47, "See You Next Fall"—Alex will soon leave for college, and Phil and Claire experience many different emotions as a result.
- *Modern Family*—Episode 56, "After the Fire"—Claire thinks Mitchell has mother issues, and Cam thinks Haley and Alex have issues with gay people. Claire and Cam ultimately realize that their own emotions are creating the issues.

PLANNING YOUR CLASS

50–60 Minute Class

Assign Worksheets 3.1 and 3.2 for homework. Debrief those. Then cover the A-E model (3.3) with students and have them work through the A-E exercise in class. If time allows, show a short clip from one of the television shows and discuss how the characters showed emotional self-awareness.

Assign Worksheets 3.1, 3.2 and 3.5 for homework. Debrief those. Then cover the A-E model (3.3) with students and have them work through the A-E exercise in class. Have students share some A-E examples with each other. Pick a TV or movie clip (3.4) that illustrates emotional self-awareness, particularly something that shows hot buttons being pushed or irrational beliefs creating emotions. Debrief the clip. Break students into small groups to work on a case study. Have them report back to the large group. If time permits, have students begin their self-development plan (3.6).

Activity List

Activity #	Activity Name	Brief Description and Activity Notes
3.1	Feelings Journal	Students learn to identify feelings as they are happening and begin to see patterns in what triggers their emotions.
3.2	Hot Buttons	Students identify issues or values that trigger their "hot buttons" and learn how they tend to react when a hot button is triggered.
3.3	ABCDE Exercise—The Impact of Thoughts on Emotions and Behaviors	Students learn how their thoughts can dramatically affect both their emotional and behavioral responses; they also learn how to challenge irrational thoughts that can stir negative emotions and behaviors.
3.4	Hot Buttons on Reality TV	Students observe behaviors of participants from *The Amazing Race, Survivor,* or *The Bachelor.*
3.5	Positive and Negative Affect	Students complete a self-report survey designed to help them understand whether they experience more positive or negative affect.
3.6	Self-Development Plan for Self-Awareness (*See Appendix D for the template that students will use*)	Students develop specific strategies to improve their self-awareness that they can practice independently. Have them consult Appendix A in *The Student EQ Edge: Student Workbook* for specific strategies.
3.7	Case Study—Emotional Self-Awareness	Students analyze a case student and identify the presence or absence of emotional intelligence in the situation.

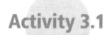

Activity 3.1
Feelings Journal

EI Dimensions Targeted: Emotional Self-Awareness

Brief Description: Students learn to identify feelings as they are happening and begin to see patterns in what triggers their emotions.

Planning the Activity

Time Expected
- Worksheet: One hour total over three to five days
- Reflection Questions: 10 minutes per written answer
- In-Class Debrief: 10 minutes

Materials
- Worksheet 3.1 from *The Student EQ Edge: Student Workbook*
- The *Student EQ Edge: Emotional Intelligence and Your Academic and Personal Success*

Facilitating the Activity

Directions
- Make sure students understand the seven basic emotions (happy, sad, angry, fearful, ashamed, disgusted, and surprised) and the variations in intensity within each (for example, *anxious* and *terrified* represent different intensity levels of *fear*).
- Encourage them to pay attention to the strength of their emotion (for example, *irritated* and *furious* are both forms of being *angry*); use the label that most closely matches the emotion and its intensity.
- Make sure they understand that feeling terms like "tired" are not emotions.

Debriefing Questions
- What was your biggest surprise after tracking your emotions for several days?
- What impact did tracking your emotions have on the type and frequency of emotions you experienced?
- See the reflection questions at the end of the worksheet.

Worksheet 3.1: Feelings Journal

Name:

At least three times per day on four different days, fill in the following form to chart your feelings. Some examples are provided to help you get started.

Date	Location	Feeling	Possible triggers
1/11	Class	Anxious	Professor announced a test next week.
1/11	Cafeteria	Calmer	Joe asked if we could study together for the test.
1/11	Hallway	Excited	Got asked to a party Friday night.
1/11	Class	Proud	Professor quoted from my paper in class.

Reflection Questions

1. Count the number of positive and negative emotions and then divide positive/negative. By definition, every emotion is either positive or negative, so classify each one! If you experience more positive emotions, your final number will be higher than one; if more negative, less than one.
   a. What is your ratio of positive to negative emotions?
   b. How do you think this affects you throughout your day?
2. What other patterns do you see in your journal? Look for types of situations or certain people that trigger similar emotions and explain what you find.
3. Which emotions are most easily triggered for you? Explain why you think this occurs.

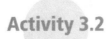

Activity 3.2
Hot Buttons

EI Dimensions Targeted: Emotional Self-Awareness, Impulse Control

Brief Description/Objective: Students will identify issues or values that trigger their hot buttons and learn how they tend to react when a hot button is triggered.

Planning the Activity

Time Expected
- Worksheet: 15 minutes
- Reflection Questions: 10 minutes per question
- In-Class Debrief: 15–20 minutes

Materials
- Worksheet 3.2 from *The Student EQ Edge: Student Workbook*
- *The Student EQ Edge: Emotional Intelligence and Your Academic and Personal Success*

Facilitating the Activity

Directions
- Before asking the students to complete Worksheet 3.2, explain that "hot buttons" involve any issue that triggers a strong negative emotional reaction. Hot buttons are not necessarily a bad thing. For example, discrimination against handicapped individuals could trigger a strong feeling of sadness or anger in us. Seeing a child being screamed at by an adult could trigger similar reactions. Our hot buttons develop because of personal experiences and values we have adopted. It's usually very helpful to students to share an example of one of your own hot buttons and how you developed it.
- If desired, have the class generate a list of values that can trigger hot buttons when they are violated by others. Keep in mind that significant personal experiences can also create hot buttons in us.
- Ask the students to complete Worksheet 3.2.
- The worksheet directs students to think about a recent time when *anger* was triggered; everyone can then hear about the variety of responses to anger. You can also do the same activity substituting other emotion words, even positive ones.

Debriefing Questions
- Ask students who think they have underreacted or overreacted to a hot button to share their reactions. What are some reasons for under- or overreaction?

- What kinds of suggestions did you make to yourself for how you could have handled the situation differently? Have the group pick the suggestions they believe are most likely to result in an effective, just, and humane resolution.
- Do you react the same way when your sadness, fear, or anxiety hot buttons get pushed? Can you see patterns in your reactions that model how your family members reacted to situations?
- See the reflection questions at the end of the worksheet.

Worksheet 3.2: Hot Buttons

Name:

All of us have hot buttons—situations we react to with strong emotion. Hot buttons develop in many ways; they can be based on past experiences or values that you've learned. Some common hot buttons are:

- Lack of fairness
- Lack of acceptance
- Criticism
- Lack of respect
- Being teased by someone (parent, teammate)
- Sensitivity about some aspect of who you are (for example, appearance, ethnicity, intelligence, lack of skill in an area)
- Negativity

List other possible hot buttons here:

1. Think about the last incident at home or school when you got really *angry*. Identify the two or three buttons that could have been "pushed." List them here.
2. Analyze what happened once the button got pushed. Did you withdraw? Overreact? Lash out? Become stressed? Describe both your *internal feelings* and your *external behaviors*.

   Internal feelings:

   External behaviors:

3. Name two specific things you could have done to manage your emotions or behavior better.
   a.
   b.

Reflection Questions

1. What will need to change for you to be able to handle the situation differently the next time your *anger* hot button gets pushed?
2. What can you do now to prepare for that?

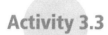

Activity 3.3

ABCDE Exercise—The Impact of Thoughts on Emotions and Behaviors

EI Dimensions Targeted: Emotional Self-Awareness, Impulse Control

Brief Description/Objective: Students will learn how their thoughts can dramatically affect both their emotional and their behavioral responses; they will also learn how to challenge their destructive thoughts.

Planning the Activity

Time Expected
- Mini-Lecture: 20 minutes to cover Ellis's A-E theory
- Worksheet: 10–15 minutes
- Reflection Questions: 10–15 minutes
- In-Class Debrief: 15–20 minutes to debrief

Materials
- Worksheet 3.3 from *The Student EQ Edge: Student Workbook*
- Information about Albert Ellis's theory (see the following links for good sources of information)
- *The Student EQ Edge: Emotional Intelligence and Your Academic and Personal Success*

Facilitating the Activity

Directions
- Cover Ellis's paradigm related to rational and irrational beliefs and how our beliefs—rather than the events that happen to us—trigger our emotional and behavioral responses. If you are not already familiar with Ellis's Rational-Emotive Behavior Therapy (REBT) and specifically the A-E paradigm, a good summary can be found at the following sites (the second includes a biography of Ellis and explains the addition of D and E to his model):
    - http://www.stressgroup.com/articles/article/1228898/11306.htm
    - http://webspace.ship.edu/cgboer/ellis.html
- Assign Worksheet 3.3. If you assign this worksheet during class time, have students who finish quickly help a classmate who has not.
- Ask several students to share their A-E scenarios with the class. Make sure to correct any misunderstandings about the A-E model.

Debriefing Questions
- Draw three columns on the board for academic achievement, relationships, and happiness. Write irrational beliefs for each category on the board.
- See the reflection questions at the end of the worksheet.

Worksheet 3.3: ABCDE Exercise—The Impact of Thoughts on Emotions and Behaviors

Name:

Read through the following example. Then identify a recent episode (*activating event, A*) in which you engaged in *irrational beliefs* (B). Please keep your answers simple. Do not tell the whole story; rather, summarize with statements; for example, "My coach yelled at me" or "I made a C on an important test."

Example:

A = **A**ctivating Event: I found out my friend is going out with someone I used to want to go out with in the past.

B = (irrational) **B**elief: My friend does not care about me or my feelings.

C = **C**onsequences of the irrational belief:

    Emotional: feeling sad, angry at friend

    Behavioral: refuse to respond to friend's text

D = **D**ispute (the irrational belief): I have not talked about wanting to go out with that person in over a year. I'm dating someone else now.

E = (New) **E**ffect:

    Emotional: Less sad (although I would still like to have dated that person); not angry

    Behavioral: Answer friend's text

Now it's your turn! Think about a time when you may have overreacted to a situation or handled a situation poorly. Using the example as a model, fill in the blanks.

1. What was the *activating* event (A)?
2. What was your *irrational belief* or beliefs (B)?
3. What *consequences* (C) were caused by your irrational belief?
    a. Emotional consequences
    b. Behavioral consequences
4. What are some ways to *dispute* (D) your irrational belief?
    a. Provide at least two other explanations for the cause of the activating event or how you can interpret it in a more rational way than your response to #2.
    b. Provide at least one piece of disputing evidence from your past interactions with this person.

5. What would be the new *effects* (E) for you if you replaced your irrational belief with a more rational one?
    a. Emotional effects
    b. Behavioral effects

Reflection Questions

Most of our irrational beliefs fall into broad categories related to assumptions we make about . . .

1. Competence or achievement: "I must always make an A" or "I should be a starting player."
2. Relationships: "Everybody should like me" or "Others should always treat me well and look after me" or "I need to be popular."
3. Our right to happiness: "Other people should ensure my happiness, and if they don't, I have a right to be miserable" or "My needs are more important than others' needs" or "If only *x* would change, then I would be happy."

Look back at the recent episode you described earlier. Does your irrational belief relate more to competence, relationships, or happiness? Explain. If you think it doesn't relate to any of these, identify an alternative reason behind your irrational belief.

Suppose some part of your irrational belief is true. For example, none of us is liked by everyone! What is a more rational statement to tell yourself when you know someone doesn't like you?

Why do people hold on to their irrational beliefs? What do they gain by doing this? What is gained by disputing your irrational beliefs?

Activity 3.4

Hot Buttons on Reality TV

EI Dimension Targeted: Emotional self-awareness; impulse control

Brief Description/Objective: Students identify issues or values that trigger other people's hot buttons and what emotions and behaviors the person displays when a hot button is triggered.

Planning the Activity

Time Expected
- Worksheet and Media Viewing: 10–20 minutes
- Reflection Questions: 5–10 minutes
- In-Class Debrief: 15–20 minutes

Materials
- Worksheet 3.4 from *The Student EQ Edge: Student Workbook*
- Media clip of your choice, such as *The Amazing Race or Survivor;* go to www.hulu.com to find clips.
- Alternative: Assign this activity to students for homework and then use one of the clips they found to show in class.
- *The Student EQ Edge: Emotional Intelligence and Your Academic and Personal Success*

Facilitating the Activity

Directions
- Cue the media clip to a scene just before one of the characters begins to lose emotional control; show as many of these scenes as you would like.
- In small or large groups, ask students to answer the following questions and write their answers on a chart or board:
    - Which character had a hot button pushed and what situation pushed his or her button?
    - What emotions did the person display when the button got pushed?
    - What behaviors did the person display when the button got pushed?
    - How did other people who were around the person react?

Debriefing Questions
- Overall, do you think the person's reaction to getting a hot button pushed was positive, neutral, or negative? Explain.
- How was the person's performance affected after the hot button got pushed?
- Have the students analyze the scenario using the steps of the A-E model learned previously.
- See the student reflection questions on the worksheet.

Worksheet 3.4: Hot Buttons on Reality TV

Name:

Pick a reality TV show (such as *The Amazing Race*, *Survivor*, *The Bachelor*, *Top Chef*, or any other one of your choosing) or a comedy (such as *The Office*, *30 Rock*, or *Modern Family*). Find a scene where one of the characters has a hot button pushed.

Write down the episode title, date, or number:

- Summarize the scene you watched. Include which character had a hot button pushed and what situation pushed it.
- What emotions did the person display when the button was pushed?
- What behaviors did the person display when the button was pushed?
- How did other people who were around the person react?
- Was the person more or less effective in interactions after the hot button got pushed? Explain.

Reflection Questions

1. It's often easier to identify when others' hot buttons get pushed rather than our own. What signals can you cue into to better recognize when your hot buttons have been pushed?

2. Ask a good friend or family member how he or she knows when one of your hot buttons has been pushed. Compare that person's answer to your answer to question 1.

Activity 3.5
Positive and Negative Affect

EI Dimension Targeted: Emotional Self-Awareness; Impulse Control

Brief Description: Students will complete a self-report survey related to their amount of positive and negative affect.

Planning the Activity

Time Expected
- Worksheet and Survey: 5–10 minutes
- Reflection Questions: 10–15 minutes
- In-Class Debrief: 10 minutes

Materials
- Worksheet 3.5 from *The Student EQ Edge: Student Workbook*
- www.authentichappiness.com
- *The Student EQ Edge: Emotional Intelligence and Your Academic and Personal Success*

Facilitating the Activity

Directions
- Assign Worksheet 3.5.
- Be sure to let students know that they will have to register on the site but that their data will remain confidential. The site is sponsored by the University of Pennsylvania and renowned psychologist Dr. Martin Seligman.

Debriefing Questions
- What is the impact on you of being around people with positive affect? Being around those with negative affect?
- See the reflection questions at the end of the worksheet.

Worksheet 3.5: Positive and Negative Affect

Name:

Go to www.authentichappiness.com and create a user profile. All of your information will remain confidential. On the home page, scroll through the Questionnaires Menu to find this link:

PANAS Questionnaire

Log in and take the PANAS (Positive and Negative Affect Survey) questionnaire.

Reflection Questions

1. What was your level of positive and negative affect? Were you surprised by your level of positive or negative affect? Explain.
2. All of us have ups and downs and will experience positive and negative emotions. What do you consider an acceptable balance of positive and negative affect for you? Explain.

Activity 3.6
Self-Development Plan for Emotional Self-Awareness

The directions and template for students to use to create a self-development plan appear in Appendix D of this *Facilitation and Activity Guide*. Each chapter in *The Student EQ Edge: Student Workbook* contains a self-development template related to improving EI skills *for that scale.*

Activity 3.7
Case Study—Emotional Self-Awareness

See Chapter 2 of this book to assign a case study relevant to emotional self-awareness. Chapter 2 of *The Student EQ Edge: Student Workbook* contains all of the same case studies.

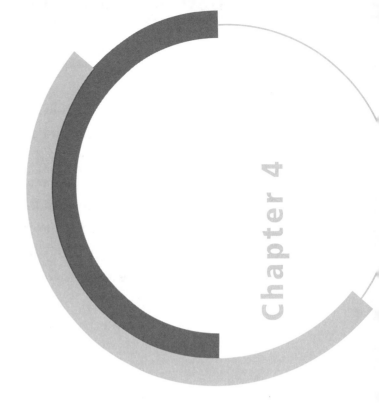

Chapter 4

Self-Regard

Self-regard involves three fundamental components: awareness of strengths and weaknesses, self-acceptance and respect for who you are as you are, and the resulting level of confidence. Self-regard can be difficult to achieve and maintain. There are multiple pressures in our society to achieve, look beautiful, and be the best in everything—and feel like a failure if you fall short of this. Organized sports competitions, which begin as young as four years of age, always have winners and thus losers. We all earn grades in school, hear comments made about us by others, and experience successes and failures. All of these experiences affect the development of our self-regard.

How can we be aware of our strengths and weaknesses, accept and respect ourselves as we are, and also remain confident? For some, this delicate balance can be disrupted in at least three ways:

- Thinking about only our strengths and ignoring our weaknesses can lead us to develop blind spots and sometimes appear overly confident or even cocky.
- Focusing too much on weaknesses can lead to a lack of self-acceptance or confidence.
- Understanding both strengths and weaknesses but not feeling good about ourselves as we are can harm our self-respect and self-confidence.

A key role for the facilitator while teaching this unit is to model healthy self-understanding and self-acceptance. At the beginning of each session with students, share some information about your own strengths and weaknesses. Modeling self-acceptance and confidence while also acknowledging weaknesses shows students how others manage this sometimes challenging balance.

Can someone have self-regard that is too well-developed? The answer would typically be "no." Even so, if someone is very high in self-regard and assertiveness and is *not* skilled in empathy or interpersonal relationships, that person may come across to others as "cocky." So high self-regard is great; it's only when self-regard is not balanced by other EI strengths that problems can occur.

STUDENT LEARNING OUTCOMES

Students will:

- Become more aware of their strengths and limitations
- Understand how their self-acceptance and respect are influenced by their awareness of and reaction to their strengths and limitations
- Understand how confidence is affected by our awareness and acceptance of our strengths and limitations

SUGGESTED READINGS, MOVIES, AND TELEVISION SHOWS

- *The Student EQ Edge: Emotional Intelligence and Your Academic and Personal Success,* Chapter 4

Movies
- *Odd Girl Out*—about 30 minutes into the movie (begin with the lunchroom scene where she is prevented from sitting at the table with her "friends")—Vanessa, the bullied girl, experiences a series of rejections from her friends and, in a desperate move, cuts her hair because they've made fun of it.

- *Patch Adams*—Scene 1, "Troubled Mind," and Scene 2, "Look Beyond"—Patch playfully gets the patients to laugh at their infirmities; a genius, hospitalized because of mental problems, teaches Patch important lessons about self-acceptance.
- *The Rookie*—Scene 4, "The Deal"—Jim, the coach, recognizes that the players don't feel good about themselves and are not confident enough to win. In return, they recognize that he might lack the confidence to pursue his dream of playing major league baseball.

Television Shows

- *30 Rock*—Episode 6, "Jack Meets Dennis"—Jack points out to Liz that she struggles with self-regard.
- *Glee*—Episode 3, "Acafellas"—Mr. Schuster, Finn, and others struggle with confidence.
- *Modern Family* provides a look at three interconnected families in a sitcom. Characters display various levels of self-awareness of strengths and limitations, self-acceptance, and confidence.
- Reality TV shows such as *The Amazing Race, Survivor, or The Bachelor*—Choose parts of episodes that portray the participants as too confident, unaware of weaknesses (blind spots), or too aware of weaknesses and thus lacking confidence. Analyze the impact of these different patterns as the show progresses.

PLANNING YOUR CLASS

50–60 Minute Class

Assign Worksheets 4.1, 4.2, and 4.4 for homework. Begin class with a mini-lecture to make sure students understand the meaning and components of self-regard. Then debrief Worksheets 4.1, 4.2, and 4.4. Generate positive and negative self-talk statements with the class and have them complete Worksheet 4.3. If time allows, have them pair up with a friend to share insights they gained from Worksheet 4.3.

Assign Worksheets 4.1, 4.2, and 4.4 for homework. Begin class with a mini-lecture to make sure students understand the meaning and components of self-regard. Then debrief Worksheets 4.1, 4.2, and 4.4. Generate positive and negative self-talk statements with the class and then have them complete Worksheet 4.3, pairing with a friend to share one or two insights from the activity. Next, show a TV program or part of a movie in which the characters have varying levels of self-regard (Worksheet 4.5) and discuss the episode using the debriefing questions. Assign a case study related to self-regard (Activity 4.7). Close with everyone working on a self-development plan for self-regard (Activity 4.6).

Activity List

Activity #	Activity Name	Brief Description and Activity Notes
4.1	Who Am I?	Students identify strengths, weaknesses, times they feel most confident, and what they like most about themselves.
4.2	Locus of Control Scale (Rotter, 1966)	Students complete Rotter's internal-external locus of control scale and understand how locus of control and self-regard are related.
4.3	Positive and Negative Self-Talk	Students think about successes and failures and what internal self-talk probably accompanied those experiences.
4.4	360° Feedback	Students seek input from others about their strengths and weaknesses.
4.5	*Modern Family*	Students watch an episode of *Modern Family* and analyze the self-regard of the major characters.
4.6	Self-Development Plan for Self-Regard	Students develop a plan to help them improve their self-regard. Have them turn in a progress report in one to two months.
4.7	Case Study— Self-Regard	Students analyze the presence or absence of EI skills through a case study. All case studies appear in Chapter 2 of both *The Student EQ Edge: Facilitation and Activity Guide* and *The Student EQ Edge: Student Workbook*.

Activity 4.1

Who Am I?

EI Dimensions Targeted: Self-Regard, Emotional Self-Awareness

Brief Description/Objective: Students will identify their strengths and weaknesses as well as what they like best about themselves and what makes them feel most confident.

Planning the Activity

Time Expected
- Introduction: 5 minutes
- Worksheet: 10 minutes
- Reflection Questions: 10–15 minutes
- In-Class Debrief: 15–20 minutes

Materials
- Worksheet 4.1 from *The Student EQ Edge: Student Workbook*
- Board or flip chart, markers
- *The Student EQ Edge: Emotional Intelligence and Your Academic and Personal Success*

Facilitating the Activity

Directions
- Before you assign Worksheet 4.1, let students know that everyone has weaknesses and that it is healthy to acknowledge those without overreacting (beating ourselves up about them) or underreacting (pretending we don't have weaknesses). Likewise, we all have strengths and need to acknowledge those. You may want to share an example or two from your own strengths and weaknesses to model this skill.
- Assign Worksheet 4.1.
- Have students take their completed charts and pair with a classmate. Suggest they share any two of the quadrants with each other. Note: The vast majority of students will choose to share their strengths and one of the other positive quadrants. If this is the case, begin a discussion with students about why we have difficulty sharing our weaknesses. See the following debriefing questions for some ideas.

Debriefing Questions
- What elements in our society make it easier for us to talk about strengths rather than weaknesses?
- Are some weaknesses more acceptable to acknowledge than others?
- How can we acknowledge our strengths and be confident without seeming cocky?
- See the reflection questions at the end of the worksheet.

Worksheet 4.1: Who Am I?

Name:

Fill in each quadrant in the table. Listing is fine. Be honest about your limitations!

My strengths are . . .	My weaknesses (areas to improve) are . . .
I feel most confident when . . .	I feel least confident when . . .

Reflection Questions

1. What surprises you the most, looking at your completed chart?
2. What connections do you see between your strengths and your areas of confidence?
3. What connections do you see between your weaknesses and your confidence?
4. How can you strengthen your areas of weakness?

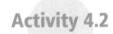

Activity 4.2
Locus of Control Scale (Rotter, 1966)

EI Dimensions Targeted: Self-Regard

Brief Description/Objective: Students will complete Rotter's (1966) original measure of locus of control and learn how locus of control is related to self-regard. If you are not familiar with locus of control, you can learn more at: http://www.mindtools.com/pages/article/newCDV_90.htm or http://wilderdom.com/psychology/loc/LocusOfControlWhatIs.html.

Planning the Activity

Time Expected
- Worksheet: 15 minutes
- Reflection Questions: 10–15 minutes
- In-Class Debrief: 10–20 minutes

Materials
- Worksheet 4.2 from *The Student EQ Edge: Student Workbook*
- *The Student EQ Edge: Emotional Intelligence and Your Academic and Personal Success*

Facilitating the Activity

Directions
- In-class mini-lecture (optional)—Explain locus of control in more detail. Whereas internals look to their ability or effort to explain their successes and failures, externals look outside themselves to other people, luck, or circumstances. Explain how a tendency to externalize may make it more difficult to identify and accept our strengths, our weaknesses, or both. For more information about locus of control, go to http://www.mindtools.com/pages/article/newCDV_90.htm. This website also has an electronic version of the Rotter scale.
- Students generally enjoy self-assessment activities, but they can become stressed if their score doesn't match the ideal. Point out that we can change our locus of control if we choose to do so.
- Assign Worksheet 4.2.

Debriefing Questions
- What could be some of the advantages and disadvantages of an internal locus of control?
- What could be some of the advantages and disadvantages of an external locus of control?
- Do you tend to be more internal about some issues (for example, social relationships, academics, health, sports) and more external about others? Explain why.
- Do you tend to be more internal about your successes or your failures? Explain why you think this pattern occurs.
- See the reflection questions at the end of the worksheet.

Worksheet 4.2: Locus of Control Scale (Rotter, 1966)

Name:

For each item, circle either a or b. Do not skip any items.

1. a. Children get into trouble because their parents punish them too much.
   b. The trouble with most children nowadays is that their parents are too easy with them.
2. a. Many of the unhappy things in people's lives are partly due to bad luck.
   b. People's misfortunes result from the mistakes they make.
3. a. One of the major reasons why we have wars is because people don't take enough interest in politics.
   b. There will always be wars, no matter how hard people try to prevent them.
4. a. In the long run people get the respect they deserve in this world.
   b. Unfortunately, an individual's worth often passes unrecognized no matter how hard he tries.
5. a. The idea that teachers are unfair to students is nonsense.
   b. Most students don't realize the extent to which their grades are influenced by accidental happenings.
6. a. Without the right breaks one cannot be an effective leader.
   b. Capable people who fail to become leaders have not taken advantage of their opportunities.
7. a. No matter how hard you try, some people just don't like you.
   b. People who can't get others to like them don't understand how to get along with others.
8. a. Heredity plays the major role in determining one's personality.
   b. It is one's experiences in life that determine what one is like.
9. a. I have often found that what is going to happen will happen.
   b. Trusting to fate has never turned out as well for me as making a decision to take a definite course of action.
10. a. In the case of the well-prepared student, there is rarely, if ever, such a thing as an unfair test.
    b. Many times exam questions tend to be so unrelated to course work that studying is really useless.
11. a. Becoming a success is a matter of hard work; luck has little or nothing to do with it.
    b. Getting a good job depends mainly on being in the right place at the right time.
12. a. The average citizen can have an influence in government decisions.
    b. This world is run by the few people in power, and there is not much the little guy can do about it.
13. a. When I make plans, I am almost certain that I can make them work.
    b. It is not always wise to plan too far ahead because many things turn out to be a matter of good or bad fortune anyhow.

14. a. There are certain people who are just no good.
    b. There is some good in everybody.
15. a. In my case, getting what I want has little or nothing to do with luck.
    b. Many times we might just as well decide what to do by flipping a coin.
16. a. Who gets to be the boss often depends on who was lucky enough to be in the right place first.
    b. Getting people to do the right thing depends on ability; luck has little or nothing to do with it.
17. a. As far as world affairs are concerned, most of us are the victims of forces we can neither understand nor control.
    b. By taking an active part in political and social affairs, the people can control world events.
18. a. Most people don't realize the extent to which their lives are controlled by accidental happenings.
    b. There really is no such thing as "luck."
19. a. One should always be willing to admit mistakes.
    b. It is usually best to cover up one's mistakes.
20. a. It is hard to know whether or not a person really likes you.
    b. How many friends you have depends on how nice a person you are.
21. a. In the long run the bad things that happen to us are balanced by the good ones.
    b. Most misfortunes are the result of lack of ability, ignorance, laziness, or all three.
22. a. With enough effort we can wipe out political corruption.
    b. It is difficult for people to have much control over the things politicians do in office.
23. a. Sometimes I can't understand how teachers arrive at the grades they give.
    b. There is a direct connection between how hard I study and the grades I get.
24. a. A good leader expects people to decide for themselves what they should do.
    b. A good leader makes it clear to everybody what their jobs are.
25. a. Many times I feel that I have little influence over the things that happen to me.
    b. It is impossible for me to believe that chance or luck plays an important role in my life.
26. a. People are lonely because they don't try to be friendly.
    b. There's not much use in trying too hard to please people; if they like you, they like you.
27. a. There is too much emphasis on athletics in high school.
    b. Team sports are an excellent way to build character.
28. a. What happens to me is my own doing.
    b. Sometimes I feel that I don't have enough control over the direction my life is taking.
29. a. Most of the time I can't understand why politicians behave the way they do.
    b. In the long run the people are responsible for bad government on a national level, as well as on a local level.

Scoring: Note that there are 6 unscored items (1, 8, 14, 19, 24, and 27) and 23 items for scoring.

Score 1 point for each of the following:

2b	16b
3a	17b
4a	18b
5a	20b
6b	21b
7b	22a
9b	23b
10a	25b
11a	26a
12a	28a
13a	29b
15a	

My total score is _____ (0–23)

External = 11 and below with a lower score (closer to 0) reflects more externality; people with an external locus of control are more likely to believe that external circumstances—ranging from other people's behavior to fate or luck—are the primary explanation for what happens to them in life.

Internal = 13 or higher with a higher score (closer to 23) reflects more internality (note that this is reverse-scored from the original Rotter scale); people with an internal locus of control tend to explain events based on their ability, skill, or effort; in other words, they take responsibility for what happens.

Reflection Questions

1. What is your reaction to your results?
2. What do you believe are some of the benefits and consequences of having an external locus of control?
3. What do you believe are some of the benefits and consequences of having an internal locus of control?
4. What connection do you see between your self-regard and locus of control?

Activity 4.3
Positive and Negative Self-Talk

EI Dimensions Targeted: Self-Regard, Emotional Self-Awareness, Optimism

Brief Description/Objective: Students will identify times when they use positive and negative self-talk and will understand the connection between self-talk and confidence levels. Students also learn how to convert negative self-talk into something more helpful.

Planning the Activity

Time Expected
- Introduction: 5 minutes
- Worksheet: 15 minutes
- Reflection Questions: 10 minutes
- In-Class Debrief: 15 minutes

Materials
- Worksheet 4.3 from *The Student EQ Edge: Student Workbook*
- Flip chart or board; markers for students to use on the chart or board
- *The Student EQ Edge: Emotional Intelligence and Your Academic and Personal Success*

Facilitating the Activity

Directions
- To prepare the students, you may need to generate a list of positive and negative self-talk items *prior to assigning the worksheet*. Once students understand how to identify self-talk, they will be able to add to the following list:
  - Some common examples of positive self-talk are:

    I'm really good at . . .

    I've done this before, so I know I can do it again

    Things always work out if I stay calm

  - Likewise, some good examples of negative self-talk are:

    I never do well at . . .

    I won't be well liked if I don't. . . .

    I'm not very smart if I can't do . . .

- Assign Worksheet 4.3.
- After students have completed the worksheet, draw three vertical lines on the board. In the left column, place all of the positive self-talk items. Try to get each student to contribute at least one item to the positive list.
- In the middle column, record negative self-talk items. Again, get as many students as possible to contribute a negative self-talk item.
- Then, divide students into groups. Assign each group one to three of the negative self-talk items. Ask them to turn each negative statement into a form of positive self-talk. For example, "I'm no good at _____," can be turned into "I can get better at _____ by _____."
- Ask students to put their revised statements on the board in the third column.
- Encourage interested students to key some of the positive self-talk items into their phone or computers for easy access.

Debriefing Questions

- How difficult was it to replace negative self-talk with more hopeful and positive messages?
- How can you train yourself to replace your negative messages with the ones the class came up with?
- See the reflection questions at the end of the worksheet.

Worksheet 4.3: Positive and Negative Self-Talk

Name:

Positive self-talk and negative self-talk are internal messages we give ourselves, sometimes without even knowing that we do it! A good way to cue into your positive and negative self-talk is to pay attention to behaviors related to either persisting or giving up, then analyze your internal self-talk that accompanied the behavior. Fill in the following chart.

Constructive Behaviors: The last time I kept trying to master something hard in my academic work, a sport, or an activity was . . . The last time I did something I was scared to do was . . .	**Related Positive Self-Talk:** And what I said to myself to help me keep trying was . . . And what I said to myself to help me overcome my fear was . . .
Destructive Behaviors: The last time I gave up while trying to master academic work was . . . The last time I did not try to do something because I lacked confidence was . . .	**Related Negative Self-Talk:** And what I said to myself was . . . And what I said to myself that held me back was . . .

Reflection Questions

1. How aware were you before this assignment of your self-talk? How has your awareness level changed as you go through your day?

2. Do your negative messages follow a pattern of criticizing some aspect of yourself, such as your physical appearance, your intelligence, or your popularity? If so, explain what causes this.

3. Which of your positive messages is most helpful to you? How can you use this message more frequently?

4. What is your ratio of positive self-talk to negative self-talk? What is the consequence to you of your current ratio?
   a. I use much more positive self-talk than negative self-talk.
   b. I use more positive self-talk than negative self-talk.
   c. I use them about the same amount.
   d. I use more negative self-talk than positive self-talk.
   e. I use much more negative self-talk than positive self-talk.

Activity 4.4
360° Feedback

EI Dimensions Targeted: Self-Regard, Emotional Self-Awareness, Interpersonal Relationships

Brief Description/Objective: Students will understand how others view their strengths and weaknesses.

Planning the Activity

Time Expected
- Worksheet: 20 minutes
- Reflection Questions: 15 minutes
- In-Class Debrief: 1 minute per student in the class

Materials
- Worksheet 2.7 and Worksheet 4.4 from *The Student EQ Edge: Student Workbook*
- Board or flip chart and markers
- *The Student EQ Edge: Emotional Intelligence and Your Academic and Personal Success*

Facilitating the Activity

Directions
- Assign Worksheet 4.4.
- After students have completed their worksheets, ask each student to pick one person on his or her list and what that person said about his or her strengths and weaknesses. Also, have each student mention the answer that most surprised him or her.

Debriefing Questions
- What emotional reactions did you experience as others described your strengths? Your weaknesses?
- How often did you find yourself defending yourself or explaining something when someone mentioned a weakness? In contrast, what did you do when strengths were mentioned?
- See the reflection questions at the end of the worksheet.

Worksheet 4.4: 360° Feedback

Name:

People who know you well will know your strengths and weaknesses. Ask three people who know you well to give you a list of three to five of your strengths and three to five of your weaknesses. Record them in the following chart.

Name of person giving you feedback	Strengths	Weaknesses

Reflection Questions

1. What are the common themes about your strengths? Weaknesses?
2. What strengths and weaknesses surprised you the most?
3. How did it feel to have others comment on your strengths? Your weaknesses?

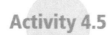

Activity 4.5
Modern Family

EI Dimensions Targeted: Self-Regard

Brief Description/Objective: Students will look for examples of characters' self-regard through their statements and behaviors.

Planning the Activity

Time Expected
- Worksheet and episode of *Modern Family*: 30 minutes
- Reflection Questions: 5 minutes
- In-Class Debrief: 1 minute per student in the class

Materials
- Worksheet 4.5 from *The Student EQ Edge: Student Workbook*
- Board or flip chart and markers
- *The Student EQ Edge: Emotional Intelligence and Your Academic and Personal Success*

Facilitating the Activity

Directions
- Watch an episode of *Modern Family* in class (most episodes will have at least two or three examples of the behaviors students are supposed to observe).
- Assign Worksheet 4.5 from *The Student EQ Edge: Student Workbook.*

Debriefing Questions
- Which character would you most want to be in terms of self-regard?
- Open a discussion with students about why they picked the character they did. What challenges does this character face personally and interpersonally because of his or her self-regard? What advantages does this person have because of his or her self-regard?
- See the reflection questions at the end of the worksheet.

Worksheet 4.5: *Modern Family*

Name:

Watch an episode of *Modern Family* (or another show assigned by your instructor) and record specific comments made by the characters or behaviors they engaged in that reflected self-awareness of strengths and/or weaknesses.

Character	Incident or Comment	Strength or Weakness?

Reflection Questions

1. Which character do you believe has the most well-developed self-regard? Explain.
2. Which character do you believe has the least well-developed self-regard? Explain.

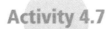

Activity 4.6

Self-Development Plan for Self-Regard

The directions and template for students to create a self-development plan appear in Appendix D of this *Facilitation and Activity Guide*. *The Student EQ Edge: Student Workbook* contains a template for developing self-regard in chapter 4.

Activity 4.7

Case Study—Self-Regard

See the case studies in chapter 2 and assign a case study relevant to emotional self-regard. Chapter 2 of *The Student EQ Edge: Student Workbook* contains all of the same case studies.

Self-Actualization

Self-actualization involves setting goals, making good use of one's abilities to accomplish those goals, and being motivated to achieve those goals. People who have higher levels of self-actualization will be driven to achieve, will be involved in activities that allow for self-improvement, and will receive meaning and satisfaction from whatever they do. A lack of self-actualization can lead us to flounder or experience our daily activities with less enjoyment or meaning. Research with college students indicates that those who have a defined purpose for being in college make better grades and are more likely to persist with their education (Pascarella & Terenzini, 2005). Can you imagine most students studying hard without a clear sense of purpose for pursuing higher education?

It's hard to imagine someone who is too self-actualized. Wouldn't that mean that goal setting and satisfaction can be overdone? There is something to be cautious about, though. Highly self-actualized people may have a difficult time understanding why others don't seem interested in goal setting or achievement. Thus we must realize that not everyone is as self-actualized as we may be, and we must practice patience while they develop their skills in this area.

STUDENT LEARNING OUTCOMES

Students will:

- Understand what self-actualization is and how to identify it in themselves and others
- Identify goals for their academic, cocurricular, and personal lives
- Identify what gives them meaning or enjoyment and what inspires them
- Understand what emotions are triggered when they are asked to think about goals
- Develop a personal mission statement

SUGGESTED READINGS, MOVIES, AND TELEVISION SHOWS

- *The Student EQ Edge: Emotional Intelligence and Your Academic and Personal Success*, Chapter 5

Movies

- *Patch Adams*—Scene 11, "Gesundheit"—Patch identifies the site where he will build his free health care clinic.
- *The Pursuit of Happyness*—Final scene, "The Job Offer"—After enduring countless hardships, the main character achieves his goal of getting a job offer.
- *The Rookie*—Scene 12, "Jimmy's Dream," and Scene 13, "The Major Leagues"—Jimmy struggles with whether to stick with his dream of playing baseball or to go home; he chooses to continue to follow his dream and earns a spot in the major leagues.

Television Shows

- Reality TV shows such as *The Amazing Race*, *Survivor*, or *The Bachelor*—These shows attract a variety of participants, some seeking the experience, some the fame, others a financial payoff, and still others a new challenge. No matter what type of reality show it is, there is always some type of "winner" and thus many "losers." Ask questions similar to these:

- Do participants talk about any life or career goals other than "winning" the show?
- Compare and contrast participants' goals related to the show and those they talk about for their lives and careers.
- Compare and contrast two people on the show who vary in their levels of self-actualization. What differences do you see in how these people approach the goal of being the winner?

PLANNING YOUR CLASS

50–60 Minute Class

Assign Worksheets 5.1, 5.2, and 5.4 for homework. Begin the class by asking each student to share either one goal or his or her mission statement. Then, using the debriefing questions associated with Worksheet 5.2, discuss students' emotional reactions to identifying goals. Show a short clip from *The Amazing Race* and have students fill out Worksheet 5.5 as they are watching the program. Debrief by having the students compare their emotions to the emotions of the *Amazing Race* participants when (1) no goals are obvious, (2) goals are stated and achieved, or (3) goals are stated but not achieved.

3–4 Hour Workshop

Assign Worksheets 5.1, 5.2, and 5.3 for homework. Begin class by having each student share a goal or something that inspires him or her. Now, using the debriefing questions associated with Worksheet 5.2, discuss emotional reactions to identifying goals. Help students explore more about the source of their feelings; if they feel anxious about setting goals, have them identify the cause or source of the anxiety. Assign small groups to complete the case study (Activity 5.6) and report out their analysis. Help students craft a personal mission statement (Activity 5.4) for right now or for 15 years from now and share those with the class. Next, have students complete the self-development plan (Activity 5.6). Play a clip of *The Amazing Race* and have students complete Worksheet 5.5.

Activity List

Activity #	Activity Name	Brief Description and Activity Notes
5.1	Who Am I? (continued)	Students examine their *purpose* and *goals* and what gives them *meaning* and *enjoyment*. Make sure students know it is okay to list any goal—education related or not.
5.2	Emotions Meter	Students identify which emotions they feel when asked to think about goals for their academic work, cocurricular activities, and personal life.
5.3	Quotes, Sayings, and Songs—A Window into You!	Students identify song titles, quotes, and sayings that inspire them.
5.4	Defining Your Personal Mission Statement	Students draft a personal mission statement. This activity will take about 15 minutes of introduction time.
5.5	*The Amazing Race*	In this reality TV show, people team with a friend, partner, or family member to race around the globe against other teams. Every show presents obstacles and challenges the teams must overcome.
5.6	Self-Development Plan for Self-Actualization	Students develop two strategies for improving their self-actualization.
5.7	Case Study—Self-Actualization	Students identify how self-actualization affects behaviors and decisions (see Chapter 2).

Activity 5.1
Who Am I? (continued)

EI Dimensions Targeted: Self-Actualization, Self-Regard

Brief Description/Objective: Students will examine their *purpose* and *goals*, and what gives them *meaning* and *enjoyment*.

Planning the Activity

Time Expected
- Worksheet: 15 minutes
- Reflection Questions: 10 minutes
- In-Class Debrief: 20 minutes

Materials
- Worksheet 5.1 from *The Student EQ Edge: Student Workbook*
- Markers, board or flip chart
- *The Student EQ Edge: Emotional Intelligence and Your Academic and Personal Success*

Facilitating the Activity

Directions
- Assign Worksheet 5.1 from *The Student EQ Edge: Student Workbook.*
- After students have completed their worksheets, ask each to share one goal from either his or her personal or academic side as well as one thing that gives the student meaning or enjoyment.

Debriefing Questions
- How did you react to hearing others' goals?
- Students probably listed a variety of things that give their lives meaning or enjoyment. Ask students what conclusions they can reach from this.
- See the reflection questions at the end of the worksheet.

Worksheet 5.1: Who Am I? (continued)

Name:

Complete the following sentence:

My favorite song title, quote, or saying is:

Now complete each quadrant of the worksheet.

My goals for my personal life are . . .	My goals for my academic work are . . .
I receive the most *enjoyment* from . . . (for example, being with friends, working on computers, playing basketball)	I receive the most *meaning* from . . . (for example, playing on a team, doing volunteer work)

Reflection Questions

1. Does your favorite song title express something about who you are or what goals you have? If so, explain. If not, make up a song title that describes you.
2. What experiences or people have shaped your goals?
3. Identifying goals is easier than accomplishing them. Pick your most important goal and identify what you need to do to accomplish that goal.
    a. This week?
    b. This month?
    c. This year?

Activity 5.2
Emotions Meter

EI Dimensions Targeted: Self-Actualization, Emotional Self-Awareness

Brief Description/Objective: Students will identify which emotions they feel when asked to think about goals for their academic work, cocurricular activities, and personal life.

Planning the Activity

Time Expected
- Worksheet: 5 minutes
- Reflection Questions: 15 minutes
- In-Class Debrief: 10–15 minutes

Materials
- Worksheet 5.2 from *The Student EQ Edge: Student Workbook*
- Markers, board or flip chart
- *The Student EQ Edge: Emotional Intelligence and Your Academic and Personal Success*

Facilitating the Activity

Directions
- Assign Worksheet 5.2.
- After students complete the worksheet, take a tally of how many students listed each emotion for academic, cocurricular, or personal goals.

Debriefing Questions
- What are the trends and patterns in your emotional responses to setting academic, cocurricular, and personal goals?
- Is there a wider variety of emotional reaction to one type of goal than to another? Do you tend to react with negative emotions to one type of goal and with positive emotions to other types of goals?
- See the reflection questions at the end of the worksheet.

Worksheet 5.2: Emotions Meter

Name:

Thinking about your goals and what gives your life meaning can create many different emotions. Circle the clip art picture(s) in Figure 5.1 that best convey(s) how you feel when thinking about your *academic, cocurricular,* and *personal* goals. Write the word *academic, cocurricular,* or *personal* for each picture you circle.

Figure 5.1. **Goals Trigger Emotions**

BORED   CONFUSED   STRESSED OUT

ANGRY   THOUGHTFUL   HAPPY, EXCITED

SAD   MOTIVATED

Reflection Questions

1. Pretend you are talking to your best friend. Write a brief message that summarizes what you would say to your friend about why you circled the pictures you chose.
2. Which type of goal produced your strongest emotional reaction? Explain why that goal is so important to you.
3. How do your emotional reactions affect your ability to accomplish the goal? Explain.

Activity 5.3

Quotes, Sayings, and Songs—A Window into You!

EI Dimensions Targeted: Self-Actualization

Brief Description/Objective: Students will identify sources of inspiration or motivation by thinking about quotes, sayings, and song titles.

Preparing the Activity

Time Expected
- Worksheet: 10–20 minutes (some students will readily identify things that inspire them; others will take much longer)
- Reflection Question: 15 minutes
- In-Class Debrief: 15 minutes

Materials
- Worksheet 5.3 from *The Student EQ Edge: Student Workbook*
- Markers, flip chart or board
- *The Student EQ Edge: Emotional Intelligence and Your Academic and Personal Success*

Facilitating the Activity

Directions
- Assign Worksheet 5.3 to be completed outside of class time.
- Place the students into small groups of three or four and ask them to share one item from their list and why they find it inspiring.

Debriefing Questions
- What types of common themes about what inspires you did you find in your small group?
- What person inspires you the most? What have you done that you might not have tried without support or inspiration from this person?
- What did you learn about yourself from completing this activity?
- See the reflection question at the end of the worksheet.

Worksheet 5.3: Quotes, Sayings, and Songs—A Window into You!

Name:

In the chart, write three or four meaningful sayings, quotes, song titles, song lyrics, or other words that describe or inspire you. Then write a brief description about why you chose to include each in your list.

Saying, Song Title, Lyric, or Quote	Why I like this or why it motivates me
Example: "Edge of Glory" by Lady Gaga	This is how I felt when I almost made an A in a really difficult class; the B was good, but I knew I could have made an A if I just worked a little harder.

Reflection Question

What did you learn about yourself and your motivations by doing this exercise?

Activity 5.4
Defining Your Personal Mission Statement

EI Dimensions Targeted: Self-Actualization

Brief Description/Objective: Students will draft a personal mission statement.

Planning the Activity

Time Expected
- Introduction to the Activity: 10 minutes (directions follow)
- Worksheet: 10–20 minutes
- Reflection Questions: 10–15 minutes
- In-Class Debrief: 10–15 minutes

Materials
- Worksheet 5.4 from *The Student EQ Edge: Student Workbook*
- *The Student EQ Edge: Emotional Intelligence and Your Academic and Personal Success*

Facilitating the Activity

Directions
- *Before* assigning the worksheet, go over the definition and purpose of a mission statement.
- Ask the students to read the mission statements on the student worksheet and comment on their clarity.
- Ask the students to begin developing their own mission statement by brainstorming a list of words that describe them now and also a list that describes what they hope to accomplish.
- Have students craft their own mission statement and share it with others.

Debriefing Questions
- What did you find most challenging about developing a mission statement?
- What level of congruence exists between your mission statement and your behaviors?
- See the reflection questions at the end of the worksheet.

Worksheet 5.4: Defining Your Personal Mission Statement

Name:

Almost every major company, educational institution, or organization has a mission statement.

The purpose of a mission statement is to describe—in one sentence—the organization and what it hopes to accomplish or provide. For example, here are mission statements from organizations you've probably heard of:

Amazon: "Our vision is to be earth's most customer centric company; to build a place where people can come to find and discover anything they might want to buy online." http://phx .corporate-ir.net/phoenix.zhtml?c=97664&p=irol-faq#14296

McDonald's: Our mission is to be our customers' favorite place and way to eat." http://www .aboutmcdonalds.com/mcd/student_zone/company_information.html

Twitter: "To instantly connect people everywhere to what's most important to them." http:// www.twitterrati.com/2011/01/11/twitters-new-mission-statement/

United States Department of State: "Create a more secure, democratic, and prosperous world for the benefit of the American people and the international community." http://www .state.gov/s/d/rm/rls/dosstrat/2004/23503.htm

Now it's your turn. Craft a personal mission statement. Think about the questions "What do I want to do?" "For whom?" and "Why is this important?" Fulfilling your mission statement should produce enjoyment and meaning for you. Look at your answers on Worksheets 5.1 and 5.3 to help you get ideas.

My mission is . . .

Reflection Questions

1. If someone else observed your behavior for a week, would they agree that your behavior matches your mission statement? Explain your answer.
2. What are the key values reflected in your mission statement and why did you choose those?

Activity 5.5

The Amazing Race

EI Dimensions Targeted: Self-Actualization

Brief Description/Objective: After watching an episode of *The Amazing Race*, students will be able to identify the goals of various participants and how motivated they were to achieve them.

Planning the Activity

Time Expected
- Introduction to the Activity: 5 minutes (see directions that follow)
- Worksheet (watching an episode): 45–60 minutes
- Reflection Questions: 10 minutes
- In-Class Debrief: 10–15 minutes

Materials
- Worksheet 5.5 from *The Student EQ Edge: Student Workbook*
- Any episode of *The Amazing Race* (every episode has different participants revealing different goals and levels of motivation)
- *The Student EQ Edge: Emotional Intelligence and Your Academic and Personal Success*

Facilitating the Activity

Directions
- Many old episodes of TV programs can be found in the public domain or can be rented cheaply (go to www.hulu.com). If possible, provide students with the exact link of the episode you want them to watch or show the episode in class.
- Assign Worksheet 5.5. Ask them to focus on one or two characters in the chosen episode and record what the character says or does that reflect goals and motivations. Also ask students to observe what gives participants enjoyment—is it accomplishing goals or something else?

Debriefing Questions

- Who do you think showed the most well-developed goals? What did that person do or say to demonstrate those goals?
- Who do you think showed the least well-defined goals? What happened to that person as the episode progressed?
- What was the relationship between reaching goals successfully and various emotions? Did success guarantee happiness? Explain.
- See the reflection questions at the end of the worksheet.

Worksheet 5.5: *The Amazing Race*

Name:

Watch an episode of *The Amazing Race* (or another show assigned by your instructor) and record specific comments made by the characters or behaviors they engaged in that reflected self-actualization. Not all contestants are motivated just by the money. Listen and watch for other motivations!

Participant	Comment or Behavior	Self-Actualization Anaiysis

Reflection Questions

1. What goal statement did you find most inspiring? Explain why you chose this one.
2. If you had a chance to be on *The Amazing Race* (or other show you watched) and there was not a million-dollar prize, would you participate? Why or why not?

Activity 5.6

Self-Development Plan for Self-Actualization

The directions and template for students to create a self-development plan appear in Appendix D of this *Facilitation and Activity Guide. The Student EQ Edge: Student Workbook* contains a template for developing self-actualization in Chapter 5.

Activity 5.7

Case Study—Self-Actualization

See Chapter 2 to assign a case study relevant to emotional self-actualization. Chapter 2 of *The Student EQ Edge: Student Workbook* contains all of the same case studies.

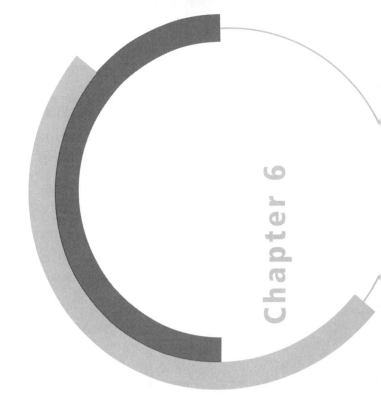

Chapter 6

Emotional Expression

What is emotional expression? We can express our emotions verbally with the use of emotion words such as "angry," "sad," or "happy." Most often, though, emotion is expressed nonverbally, through our facial expressions, body language, gestures, and tone of voice. Nonverbal communication reveals as much about what we're feeling as our words do—or more. In fact, most of us put much more weight on an individual's nonverbal expression of emotion than on the person's verbal expressions. Why? Because we seldom express our emotions through words! Instead, we use smiling or frowning, uncrossing or crossing our arms, leaning forward or backward, nodding or sighing, talking softly or loudly, making or refusing eye contact, and a myriad of other nonverbal cues to express our emotions nonverbally.

All of us learned "rules" for emotional expression as we were growing up. Perhaps your family yelled when angry—or withdrew silently. All families have family belief systems, usually unspoken, about how kids should be reared and how the family should function. Perhaps verbal expressions of anger weren't tolerated in any form. Or maybe it was okay for males to express anger but not sadness. Maybe you could tell family members if you were happy or excited, but if you happened to feel sad or anxious, you kept your feelings to yourself. Unfortunately, trying to ignore our emotions doesn't make them go away. In fact, that makes our emotions more powerful because they build up in intensity.

Can someone be too high in emotional expressiveness? People high in emotional expressiveness can create a very intense emotional environment, which can be uncomfortable for others who may be less expressive or who don't know how to react to an expressive person. Empathy is needed to help balance expressiveness.

STUDENT LEARNING OUTCOMES

Students will:

- Become more aware of both verbal and nonverbal methods of expressing emotion
- Understand their own emotional expression patterns and tendencies
- Understand how their emotional expression affects others
- Learn how to use "I" messages as a way to express emotions verbally

SUGGESTED READINGS, MOVIES, AND TELEVISION SHOWS

- *The Student EQ Edge: Emotional Intelligence and Your Academic and Personal Success*, Chapter 6

Movies
- *Erin Brockovich*—Scene 43—Erin ranges from furious (when she thinks she will get an unfair bonus) to quietly joyful when the amount is higher than she expected.
- *Odd Girl Out*—about 55 minutes into the movie—Vanessa and her mom express joy and excitement over the party she's been invited to, but despair and anger when they find out she's been tricked.

- *Patch Adams*—Scene 13, "The Last Sonnet"—Patch expresses his despair about Carin's death.
- *The Blind Side*—Scene 26, "Where My Family Goes"—Leigh Ann fights her emotions when it's time to say goodbye, but Michael openly expresses his, a rare circumstance.

Television Shows

- *Modern Family* provides a look at three interconnected families in a sitcom. Characters display various levels of emotional expression, both verbal and nonverbal.
- Reality TV shows such as *Scare Tactics*, *The Amazing Race*, *Survivor*, *The Bachelor*, *The Apprentice*, or *Top Chef* always contain examples of emotional expression. Most reality TV shows are designed to elicit strong emotional reactions from the participants—and they do!

PLANNING YOUR CLASS

50–60 Minute Class

Assign Worksheets 6.1 and 6.5 for homework. Begin the class by asking students to share general observations of verbal and non-verbal emotional expression in real life and on TV. Then, teach students the basic structure of an "I" message and have them complete Part 1 of Worksheet 6.4. Ask for volunteers to share some of their "I" messages and make sure they are using the correct format. (The most common mistake is that people fail to use an emotion word at the beginning of their "I" message and instead say something like "I feel you shouldn't have left those dirty dishes in the sink" rather than "I'm mad that you left those dirty dishes in the sink.") Finally, role play using "I" messages with an example a student provides. You should play the role of the person receiving the "I" message and react the way you think someone would react. If the "I" message is delivered effectively, respond with more cooperation and maybe by divulging some of your own feelings. Likewise, if the "I" message is not delivered effectively, then react accordingly.

Assign Worksheets 6.1, 6.2, and 6.3 for homework. Begin by debriefing Activity 6.2 according to the activity instructions. Challenge students to think about the implications of their verbal and nonverbal expressions of emotion and where they learned their patterns of expression. Then debrief Activity 6.3, which relates to emotional contagion. Next, show a 30-minute comedy TV show in class and have students complete Worksheet 6.5. Make sure different students are watching different characters in the show. Debrief Worksheet 6.5. Then teach students the basic structure of an "I" message and have them complete Part 1 of Worksheet 6.4. Ask for volunteers to share some of their "I" messages and make sure that they are using the correct format. (The most common mistake is that people fail to use an emotion word at the beginning of their "I" message and instead say something like "I feel you shouldn't have left those dirty dishes in the sink" rather than "I'm mad that you left those dirty dishes in the sink."). Finally, role play using student examples of "I" messages. You should play the role of the person receiving the "I" message and react the way you think someone would react. If the "I" message is delivered effectively, respond with more cooperation and maybe by divulging some of your own feelings. Likewise, if the "I" message is not delivered effectively, then react accordingly. Next, break students into small groups to analyze a case study. If time permits, have students create a self-development plan for emotional expression.

Activity List

Activity #	Activity Name	Brief Description and Activity Notes
6.1	Observing Emotions	Students learn to distinguish between verbal and nonverbal expression of emotion. Stress that verbal expression must involve an emotion word such as "angry" or "excited."
6.2	Observing Your Emotions	Students self-monitor their own emotional expression for one day.
6.3	Follow the Leader	Students try to influence the emotional expression of others by expressing either positive or negative nonverbal emotions.
6.4	"I" Messages	Students learn how to construct and deliver an "I" message.
6.5	TV Emotions	Students observe verbal and nonverbal expression of emotion of a main character on a television show and compare that to real life.
6.6	Self-Development Plan for Emotional Expression	Students create a plan to improve their emotional expression.
6.7	Case Study—Emotional Expression	Students analyze how emotional expression or the lack of it affects behaviors and relationships.

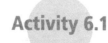

Activity 6.1
Observing Emotions

EI Dimensions Targeted: Emotional Expression

Brief Description/Objective: Students will learn to differentiate between verbal and nonverbal expression of emotion by observing another person.

Planning the Activity

Time Expected
- Worksheet: 20 minutes throughout one day
- Reflection Questions: 15 minutes
- In-Class Debrief: 10 minutes

Materials
- Worksheet 6.1 from *The Student EQ Edge: Student Workbook*
- Board or flip chart and markers
- *The Student EQ Edge: Emotional Intelligence and Your Academic and Personal Success*

Facilitating the Activity

Directions
- Before assigning the worksheet, make sure that students understand that verbal expression of emotions must include an emotion word (for example, happy, excited, sad, angry, frustrated). All other forms of expression would be considered nonverbal expressions of emotion, including:
  - Facial expressions
  - Gestures
  - Body language
  - Tone of voice
- Assign Worksheet 6.1.

Debriefing Questions
- Put four columns on the board for listing (1) positive verbal expression, (2) positive nonverbal expression, (3) negative verbal expression, and (4) negative nonverbal expression. More than likely there will be more nonverbal expressions of negative emotions than verbal ones. If so, ask the first question shown in the following list. If not, skip to the next question.
  - Why is verbal expression of negative emotion so much more difficult than nonverbal? Do you feel more vulnerable if you acknowledge emotions with words? Do you think

it's unnecessary to use emotion words if you express emotion nonverbally? (Instructor's Note: You can use these last two questions as an "agree-disagree" activity.)

- What other patterns do you see in our data?
- Think about someone you know who is very good at expressing his or her emotions *verbally*. How do you (or others) react to that person when he or she expresses emotions verbally?
- See the reflection questions at the end of the worksheet.

Worksheet 6.1: Observing Emotions

Name:

Observe other people for one day. Watch for either verbal or nonverbal expression of the following emotions: anger, frustration, sadness, anxiety, fear, happiness, excitement, disgust, surprise. If possible, try to include some observation of children age six or younger.

Describe what the person did or said	Verbal, nonverbal, or both?	Positive or negative emotion?
Example: Student slams books down on desk (nonverbal)	Nonverbal	Negative
Example: Parent claps and yells "Great play" in an excited voice when her child scores a goal in soccer	Nonverbal (clapping); nonverbal ("great play"); for this to be verbal, the parent would have had to have said something like "I'm so excited" or "I'm so happy for you"	Positive
Example: "I'm so frustrated with my coach. She's always yelling at me."	Verbal	Negative

Reflection Questions

1. What types of patterns did you observe? For example, were there . . .
   - Differences in the frequency of verbal and nonverbal expressions?
   - Gender or age differences in verbal and nonverbal expression?
   - Differences in how positive emotions are expressed versus negative emotions?
2. How did others react to verbal versus nonverbal expression of emotion?

Activity 6.2
Observing Your Emotions

EI Dimensions Targeted: Emotional Expression, Emotional Self-Awareness

Brief Description/Objective: Students will observe and record their own verbal and nonverbal expressions of emotion throughout the day.

Planning the Activity

Time Expected
- Worksheet: 20 minutes throughout the day
- Reflection Questions: 15 minutes
- In-Class Debrief: 10 minutes

Materials
- Worksheet 6.2 from *The Student EQ Edge: Student Workbook*
- Board or flip chart and markers
- *The Student EQ Edge: Emotional Intelligence and Your Academic and Personal Success*

Facilitating the Activity

Directions
- If you did *not* assign Worksheet 6.1, make sure to go over the difference between verbal and nonverbal expression of emotion before assigning the activity.
- Assign Worksheet 6.2

Debriefing Questions
- Put four columns on the board for listing (1) positive verbal expression, (2) positive nonverbal expression, (3) negative verbal expression, and (4) negative nonverbal expression. More than likely, there will be more nonverbal expression of negative emotions than verbal. If so, ask the first question shown in the following list. If not, skip to the next question.
  - Why is verbal expression of emotion so much more difficult than nonverbal? Do you feel more vulnerable if you acknowledge emotions with words? Explore all of the reasons that students suggest.
  - What other patterns do you see in the class data?
  - What people, cultural norms, or other factors influenced how you learned to express emotions?
- See the reflection questions at the end of the worksheet.

Worksheet 6.2: Observing Your Emotions

Name:

Observe yourself for one day. Every time you hear or see yourself express an emotion, record it in the following chart.

Describe your emotional expression	Verbal, nonverbal or both?	Positive, negative, or both?
Example: "I'm so *excited* about our weekend plans" (said with a big smile)	Verbal, nonverbal	Positive
Example: Slamming a book down on the desk	Nonverbal	Negative

Reflection Questions

1. What types of patterns did you observe? For example, were there . . .
   - Differences in the frequency of verbal and nonverbal expressions?
   - Differences in how you expressed positive versus negative emotions?
   - Differences in how others reacted to verbal versus nonverbal expression of emotion? Or in how they reacted to your expressions of positive and negative emotion?
2. What was your reaction to monitoring your emotional expression for a day?

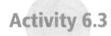

Activity 6.3
Follow the Leader

EI Dimensions Targeted: Emotional Expression, Happiness

Brief Description/Objective: Students will create emotional contagion in others, thus understanding the impact of their emotional expression on others.

Planning the Activity

Time Expected
- Worksheet (including leading the discussions): 25 minutes
- Reflection Questions: 15 minutes
- In-Class Debrief: 15 minutes

Materials
- Worksheet 6.3 from *The Student EQ Edge: Student Workbook*
- Board or flip chart and markers
- *The Student EQ Edge: Emotional Intelligence and Your Academic and Personal Success*

Facilitating the Activity

Directions
- Briefly explain the concept of emotional contagion to students. Emotional contagion occurs whenever one person's expression of emotion affects the emotional reactions of others in the group. Leaders—whether formally elected or those who emerge as leaders within a group—have a significant impact on how others in the group feel. If the leader is happy and positive, the chances are much better that the group will take on this emotion. Unfortunately, the opposite is also true.
- If you choose to do this activity in class instead of assigning it for homework, do not discuss emotional contagion first. Instead, ask one student to be the discussion leader and another to be the observer and give only those two students the instructions. Other students in the class will be unaware of the purpose of the activity and therefore react the way they normally would to others' emotional expressions.
- Assign Worksheet 6.3 (If you did not assign Worksheet 6.1 or 6.2, review the difference between verbal and nonverbal expression of emotion as covered in the directions to Activity 6.1).

Debriefing Questions
- What implications does emotional contagion have for leaders and followers? Think of specific examples such as teacher-student, boss-employee, president-citizen, chair–committee member, or coach-player.
- How do you think positive emotional contagion relates to performance or productivity?
- See the reflection questions at the end of the worksheet.

Worksheet 6.3: Follow the Leader

Name:

Part 1

Because emotions are contagious, we can influence others to have more positive or negative emotions by our expressions of emotion. Pair up with a classmate; one of you will be the *discussion leader* and the other will be the *observer.* Then gather two or three additional friends and ask them to help you for 10 minutes with a class project. Explain that all they have to do is talk with you about their summer plans or what courses they plan to take next semester. Or pick a different topic of your choice. You should pick a topic that is neutral (strong feelings one way or the other are not likely) and a topic that would be easy for your group to discuss.

Discussion Leader. *Your job is to try to positively influence the emotion of the group.* During the 10 minutes, you should smile frequently, talk with an excited tone of voice, sit with open body language, make positive comments about your friends' comments, and use words like "happy" and "excited." Make sure your verbal and nonverbal emotions are congruent!

Observer. *Your job is to record the facial expressions and verbal emotional expressions of the other group members.* Sit where you can observe their faces and hear what they say but they cannot see what you are writing down. At one-minute intervals during the conversation, record people's facial expressions in the charts that follow. Also, record anything people say that is positive or negative; for example, "That sounds like fun" or "That sounds bad." Record both positive and negative expressions of emotion throughout the conversation.

Directions for the Conversation

1. The *discussion leader* should *open the conversation with a neutral tone* of voice and facial expression. Explain that you will have a 10-minute conversation about everyone's summer plans (or what courses they will take next semester). Let them know that the observer will be taking notes and that you'll let them know more about what you are doing after the discussion. (The observer should record verbal and nonverbal expressions of emotion during this time of introducing the activity.)

2. Then tell the group members you'll begin by sharing your plans. *Change your emotional expression at this point to positive!* As you tell them your plans, smile, use an excited tone of voice, and use emotion words like "excited" and "happy." Make sure you are sitting with open body language and leaning slightly forward. (The observer should be recording other people's reactions as you talk.)

3. Then ask someone else to share his or her plans. *Again, use positive emotional expression*, both verbal and nonverbal—nod in agreement, smile, sit with open body language, and say things like "That sounds like fun" (but only if that's true!). In other words, at every opportunity when you can genuinely do so, convey positive emotions. (The observer should be scanning the group members during this time and recording their reactions.)

4. Continue the conversation in this manner for about 10 minutes or until the conversation reaches a natural end. (The observer should be recording emotional expression this whole time.)

Part 2

5. Repeat the entire activity, but this time *change your emotional expression to negative* (frustrated, angry, scared, and sad). You can use the same group of people as participated earlier or you can gather a new group of friends for the second conversation. *If you use the same group, choose a new topic.*

Directions for the Conversation

1. The *discussion leader* should *open the conversation with a neutral tone* of voice and facial expression. Explain that you will have a 10-minute conversation about everyone's summer plans (or what courses they will take next semester). Let them know that the observer will be taking notes and that you'll let them know more about what you are doing after the discussion. (The observer should record verbal and nonverbal expressions of emotion during this time of introducing the activity.)

2. Then tell the group members you'll begin by sharing your plans. *Change your emotional expression at this point to negative.* As you tell them your plans, frown, use an angry or frustrated tone of voice, and use emotion words like "frustrated," "mad," or "scared." Sit with your arms folded, lean slightly back, and frown. Use negative phrases such as "I dread . . ." (The observer should be recording other people's reactions as you talk.)

3. Then ask someone else to share his or her plans. *Again, use negative emotional expression*, both verbal and nonverbal—shake your head as if saying "No" or "That's no good," sit with closed body language, and say things like "That's no fun" or "That sounds bad" (but only if that's true!). In other words, at every opportunity when you can *genuinely* do so, convey some type of negative emotion. (The observer should be scanning the group members during this time and recording their reactions.)

4. Continue the conversation in this manner for at least 10 minutes or until the conversation reaches a natural end. (The observer should be recording emotional expression this whole time.)

5. At the end of the second discussion, tell your friends the purpose of the activity and note their reactions.

Emotional Reactions to Positive Emotions: Verbal and Nonverbal

Time	Friend #1	Friend #2	Friend #3
During directions			
At first expression of positive emotion by group leader			
1 minute later			
1 minute later			

Emotional Reactions to Negative Emotions: Verbal and Nonverbal

Time	Friend #1	Friend #2	Friend #3
During directions			
At first expression of negative emotion by group leader			
1 minute later			
1 minute later			

Reflection Questions

1. Compare and contrast the data on your two charts.
   a. How many total positive and negative expressions did you have during the positive and negative conversations?
   b. How long did it take other group members to begin responding to the leader's emotions?
   c. Which type of emotion—positive or negative—was picked up faster by other group members?
   d. What other observations can you make about your data?
2. After you told people the purpose of the conversation, what reactions did they have?

Activity 6.4
"I" Messages

EI Dimensions Targeted: Emotional Expression, Assertiveness

Brief Description/Objective: Students will learn how to construct and deliver an "I" message that conveys their verbal emotions.

Planning the Activity

Time Expected
- Worksheet Part 1: 10 minutes; Worksheet Part 2: 10 minutes
- Reflection Questions: 20 minutes (10 minutes each for Part 1 and Part 2)
- In-Class Debrief: 10 minutes (possibly longer, if you assigned Part 2 of the activity)

Materials
- Worksheet 6.4 from *The Student EQ Edge: Student Workbook*
- Board or flip chart and markers
- *The Student EQ Edge: Emotional Intelligence and Your Academic and Personal Success*

Facilitating the Activity

Directions
- Make sure to review "I" messages with students prior to assigning the worksheet. Students often believe that statements such as "I feel like you are being clingy" or "I feel like you're being unfair" qualify as an "I" message. A true "I" message involves the speaker owning his or her feelings, a behavioral description of what caused the feelings, and acknowledgment of how the situation is affecting him or her. Using the pronoun "I" does not ensure that someone is using a true "I" message. See Worksheet 6.4 for more information about how to construct an effective "I" message.
- Assign Worksheet 6.4 (make sure to clarify whether you want students to complete Parts 1 and 2, or just Part 1).

Debriefing Questions
- If using "I" messages is so important, why don't more people do it?
- How can you tell if you need to use an "I" message?
- See the reflection questions at the end of the worksheet.

Worksheet 6.4: "I" Messages

Name:

Using "I" messages is an effective way to convey strong emotions in an appropriate way. The formula for effective "I" messages is simple:

"I feel [insert emotion word here] because [describe the behaviors of others or situation that made you feel this way] and the effect on me is [describe what impact that emotion is having on your emotions and behavior]."

For example, let's suppose you are angry at a family member because that person embarrassed you in front of friends by telling them you were grounded. An "I" message might sound like this:

"I'm mad at you because you told my friends that I was grounded and that embarrassed me so much it makes me not want to bring my friends home with me."

Here's another example: let's suppose you're frustrated because the directions for an assignment are unclear.

"I'm frustrated because I don't understand the instructions you provided for the assignment and that's made me not want to work on getting it done."

And let's take a positive emotion:

"I'm so happy because I got my acceptance letter today and all I want to do is go out and celebrate."

Part 1. Formulating "I" Messages

1. Think about a time you experienced each of the following emotions. Briefly describe the situation in the appropriate box.
2. Write down an "I" message related to each situation in its corresponding box. Write in the name of the person receiving your "I" message.

Anger

Situation:	"I" message:

Note: The recipient of the "I" message should be the person you were angry with.

Sadness

Situation:	"I" message:

Note: If a person did something to make you sad, you should direct your "I" message to that person. If a situation is making you sad (for example, a family member got diagnosed with a serious illness), your "I" message can be directed to a good friend, another family member, or someone else you trust.

Happiness or Excitement

Situation:	"I" message:

Note: If a person did something that made you happy, you should direct your "I" message to that person. If a situation is making you happy (for example, your team just won a big game), your "I" message can be directed to a good friend, another family member, or someone else you trust.

Reflection Questions

1. Would you be willing to deliver any or all of the "I" messages you wrote above to someone? Explain why or why not.
2. Which part of the "I" message formula did you have the most trouble developing? Why was that part more difficult for you?
3. Pretend someone is mad at you about something. Which of the following reactions would you want the person to choose?
   a. Give me the silent treatment for a few days and then pretend like nothing is wrong.
   b. Yell at me until all the person's anger was vented but without an opportunity for us to talk through the situation.
   c. Try to pretend like nothing is wrong, but it comes through anyway through sarcasm, facial expressions, and such.
   d. Talk to me about why he or she is mad but without yelling at me. (Note: If you choose this option, you should assume the person begins the conversation with some type of "I" message.)

Explain why you picked your chosen option. What strategy do you use with others?

Part 2. Using Your "I" Messages

Take one of the "I" messages you developed for Part 1 of this worksheet and deliver the "I" message to the appropriate person. Deliver the message in person rather than by text, email, or phone. (Remember how important nonverbal expression of emotion is? It's much harder to understand someone else's nonverbal expression of emotion unless we are interacting face-to-face!) If you are not comfortable delivering one of the messages you developed for Worksheet 6.4, then develop a new "I" message and write it here.

Reflection Questions

1. What emotions did you feel *before* you opened a conversation using an "I" message? What about *after* you had done so?
2. Analyze how the conversation went. How was the "I" message received by the other person? What type of conversation followed? Were you satisfied with how things went?

Activity 6.5
TV Emotions

EI Dimensions Targeted: Emotional Expression

Brief Description/Objective: Students will observe the verbal and nonverbal expression of emotion of a main character on a television show and compare that to real life.

Planning the Activity

Time Expected
- Worksheet: 25 minutes
- Reflection Questions: 10 minutes
- In-Class Debrief: 10 minutes

Materials
- Worksheet 6.5 from *The Student EQ Edge: Student Workbook*
- Board or flip chart and markers
- *The Student EQ Edge: Emotional Intelligence and Your Academic and Personal Success*
- TV and VCR/DVD player if you want to show a television clip in class
- TV clip identified if you plan to do this activity in class

Facilitating the Activity

Directions
- Assign Worksheet 6.5.
- Remind students about the differences between verbal and nonverbal expressions.

Debriefing Questions
- What types of differences did you identify between observing another person (see Activity 6.1) and observing a TV character? What elements of a TV show might make it easier for characters to express emotion?
- See the reflection questions at the end of the worksheet.

Worksheet 6.5: TV Emotions

Name:

Watch a comedy (sitcom) on TV such as *Glee*, *Modern Family*, *30 Rock*, or *The Office*. Pick one of the main characters from the show, and as you watch, tally the times the character engages in each of the verbal or nonverbal expressions of emotion in the following charts. Fill in the blank cells with any additional behaviors observed and the number of times each occurred.

Character's Name/TV Show:

Nonverbal Expressions of Emotion

Positive Expression	Tally	Negative Expression	Tally
Smiles, laughs		Frowns	
Nods approval		Makes other type of negative facial expression	
Leans toward the other person		Rolls eyes	
Sits or stands with open body posture		Sits or stands with closed body posture (arms folded in front, hands on hips)	
Uses pleasant tone of voice (warm, appropriate volume)		Uses unpleasant tone of voice (for example, shrill, too loud, or sarcastic)	
Makes eye contact when talking to someone		Looks away when talking to someone	
Touches the person (for example, a hug or hand on shoulder)		Interrupts	

Verbal Expressions of Emotion (listen for emotion words!)

Positive Expression	Tally	Negative Expression	Tally
Happiness		Angry, irritated, upset	
Excitement		Frustrated	
Joy or love		Sad, depressed, down	
		Nervous, scared, anxious, afraid, worried	
		Disgusted	

Reflection Questions

1. Count how many tally marks you have in each of the four areas and record your results here:
   - Positive nonverbal
   - Negative nonverbal
   - Positive verbal
   - Negative verbal
2. What is your reaction to the patterns you found? How do they compare to estimates that about 90 percent of emotional expression is communicated nonverbally and 10 percent or less is communicated verbally?
3. Why do you think it's easier for most people to express emotions nonverbally than verbally?

Activity 6.6

Self-Development Plan for Emotional Expression

The directions and template for students to create a self-development plan appear in Appendix D of this *Facilitation and Activity Guide*. *The Student EQ Edge: Student Workbook* contains a template for developing emotional expression in Chapter 6.

Activity 6.7

Case Study—Emotional Expression

See Chapter 2 to assign a case study relevant to emotional expression. Chapter 2 of *The Student EQ Edge: Student Workbook* contains all of the same case studies.

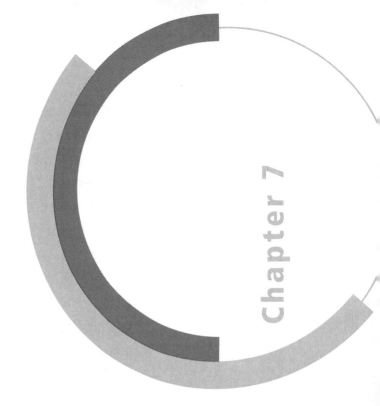

Chapter 7

Independence

What is independence? Independence involves being willing to act on your own, make your own decisions, and generally be free of relying too much on others. Independence does *not* require students to ignore others' advice or never seek their opinion. Instead, students should seek others' opinions purposefully, particularly when the decision has long-term implications or when their academic or personal well-being is at stake. Emphasize the value of taking advantage of the resources the school offers, whether it be a research librarian or a counselor. Independence also involves the willingness to assume responsibility, freeing yourself from overdependence on others to approve decisions, take action for you, or provide more support than needed. Some students ask for or expect too much support, such as in asking a faculty member to email their grades when the students could look them up online.

By understanding different ways they can be dependent or independent, students can realize many benefits—academic, financial, emotional, social, and physical. Many high school and college students seek different levels of independence across these areas. For example, a high school senior may yearn to leave home to go to college, often reminding parents that he or she "can't wait" to leave home (physical independence), yet still want parents to provide spending money (financial dependence).

The student may seek emotional independence one day (instructing parents not to ask questions about what the student is doing) and the next day call asking for support to make a minor decision. An adult student often is completely financially independent but still may rely on family for emotional support. The appropriate level of independence in each area changes as we age and as our circumstances change. *The Student EQ Edge: Emotional Intelligence and Your Academic and Personal Success* (Stein, Book, & Kanoy, 2013) deals mainly with social and emotional forms of independence, but students will benefit by considering other areas as well.

Can a student be too independent? Very high levels of independence come with certain consequences. In fact, research by Mann and Kanoy (2010) found that independence negatively correlated with student success in college! By not asking for help even when they need it, not taking advantage of the resources available to support them, and not seeking the advice of faculty members, highly independent students harm their chances of success.

STUDENT LEARNING OUTCOMES

Students will:

- Identify their tendencies to work alone or be supported by others
- Take action by themselves and examine how they react
- Identify the short-term and long-term costs of excessive dependency on others
- Create a plan for individual improvement related to independence

SUGGESTED READINGS, MOVIES, AND TELEVISION SHOWS

- *The Student EQ Edge: Emotional Intelligence and Your Academic and Personal Success*, Chapter 7

Movies

- *Erin Brockovich*—Scene 11, "Researching the Pro Bono Case"—Erin strikes out on her own to investigate why health care information is included in a real estate contract.
- *Odd Girl Out*—Throughout the movie, Vanessa clings to her best friend Stacey even though Stacey is rejecting her; also, an African-American girl who befriends Vanessa models healthy independence throughout the movie.
- *The Blind Side*—Scene 4, "Family News," and Scene 5, "Just for One Night"—These two scenes show Michael taking care of himself by going to the laundromat and finding a warm place to sleep when he is homeless.

Television Shows

- *Modern Family*– Episode 54, "Go Bullfrogs"—Phil and Haley visit Phil's alma mater. Haley tests her independence, and Phil recognizes that she is growing up.
- Reality TV shows designed to create stress (for example, *The Amazing Race*, *Survivor*, *The Bachelor*, *Top Chef*, and *Celebrity Apprentice*) are good choices. Focus on parts of episodes in which participants have to make decisions or take action. Do they ponder too long, seeking lots of advice? Or do they wait for someone else in the group to take charge? Maybe they act too frequently by themselves, creating too much distance between themselves and other group members.

PLANNING YOUR CLASS

50–60 Minute Class

Assign Activities 7.1 and 7.2 for homework. Make sure students understand the different categories of action or decision for Activity 7.1. Have them complete both activities before talking about independence in class. Debrief Activities 7.1 and 7.2. Begin class with a discussion of four types of independence: academic, social/emotional, physical, and financial. Then show the YouTube clip that is part of Activity 7.3 and debrief it. Challenge students to reflect on the relative amount of independence they want and the advantages of independence and disadvantages of dependence.

3–4 Hour Workshop

Assign Activities 7.1 and 7.2 to do for homework. Make sure students understand the different categories of action or decision for Activity 7.1. Have them complete both activities before talking about independence in class. Debrief Activities 7.1 and 7.2. Then begin a discussion of four types of independence: academic, social/emotional, physical, and financial. If your students are typical young adults, they see little correlation among these areas of independence—that is, they sometimes want full physical independence and as much financial dependence as adults are willing to offer! Activity 7.3 helps make this point. Focus on the long-term consequences of dependence. Then have them watch a TV show (Activity 7.4) and analyze the implications of various actions. Activity 7.6 should be completed next to ensure adequate time for completion. Then wrap up with Activity 7.5. This will generate lots of discussion about parenting styles and how adults treat male and female children differently with regard to physical independence, and much more!

Activity List

Activity #	Activity Name	Brief Description and Activity Notes
7.1	Private Eye	Students gain awareness of their tendencies related to independence, including physical, emotional, social, and financial.
7.2	By Yourself	Students complete an activity by themselves that they would normally complete with others.
7.3	Please Do This for Me!	Students watch a YouTube clip (link provided) and analyze the dependency of 18-year-old Anthony on his mother.
7.4	Reality TV—Too Needy, Too Alone, or Just Right?	Students watch a sitcom and determine the independence level of various characters. Do characters gain some short-term benefit from dependence? What do the adults do to foster dependence versus independence?
7.5	On My Own	Students analyze various scenarios and decide how much independence is age appropriate. The reasoning provided is more relevant than the age chosen.
7.6	Self-Development Plan for Independence	Students create strategies for self-development related to independence skills.
7.7	Case Study—Independence	Students analyze the behavior of a student who faces challenges related to independence.

Activity 7.1
Private Eye

EI Dimensions Targeted: Independence, Emotional Self-Awareness

Brief Description/Objective: Students will observe and record their levels of independence in different types of situations.

Planning the Activity

Time Expected
- Worksheet: 15 minutes
- Reflection Questions: 10 minutes
- In-Class Debrief: 10 minutes

Materials
- Worksheet 7.1 from *The Student EQ Edge: Student Workbook*
- Board or flip chart and markers
- *The Student EQ Edge: Emotional Intelligence and Your Academic and Personal Success*

Facilitating the Activity

Directions
Assign Worksheet 7.1. Go over the different types of situations that call for independence; these different types of independence are outlined on Worksheet 7.1

Debriefing Questions
- Conduct an agree-disagree exercise with students based on the following question: "Parents should let me be physically independent before I am ready to be financially or emotionally independent." Have students representing the two sides converse with each other. Redo the activity and have students pretend they are parents answering the same question. More than likely the students will understand that adults may have different views. This can lead to a fruitful conversation, which may help the students see the need for gradual change in independence levels.
- See the reflection questions at the end of the worksheet.

Worksheet 7.1: Private Eye

Name:

Pretend you are a private investigator and your job is to observe yourself. During one 24-hour period, write down all of the times you acted independently or dependently. Listed here are four main areas of independence and examples of independent behavior:

- *Academic.* Examples: completing projects without asking the professor for help, studying alone instead of with a tutor or study group, making class choice decisions without consulting your advisor. (Note: Students who are too independent do *not* perform as well in college as those who have more moderate amounts of independence. They don't seek help even when they clearly need it!)
- *Financial.* Examples: earning your spending money, not asking others to bail you out if you overspend or bounce a check, opening and managing your own bank account, understanding how your credit card works.
- *Physical.* Examples: driving on a long trip by yourself, spending weeks or months away from home without getting homesick, being comfortable staying by yourself.
- *Social/emotional.* Examples: making important decisions without needing approval or reassurance from others; handling challenging situations with teachers, coaches, or bosses without others doing it for you; standing up to group pressure when you disagree with members' behaviors.

Fill in the following chart, following the examples. Make sure you include at least one of each area of independence, even if you have to observe yourself for more than one day.

Situation	Type of independence	Independence or dependence?
Picked a major without getting family approval	Social/emotional	Independence
Asked parents for additional money to cover overdrawn bank account	Financial	Dependence
Found directions and drove alone to get my driver's license renewed	Physical	Independence
Went to see teacher four times for additional help on the same assignment	Academic	Dependence

Reflection Questions

1. What types of patterns do you see in terms of how much you consult others for various types of decisions?
2. Whose opinion or support is important to you, and does that vary by the type of decision?
3. What is your overall comfort level with acting independently?
4. What was your level of independence during this observation period? How much did observing your own behavior change how often you sought others' opinions or approval?
5. How did your emotional reactions to various situations relate to your level of independence?

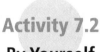

Activity 7.2

By Yourself

EI Dimensions Targeted: Independence, Emotional Self-Awareness

Brief Description/Objective: Students will engage in a behavior that they would normally rely on others to do with them or for them.

Planning the Activity

Time Expected
- Worksheet/Activity: 10 minutes to 2 hours (determined by the activity chosen)
- Reflection Questions: 15–20 minutes
- In-Class Debrief: 10 minutes

Materials
- Worksheet 7.2 from *The Student EQ Edge: Student Workbook*
- Board or flip chart and markers
- *The Student EQ Edge: Emotional Intelligence and Your Academic and Personal Success*

Facilitating the Activity

Directions
- Assign Worksheet 7.2, stressing to students that they should *not* do anything dangerous or emotionally risky; the purpose of this activity is to stretch their comfort level with independence but not to *exceed* it or engage in unsafe behavior.
- Make sure you assign this activity one week ahead of the due date.

Debriefing Questions
- Ask students to explain how they chose their activity. Were they trying to pick something very safe? Something that stretched them more? How did the potential reaction of others in the situation influence them?
- See the reflection questions at the end of the worksheet.

Worksheet 7.2: By Yourself

Name:

Do something by yourself that you would normally do with others and that will make you somewhat uncomfortable to do by yourself. Go eat in a restaurant, go shopping, or go to a movie. Go talk to a faculty member about a class if that's not something you would normally do. Do *not* tell others ahead of time why you are doing this alone. *Do not pick an unsafe activity, just one you normally would not do alone.* Then answer the reflection questions below.

Reflection Questions

1. What did you do by yourself that you would normally do with others?
2. What emotions did you experience as you were deciding what to do and right before the activity? Why do you think you experienced those emotions?
3. How did you feel after you completed the activity? Explain why you felt this way.
4. (Optional) Tell someone who knows you well what you did by yourself, but do *not* tell that person why you did the activity alone. What was the person's reaction?

Activity 7.3
Please Do This for Me!

EI Dimensions Targeted: Independence, Self-Actualization

Brief Description/Objective: Students will watch a YouTube clip of an 18-year-old who dropped out of college and sits at home playing video games. This clip illuminates the costs of too much dependence in a way that is safe for students to discuss.

Planning the Activity

Time Expected
- Worksheet and YouTube video: 5 minutes
- Reflection Questions: 10 minutes
- In-Class Debrief: 15 minutes

Materials
- Worksheet 7.3 from *The Student EQ Edge: Student Workbook*
- Board or flip chart and markers
- *The Student EQ Edge: Emotional Intelligence and Your Academic and Personal Success*
- Internet connection

Facilitating the Activity

Directions
- Determine whether you want to show the video clip in class or prefer that students view it on their own.
- Assign Worksheet 7.3 for students to use as reflection questions.

Debriefing Questions
- Ask your students to write a life scenario for Anthony at age 30. Where will he be living? What type of job will he have? What type of relationship will he have with his mother?
- Then ask them to answer the same questions about an area they identified for themselves as "too dependent" on the worksheet.
- See the reflection questions at the end of the worksheet.

Worksheet 7.3: Please Do This for Me!

Name:

Go to the following link found on YouTube, for a video called "Helicopter Parents: The lengths parents go to pamper and please their kids," http://www.youtube.com/watch?v=ufEfeDP7vBA&feature=related

Part 1

Watch the YouTube clip about Anthony. Record at least three of his actions that show dependence on his mother. Then write down the consequences of those actions for Anthony. (Note: The possible long-term consequences are not evident in the YouTube clip, so use your imagination!)

Anthony's Actions	Short-Term Results	Possible Long-Term Consequences for Anthony
1.		
2.		
3.		

Part 2

Think about behaviors you've engaged in over the past year that may have been too dependent. Maybe you asked your family members to talk with a teacher or coach for you, or fill out a form for you, or give you extra money, or take care of your car for you instead of taking care of it yourself. The action could have involved friends, such as choosing what universities to apply to based on where your friends applied or not going on a school-sponsored trip unless a friend went with you. Choose the most significant incident and answer the following reflection questions.

Reflection Questions

Describe the situation in which you acted with dependence. Then answer these questions.

1. What did you do to promote your dependence on someone else?
2. How did this benefit you in the short term?
3. How might this benefit you (or not benefit you) in the long term? Explain your answer.

Activity 7.4

Reality TV—Too Needy, Too Alone, or Just Right?

EI Dimensions Targeted: Independence; other EI scales are possible based on the TV episode selected.

Brief Description/Objective: Students will observe three different characters in a sitcom, watching for expressions of independence and dependence.

Planning the Activity

Time Expected
- Worksheet and TV Show: 30 minutes
- Reflection Questions: 10 minutes
- In-Class Debrief: 10 minutes

Materials
- Worksheet 7.4 from *The Student EQ Edge: Student Workbook*
- Board or flip chart and markers
- *The Student EQ Edge: Emotional Intelligence and Your Academic and Personal Success*

Facilitating the Activity

Directions
- Assign Worksheet 7.4.
- If you have a specific episode you want students to watch, make sure you make the link available.

Debriefing Questions:
- How well does the television program portray the likely "real world" outcomes of dependence or independence for people in a similar situation?
- See the reflection questions at the end of the worksheet.

Worksheet 7.4: Reality TV—Too Needy, Too Alone, or Just Right?

Name:

1. Watch an episode of reality TV in which people are forced to work in groups or where one person has a lot of power and control over other people. Good shows to watch include *Survivor*, *The Celebrity Apprentice*, *The Amazing Race*, *Scare Tactics*, or *The Bachelor*. Feel free to watch a different show as long as three or more people have to interact in some way.

2. Pick three characters (or three different scenarios within the episode): one time when a person was too dependent on others, one time when a person was too independent, and one time when a person exhibited appropriate independence. Summarize what each of the characters did that caused you to reach the conclusion you did.
   Person/Situation A (too dependent):

   Person/Situation B (too independent):

   Person/Situation C (appropriately independent):

3. What was the outcome for each person?
4. If you had been in this situation, which character would you most resemble? Explain your answer.

Activity 7.5
On My Own

EI Dimensions Targeted: Independence

Brief Description/Objective: Students will choose ages at which they believe it is appropriate for a child, teen, or young adult to engage in a behavior.

Planning the Activity

Time Expected
- Worksheet: 15 minutes
- Reflection Questions: 10 minutes
- In-Class Debrief: 10 minutes

Materials
- Worksheet 7.5 from *The Student EQ Edge: Student Workbook*
- Board or flip chart and markers
- *The Student EQ Edge: Emotional Intelligence and Your Academic and Personal Success*

Facilitating the Activity

Directions
- Assign Worksheet 7.5.
- Before conducting the class debrief, calculate the average age that students in the class chose for a particular activity. Look for patterns in answers based on gender, age, ethnicity, and birth order, as well as what they assumed about the child, teen, or young adult in question. For example, are male students more likely to indicate a male can drive on an interstate at an earlier age than a female? Do female students agree or disagree that a driver's gender should be a factor in determining when that person is capable of driving alone?

Debriefing Questions
- After you have calculated the class averages (include the range of answers), ask students which of the answers would be likely to change the most if everyone was asked to think about just males or just females when choosing the appropriate age. Discuss how stereotypes might affect these decisions.
- See the reflection questions at the end of the worksheet.

Worksheet 7.5: On My Own

Name:

- Fill in the following chart based on what you think would be an appropriate age for a parent to consider letting the child engage in the activity by himself or herself. Assume the child, teen, or young adult has the skill needed to do the activity or *should* have the skill by this age.
- In the space for Other #1, list something you felt capable of doing at an earlier age than you were actually allowed to do it.
- In the space for Other #2, list something you did not feel capable of doing but were forced to do at an earlier age than you would have liked.

Activity	Appropriate age	Brief explanation for the age you chose
Pay for your cell phone		
Make your own doctor's appointment		
Open and manage your own checking account		
Talk with a teacher about a bad grade you made and what you need to do differently		
Drive on an interstate highway (assuming you got your driver's license at age 16)		
Stay home alone for one hour for the first time		
Spend the night alone in your house over the weekend while your parents travel		
Choose what courses to take the next semester		
Get your car inspected		
Make your own dinner		
Do your own laundry		
Walk five minutes to a friend's house on a sidewalk in the neighborhood (assuming the neighborhood is safe)		
Other #1		
Other #2		

Reflection Questions

1. Compare the ages you listed to the decisions your family made about you. What trends do you notice?
2. Compare your answers to what a friend or classmate answered. What conclusions can you draw from the similarities and differences between your answers?
3. Consider your response for Other #1. What was your reaction to being told you could not do this yet? In retrospect, do you agree or disagree with the decision?
4. Consider your response for Other #2. What was your reaction and how did things turn out? In retrospect, do you agree or disagree with the decision?

Activity 7.6

Self-Development Plan for Independence

The directions and template for students to create a self-development plan appear in Appendix D of this *Facilitation and Activity Guide*. *The Student EQ Edge: Student Workbook* contains a template for developing independence in Chapter 7.

Activity 7.7

Case Study—Independence

See Chapter 2 to assign a case study relevant to independence. Chapter 2 of *The Student EQ Edge: Student Workbook* contains all of the same case studies.

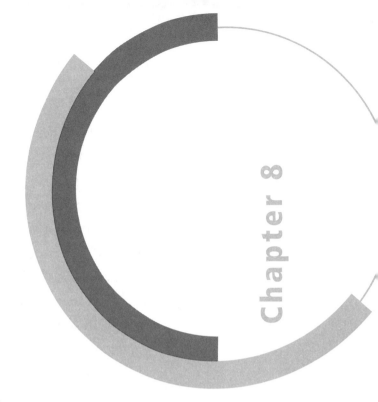

Assertiveness

What is assertiveness? There are very few other emotional intelligence skills that people might view negatively. Assertiveness, though, creates different reactions, possibly because of social, cultural, or gender messages we receive. Author Korrel taught for 30 years at an all-female college. One year Korrel had students practice being assertive by telling her one way in which she could improve a class. Several students could comfortably make eye contact and suggest an improvement. Most, though, began with a compliment about the class before providing the suggestion, did not make eye contact, or stammered a bit. One student even talked for over a minute and never even offered a suggestion for improvement! Instead, she talked about all the things she liked and just asked that we do more of them, but then corrected herself and said she couldn't think of anything to give up so she knew we couldn't do more with no additional time. So it is with assertiveness with some people. They believe that giving feedback, standing up for themselves, or stating an opinion is at worst wrong and at best destined to make others uncomfortable. Although understanding that someone else *might* become uncomfortable does show empathy, a person with lots of empathy and little assertiveness is likely to be taken advantage of by some people.

Assertiveness comprises three dimensions: expressing feelings, expressing thoughts or beliefs, and standing up for yourself. So every time you state an opinion, ask for something you need or want, give feedback to others, or say "No," you are being assertive.

Spend time helping students generate reasons why assertiveness is beneficial in each of those situations. For example, a worker who can never say "No" may get taken advantage of by colleagues or a boss. The partner in a relationship who can never state what he or she needs is destined to be less happy. The first challenge is to build comfort with assertiveness; the second is to develop assertiveness skills.

Can someone be too assertive? Remember, higher assertiveness does not equate to aggressiveness! But a person highly skilled in assertiveness could be perceived as intimidating if that assertiveness is not balanced by empathy (understanding others' perspectives) and a willingness to adapt behaviors or decisions to others' input (flexibility).

STUDENT LEARNING OUTCOMES

Students will:

- Recognize assertive, passive, or aggressive behavior in others and in themselves
- Understand their comfort level with assertiveness and situations in which they are likely to be assertive
- Practice being assertive in conversations with others
- Describe the consequences of being aggressive or passive

SUGGESTED READINGS, MOVIES, AND TELEVISION SHOWS

- *The Student EQ Edge: Emotional Intelligence and Your Academic and Personal Success*, Chapter 8

Movies
- *Erin Brockovich*—Scene 6, "Job Search"—Erin goes to Ed's office and persuades him to offer her a job.
- *Odd Girl Out*—The last scene—Vanessa finally confronts Stacey about the bullying and gets support from many of her classmates.

- *The Blind Side*—Scene 16, "Protect the Family"—Leigh Ann goes onto the field without the coach's permission, to appeal to Michael's ability to protect others.

Television Shows

- *30 Rock*—Episode 6, "Jack Meets Dennis"—Near the end of the episode, Liz has a hard time breaking up with Dennis.
- *Modern Family*—Episode 52, "Door to Door"—Claire heads to a city council meeting to request a stop sign for her neighborhood.
- *Modern Family*—Each of the three married couples on the show has a different pattern of interaction:
  - Gloria and Jay—Gloria is very assertive. Jay typically remains assertive, neither giving in to Gloria nor resorting to aggression when she strays from assertiveness and becomes demanding.
  - Claire and Phil—The husband in this partnership is more likely to be passive, especially the more assertive his wife becomes. Contrast their relationship to Gloria and Jay, who both tend to be assertive.
  - Mitchell and Cameron—This couple sometimes resorts to more indirect forms of communication that can lead to passive behavior by both. Or sometimes one is assertive and the other more passive. And occasionally you'll witness passive-aggressive behavior, but they always identify it and rectify their behavior (all within 30 minutes)!

PLANNING YOUR CLASS

50–60 Minute Class

Assign activities 8.1 and 8.5 for homework. Debrief Activity 8.1 to make sure students accurately distinguished among assertiveness, aggressiveness, and passivity. Show the YouTube clip from Activity 8.2. Choosing the third option for how to facilitate the activity will give students practice with assertive behavior. Next, have students complete two or three of the "I" messages from

Activity 8.3. If time allows, begin working on an assertiveness self-development plan (Activity 8.6).

3–4 Hour Workshop

Assign Worksheets 8.1 and 8.3 for homework. Debrief 8.1 to make sure students accurately distinguished among assertiveness, aggressiveness, and passivity. Debrief Activity 8.3—make sure students wrote appropriate "I" messages, and focus on how effectively students were able to deliver those messages. Give students more practice with assertiveness skills by showing the YouTube clips in Activity 8.2 related to assertiveness, using option 3 for how to conduct the activity. Try to have every student in the class take a turn role playing an assertive position. Have students complete the assertiveness self-assessment in Activity 8.5. Follow this by having students create an assertiveness self-development plan, Activity 8.6. If time allows, have students complete Activity 8.7, the case study analysis. Assign 8.4 for homework and debrief this with the students during the next class period.

Activity List

Activity #	Activity Name	Brief Description and Activity Notes
8.1	Assertive, Aggressive, or Passive?	Students read scenarios and decide whether characters behaved assertively, aggressively, or passively. Make sure they have a clear understanding of the differences before beginning the activity.
8.2	It Seems So Easy When Others Do It	Students watch YouTube clips of others acting assertively, aggressively, or passively.
8.3	Giving Feedback	Students write "I" messages related to different scenarios where they are asked to give someone feedback. They deliver one "I message" of their choice (review "I" messages from Chapter 6 if necessary).
8.4	Controversial Issues	Students pick a controversial topic to discuss with someone they know holds a different view.
8.5	Assertiveness Quiz	Students assess both their comfort level and their likely level of assertiveness in various situations. You may want to have students do this as the first or second activity. It's placed fifth because Activities 8.3 and 8.4 may help them gain more accurate insights about their assertiveness.
8.6	Self-Development Plan for Assertiveness	Students create strategies for self-improvement related to their assertiveness skills.
8.7	Case Study—Assertiveness	Students analyze the behavior of a student who faces challenges related to assertiveness.

Activity 8.1

Assertive, Aggressive, or Passive?

EI Dimensions Targeted: Assertiveness

Brief Description/Objective: Students will identify whether common behaviors they and others engage in are assertive, passive, or aggressive.

Planning the Activity

Time Expected
- Worksheet: 15 minutes
- Reflection Questions: 10 minutes
- In-Class Debrief: 10 minutes

Materials
- Worksheet 8.1 from *The Student EQ Edge: Student Workbook*
- Board or flip chart and markers
- *The Student EQ Edge: Emotional Intelligence and Your Academic and Personal Success*

Facilitating the Activity

Directions
- Mini-lecture: Make sure to explain the differences between assertiveness, aggressiveness, and passivity.
  - Assertiveness—stating your opinion, belief or feeling; standing up for yourself
  - Aggressiveness—physical, verbal, or emotional behavior intended to hurt others
  - Passivity—not defending your rights; not expressing your thoughts, feelings, or opinions
- Assign Worksheet 8.1.

Note: The correct answers about the behavior and what an assertive solution would be are provided in Worksheet 8.1, but these answers do not appear in *The Student EQ Edge: Student Workbook*!

Debriefing Questions
- Ask students to identify the messages they have been given about assertiveness and aggressiveness either in their families, on television, via cultural norms, or in other ways.
- See the reflection questions at the end of the worksheet.

Worksheet 8.1: Assertive, Aggressive, or Passive?

Name:

Identify which of the behaviors in the chart are assertive, passive, or aggressive, based on the definitions given earlier in this chapter. If a behavior is either passive or aggressive, describe what an assertive response or behavior would look like in that situation.

Behavior or Incident	Assertive, Passive, or Aggressive?	Assertive Solution
You share a bathroom at home with your sister. You see her headed that way, so you race past her and lock the bathroom door behind you. She screams "Jerk!" at you through the door. Your sister's behavior was . . .	aggressive	The sister should have avoided derogatory terms and expressed frustration with a clear "I" message such as "I get mad when you run by me to get to the bathroom first."
In the scenario above, your behavior of racing by her was . . .	aggressive	If you have a good reason to use the bathroom first, state it and ask to go first. Otherwise, wait your turn!
Your boss asks you to work overtime during a busy weekend. You respond by saying, "Well, I was sort of hoping to go to the beach." Your response to your boss was . . .	passive	"Well, I was sort of hoping . . ." gives a very unclear answer about whether you have definite plans. Plus, you did not say yes or no to the request.
The editor of the student newspaper asks you to write an editorial about changes in the parking policy. You are very busy but believe students are being treated unfairly, so you agree. You agree to write the article and express your opinions about the parking situation. Writing the article was . . .	assertive	You agreed without being put under pressure because the issue is important to you. You express your opinions in the article.

(continued)

Behavior or Incident	Assertive, Passive, or Aggressive?	Assertive Solution
Your dating partner asks what movie you want to see. You say, "I don't care," so your partner picks a horror movie. You hate horror movies, so you say, "Can we do something other than going to the movies?" Your response was . . .	passive	"I don't care" leaves the decision to the other person, so it's always better to state an opinion. If the other person has selected something you don't want to see, state it directly, such as, "I don't like horror movies, but I'd be willing to see a drama or comedy."
A faculty member assigns a long paper for students to complete over the weekend that had not been previously announced. You have a family wedding to attend. As you are leaving class, you mutter to your friend who's in the same class, "I hate this class." Your response to the paper assignment was . . .	passive-aggressive	Saying you hate the class is harmful to the professor and thus qualifies as aggression. Expressing displeasure indirectly to someone not involved is passive. A concern should always be stated to the other people involved.
A partner in a dating relationship breaks up with you because things are "too intense" between you. A week later, your partner asks you to go to a movie without saying anything else. You agree without asking about the purpose of getting together. Your behavior was . . .	passive	Assuming you still care about the partner in a romantic way and could be hurt further, you are not taking care of yourself without asking why the partner wants to get together, whether the partner's feelings have changed, and so on.

Reflection Questions

1. How difficult was it for you to come up with appropriately assertive responses?
2. How likely would you be to use those assertive responses if you were faced with similar situations? Explain your answer.

Activity 8.2

It Seems So Easy When Others Do It

EI Dimensions Targeted: Assertiveness

Brief Description/Objective: Students will watch 10 short scenarios on a YouTube clip that lasts about 10 minutes. Characters display either assertiveness, aggressiveness, or passivity.

Planning the Activity

Time Expected
- Worksheet and YouTube video: 25 minutes
- Reflection Questions: 10 minutes
- In-Class Debrief: 20 minutes

Materials
- Worksheet 8.2 from *The Student EQ Edge: Student Workbook*
- Board or flip chart and markers
- *The Student EQ Edge: Emotional Intelligence and Your Academic and Personal Success*
- Internet connection and YouTube clip, "Assertiveness Scenarios: 10 Examples" (http://www.youtube.com/watch?v=Ymm86c6DAF4)

NOTE: Make sure the YouTube Clip is still active before assigning this activity. If it's not active, you can alter the activity in one of two ways: conduct in-class role plays based on the following scenario descriptions or search YouTube for the key word "assertiveness" or "assertiveness training" and show a different clip.

Facilitating the Activity

There are several different ways to facilitate this activity:

1. Have the students watch the clip and complete the worksheet on their own and then debrief the activity in class.
2. Show the YouTube clip in class, pausing at the end of the scenario for students to complete their worksheets and discuss what they saw.
3. Show the YouTube clips in class, and if students agree that one or both of the characters were either too passive or too aggressive in a scenario, ask two students from the class to role play an appropriate version of the same interaction. Some of the scenarios are replayed a second time with an assertive interaction modeled so students can compare their role play interactions to what happens in the scenario.

Directions

- Choose from the three options just offered for facilitating this activity. The following list summarizes the 10 scenarios in the movie and whether the characters were assertive, passive, or aggressive.
    - Scenario #1—One person asking for help and the other person politely refusing (assertive).
    - Scenario # 2—Breaking into the lunch line—she tries to be assertive (tells him there's a queue and asks him to go to the end), but he reacts aggressively.
    - Scenario # 3—Break into the lunch line—she's very passive when he breaks into the line.
    - Scenario #4—McDonald's or Subway—she won't tell her friend where she wants to go for lunch (passive).
    - Scenario #5 -McDonald's or Subway—she is clear and assertive about where she wants to eat.
    - Scenario #6—Missing tickets—he thinks she forgot her promise to buy the tickets and yells at her; she accepts the yelling passively.
    - Scenario # 7—Breaking up—she is assertive about breaking up despite pressure from him not to break up.
    - Scenario #8—Covering for a classmate—one male gets another male he barely knows (male #2) to cover for him; male #2 is passive. [Instructor's Note: The accent of male #1 makes it very hard to understand what he's saying. You can skip this scene if necessary.]
    - Scenario # 9—Movie choice—he is commanding (aggressive) about what they will watch, she is passive.
    - Scenario #10—Movie choice—he is commanding about what they will watch, she is assertive (gives him a partial "I" message).
- Assign the YouTube clip, "Assertiveness Scenarios: 10 Examples" (http://www.youtube.com/watch?v=Ymm86c6DAF4) and Worksheet 8.2

Debriefing Questions

- What should you do if you are assertive and the other person either (1) ignores you or (2) becomes aggressive? What should guide your behavior: their reaction to you or what you want to see happen?
- See the reflection questions at the end of the worksheet.

Worksheet 8.2: It Seems So Easy When Others Do It

Name:

- Go to http://www.youtube.com/watch?v=Ymm86c6DAF4 and watch the10-minute clip, "Assertiveness Scenarios: 10 Examples." There are 10 short scenarios, as listed in the following chart.
- For each scenario, fill in the chart. In the Assertive, Aggressive, or Passive? column, list both characters and their reactions. If you think their reaction changed during the scenario (for example, passive but then becoming assertive) note this. In column #3, describe the long-term consequences for each character if his or her behavior continues in this way.

Scenario	Assertive, Aggressive, or Passive?	Long-Term Consequences for Each Character
#1 Asking for help		
#2 Breaking into line		
#3 Breaking into line (take 2)		
#4 McDonald's or Subway		
#5 McDonald's or Subway (take 2)		
#6 Missing tickets		
#7 Breaking up		
#8 Cover for me		
#9 Movie choice		
#10 Movie choice (take 2)		

Reflection Questions

1. Being appropriately assertive sometimes resulted in the other person's becoming aggressive. How does the potential for such a reaction influence your willingness to be assertive? Explain.
2. Which character reminds you the most of yourself? Now look at the long-term consequences you wrote down for that person. What is your reaction to those consequences?

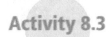

Activity 8.3
Giving Feedback

EI Dimensions Targeted: Assertiveness

Brief Description/Objective: In Part 1, students will write assertive messages related to various situations in their lives. In Part 2, they will deliver one of these messages.

Planning the Activity

Time Expected
- Worksheet: 15 minutes
- Interaction with Selected Person: 5–15 minutes
- Reflection Questions: 10 minutes
- In-Class Debrief: 15 minutes

Materials
- Worksheet 8.3 from *The Student EQ Edge: Student Workbook*
- Board or flip chart and markers
- *The Student EQ Edge: Emotional Intelligence and Your Academic and Personal Success*

Facilitating the Activity

Directions
- Assign Worksheet 8.3.
- Encourage students to complete Part 2 of the activity with someone in person.

Debriefing Questions
- Ask students to stand up if they agree with the following statements and remain seated if they disagree.
  - There are some people with whom it is inappropriate to be assertive.
  - Being assertive is likely to get me into trouble.
  - Being assertive makes me uncomfortable.
- Open a discussion about each of these items by calling on various students who agreed or disagreed to share their opinions. Your role as the facilitator is to remind students that being assertive is appropriate and thus a desirable characteristic to have.
- See the reflection questions at the end of the worksheet.

Worksheet 8.3: Giving Feedback

Name:

Giving feedback to others requires assertiveness because in giving feedback you are stating an opinion or belief. Sometimes we avoid giving feedback either because we are concerned the other person might get angry or because we don't want to hurt someone's feelings. However, withholding honest feedback prevents us from improving relationships or helping others improve their performance.

Part 1

Refer back to Chapter 6 on emotional expression and how to deliver an "I" message. Then write down "I" messages for each of the following four scenarios:

- Give feedback to a family member about something he or she has done that hurt your feelings or upset you:
- Give feedback to a friend or dating partner about a behavior he or she engages in that annoys or upsets you:
- Give feedback to a faculty member about a way to improve a class:
- Give feedback to the head of your school about something that could be done to improve the school:

Part 2

Pick one of your responses and deliver the message to the individual *in person* (or at the least via a phone call). Do *not* use text, Facebook, messaging/chat, or email!

Reflection Questions

1. Were you able to successfully deliver the feedback in an assertive way? If so, how did the interaction turn out? If you became too passive or too aggressive, what do you think caused that?
2. What was the outcome of your delivering the feedback?
3. How did you feel before, during, and after the interaction?

Activity 8.4
Controversial Issues

EI Dimensions Targeted: Assertiveness, Emotional Self-Awareness

Brief Description/Objective: Students will identify a controversial issue and someone who disagrees with them and engage in a conversation about the identified topic The goal is for the student to remain assertive, becoming neither aggressive nor passive, during a conversation.

Planning the Activity

Time Expected
- Worksheet and Conversation: 15–20 minutes
- Reflection Questions: 10 minutes
- In-Class Debrief: 10 minutes

Materials
- Worksheet 8.4 from *The Student EQ Edge: Student Workbook*
- Board or flip chart and markers
- *The Student EQ Edge: Emotional Intelligence and Your Academic and Personal Success*

Facilitating the Activity

Directions
- Assign Worksheet 8.4.
- You may want to spend a few minutes of class time helping students generate ideas about what signals they could cue into that would signal aggressiveness or passivity.

Debriefing Questions
- Many families make it "off limits" to discuss political or religious issues at family gatherings because it might create conflict. What are the possible consequences of avoiding such conversations?
- See the reflection questions at the end of the worksheet.

Worksheet 8.4: Controversial Issues

Name:

Think about a friend or family member that you differ with on some important value such as a religious or political belief. Casually bring up the topic with the person; do not let him or her know you are doing this for a class assignment. Your goal is to stay assertive without becoming passive or aggressive.

Fill in the spaces:

- The person (and their relationship to you):
- The issue:

Remaining assertive during a challenging conversation can be difficult. Answer the following questions to help you become more aware of signals that indicate you have become passive or aggressive.

- What signs can I cue into that I am becoming too aggressive? Too passive?
- What sentence can I begin the conversation with that summarizes my belief in an assertive way?

Reflection Questions

1. Analyze how well you remained assertive throughout the conversation. If you became aggressive or passive, what triggered this behavior?
2. What cultural, religious, or family values affect your level of assertiveness, aggressiveness, or passiveness?

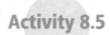

Activity 8.5
Assertiveness Quiz

EI Dimensions Targeted: Assertiveness, Emotional Self-Awareness

Brief Description/Objective: Students will complete an assertiveness questionnaire.

Planning the Activity

Time Expected
- Worksheet: 10 minutes
- Reflection Questions: 10 minutes
- In-Class Debrief: 10 minutes

Materials
- Worksheet 8.5 from *The Student EQ Edge: Student Workbook*
- Board or flip chart and markers
- *The Student EQ Edge: Emotional Intelligence and Your Academic and Personal Success*

Facilitating the Activity

Directions
- Assign Worksheet 8.5.
- Choose whether to complete the activity early in the unit (when students may believe they are more assertive than they actually are) or later in the unit after they have a better understanding of assertiveness.

Debriefing Questions
- There may be differences based on gender, culture, or ethnicity in terms of how comfortable students feel about being assertive in various situations. Talk about the costs of going against norms, even when the behavior may be seen as positive by others of a different background.
- See the reflection questions at the end of the worksheet.

Worksheet 8.5: Assertiveness Quiz

Name:

Assertiveness depends on two factors: (1) our level of (dis)comfort being assertive in that situation and (2) the situation and who is involved. Rank the situations in the following chart, circling a number score based on how you would feel and behave.

Level of comfort with being assertive

1   Very uncomfortable

2   Uncomfortable

3   Comfortable

4   Very comfortable

Level of assertiveness in that situation

1   Not at all assertive (I do not stand up for myself or state my beliefs at all; passive).

2   Somewhat assertive (I make an initial attempt to be assertive but back off if the other person challenges me).

3   Assertive (I state what I want but ultimately give in or fail to fully defend my beliefs if I am repeatedly challenged).

4   Very assertive (I continue to defend my beliefs or stand up for myself without being aggressive, no matter what the other person says or does).

0   I am likely to become aggressive (I may interrupt a lot, yell, insult the other person, throw something, or storm out).

Comfort			Assertiveness
1 2 3 4	a.	Tell a friend that he or she has done something that bothers me.	0 1 2 3 4
1 2 3 4	b.	Ask a teacher why he or she took off points for an answer on a test.	0 1 2 3 4
1 2 3 4	c.	Speak up in a class during a heated discussion.	0 1 2 3 4
1 2 3 4	d.	Speak up in a group of friends when you believe someone is doing something wrong.	0 1 2 3 4
1 2 3 4	e.	Question a rule that your family members have set for you.	0 1 2 3 4

(continued)

Comfort			Assertiveness
1 2 3 4	f.	Tell a dating partner about something that he or she has done to upset you.	0 1 2 3 4
1 2 3 4	g.	Express your opinion about a controversial topic with friends.	0 1 2 3 4
1 2 3 4	h.	Express your opinion about a controversial topic with family.	0 1 2 3 4
1 2 3 4	i.	Turn down a request to help someone when you don't want to help.	0 1 2 3 4
1 2 3 4	j.	Ask a stranger who is talking loudly during a movie to be quiet.	0 1 2 3 4

Total your comfort scores and your assertiveness. Notice that aggressiveness gets 0 points!

Reflection Questions

1. What patterns do you notice in your comfort level? In your assertiveness level?
2. Look at the items where you circled 0 for aggression. What situations are likely to promote aggression in you?
3. When you are not assertive, what do you believe is the major reason? Circle the letters for all relevant explanations.
   a. Concerned about making others angry
   b. Concerned about making things worse for myself
   c. Just don't have the energy to deal with it
   d. Don't want to risk upsetting others I care about
   e. Don't think it will change anything even if I am assertive
   f. Don't know how (don't have the skills) to be assertive
   g. Something else (explain)
4. Look at the items you circled in the previous question. What can you learn about yourself from reviewing this list?

Activity 8.6
Self-Development Plan for Assertiveness

The directions and template for students to create a self-development plan appear in Appendix D of this *Facilitation and Activity Guide. The Student EQ Edge: Student Workbook* contains a template for developing assertiveness in Worksheet 8.6.

Activity 8.7
Case Study—Assertiveness

See Chapter 2 to assign a case study relevant to assertiveness. Chapter 2 of *The Student EQ Edge: Student Workbook* contains all of the same case studies.

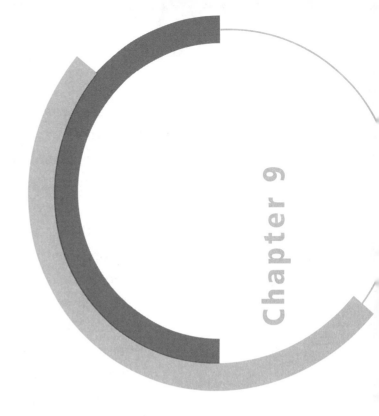

Chapter 9

Interpersonal Relationship

What is interpersonal relationship? Interpersonal relationship skills require us to care about others, to trust them with our emotions, and to be interested in getting closer to them. Life experiences can make some of us hesitant to take any kind of risk in getting to know others. Others have experienced loving, open, mutual relationships that allow us to trust others. Whatever the case for your students, developing their interpersonal skills will assure them of two things. First, they will be more likely to function more effectively in a variety of life situations, from their first job interview to healthy, loving personal relationships. Second, well-developed interpersonal skills make life richer because we get to know others better and let them get to know us better. Be sure to help students understand that interpersonal relationship skills do not mean you have to be an extrovert or the life of the party!

It's important for students to understand that there are appropriate levels of self-disclosure or personal connection, depending on the situation. With strangers, if we interact at all, we keep things at a surface level (for example, choice of a college major). With acquaintances, we get to know them better by asking questions about their weekend plans, their opinion about a musical group, and other similar questions. We can judge by their answers whether they want to get to know us better or not. With those we know well, we can share more intimate details of our lives, such as our hopes, fears, disappointments, and joys.

Many married couples complain about "growing apart" over the years. If we could observe those marriages, we'd probably see that they rarely connect on a meaningful interpersonal level anymore. Ironically, many people are afraid that if they let others in too much, they'll get hurt; in fact, it's keeping others out that leads to disconnection and broken bonds.

Can high scores on interpersonal relationship skills interfere with student success? Research cited in Chapter 1 (Sparkman, 2009) indicated that there was a relationship between high scores on interpersonal relationships and less likelihood of completing a bachelor's degree. If a student is too focused on relationships and not focused enough on academics, then graduation may be jeopardized. Again, though, balance between two EI scales—in this case interpersonal relationships and reality testing—is the key to success.

STUDENT LEARNING OUTCOMES

Students will:

- Understand the benefits of interpersonal relationships
- Analyze the impact of effective interpersonal relationships
- Identify appropriate levels of self-disclosure to use with different types of relationships
- Develop their interpersonal skills

SUGGESTED READINGS, MOVIES, AND TELEVISION SHOWS

- *The Student EQ Edge: Emotional Intelligence and Your Academic and Personal Success*, Chapter 9

Movies
- *Erin Brockovich*—Scene 16, "Miss Wichita" (sex implied)— Erin reveals she was Miss Wichita and laments her current circumstances; she shows a fear of interpersonal relationships when she asks George not to be "too nice."

- *Erin Brockovich*—Scene 21, "Ed and Erin at Jensen's"—Erin helps Ed see the value of doing little things to build relationships.
- *One Fine Day*—Scene 23, "Here's Jack," and Scene 24, "The Big Sleep"—After denying her feelings and keeping the other parent at a safe emotional distance, the single parent mother finally allows herself to form a meaningful relationship with the single parent father.
- *Patch Adams*—Scene 5, "Dr. Clown"—Patch demonstrates how to form effective relationships with adult and child patients and with the nurses.

Television Shows

- *The Office*—Episode 27, "Conflict Management"—Employees discuss their relationship issues. Dwight and Jim continue to have a challenging relationship.
- *The Office*—Episode 137, "Classy Christmas" Part 1—After Toby announces he is taking a leave to serve on a jury, he comes back to visit for a Christmas party and enjoys new and improved relationships with his coworkers.
- *The Bachelor* or *The Bachelorette*—Men and women on these dating shows consistently either reveal too much too soon about themselves, scaring away potential partners, or, more frequently, refuse to open up, even after they should be comfortable doing so because they cannot let someone else get too close. Most students will have been in some type of relationship that mimics one of these patterns.

PLANNING YOUR CLASS

50–60 Minute Class

Assign Worksheets 9.1 and 9.3 for homework. Select and debrief one. Then have students do Activity 9.2 together in class, coming up with a list of what would be appropriate interaction with a stranger, an acquaintance, and a close friend. When doing this activity, stress the meaning that interpersonal relationships give to our lives. If time allows, have students begin working on a self-development plan or a case study related to interpersonal relationships.

Assign Worksheets 9.1 and 9.4 for homework. Debrief 9.4 in class and 9.1 if you choose. Then do Activity 9.2, watching the YouTube clip about "Sharing Secrets." This is likely to promote lots of conversation about why it's best not to share personal information with others. Address these risks with the students but get them to also evaluate the consequences of staying closed to others. Activity 9.2 provides a good lead-in to Activity 9.3, which will help students understand what level of interpersonal connection is appropriate and likely to be rewarding. Next, have them complete a case study (Activity 9.7) in small groups. At this point, they should be ready to tackle a self-development plan: Activity 9.6.

Activity List

Activity #	Activity Name	Brief Description and Activity Notes
9.1	My Favorite Person	Students examine what they know about a person they feel very close to, which allows them to understand how much they tend to share with others in close relationships.
9.2.	Sharing Secrets	Students watch a brief (two minutes) video clip from the movie *Saints and Soldiers* and reflect on the personal sharing that occurred. Students are likely to have strong reactions!
9.3	Scaling the Intimacy Wall	Students identify what would be an appropriate level of personal sharing to engage in with a stranger, an acquaintance, or a close friend.
9.4	Beginning a Relationship	Students approach an acquaintance and begin a conversation as a way to practice interpersonal skills with someone they don't know very well. Students usually dread this activity but often are very excited after it's over. They have overcome a natural fear (being rejected), and the vast majority of them have a great experience.
9.5	Getting Closer	Students approach someone they feel close to and tell the person something he or she does not already know.
9.6	Self-Development Plan for Interpersonal Relationships	Students create strategies for self-improvement related to their interpersonal relationship skills.
9.7	Case Study—Interpersonal Relationships	Students analyze the behavior of a person who faces challenges related to interpersonal relationships.

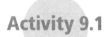

Activity 9.1
My Favorite Person

EI Dimensions Targeted: Interpersonal Relationship, Emotional Self-Awareness

Brief Description/Objective: Students will examine what they know about a person they feel very close to, allowing them to understand how much (or little) they tend to share in close relationships.

Planning the Activity

Time Expected
- Worksheet: 10 minutes
- Reflection Questions: 10 minutes
- In-Class Debrief: 10 minutes

Materials
- Worksheet 9.1 from *The Student EQ Edge: Student Workbook*
- Board or flip chart and markers
- *The Student EQ Edge: Emotional Intelligence and Your Academic and Personal Success*

Facilitating the Activity

Directions
- Assign Worksheet 9.1.

Debriefing Questions
- See the reflection questions at the end of the worksheet.

Worksheet 9.1: My Favorite Person

Name:

Part 1

Other than one of your parents or guardians, think about the person with whom you have the most meaningful relationship. Answer the following questions about that person. If you're not sure of the answer to a question, skip it for now.

What (who) is this person's . . .

- Favorite color:
- Favorite book or type of book:
- Favorite sport:
- Best friend (other than you!):
- Favorite thing to do in his or her free time:
- Greatest source of joy:
- Greatest source of sadness or anxiety:
- Biggest accomplishment in life:
- Biggest disappointment in life:

Part 2

Now contact the person and go over the answers to make sure you were correct (or close) in what you said. If you didn't know what to write down, ask the person that question.

Reflection Questions

1. What makes this person special to you?
2. How likely is it that the person knows the same amount of information about you as you did about him or her?
3. What is your reaction to what you knew about this "special" person? Was the amount you knew just right, too much, or too little, given how you feel about this person? Explain your answer.

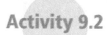

Activity 9.2

Sharing Secrets

EI Dimensions Targeted: Interpersonal Relationship, Emotional Self-Awareness

Brief Description/Objective: Students will watch a brief (two minutes) video clip from the movie *Saints and Soldiers* and reflect about the personal sharing that occurred.

Planning the Activity

Time Expected
- Worksheet and YouTube video: 2 minutes
- Reflection Questions: 15 minutes
- In-Class Debrief: 10–20 minutes

Materials
- Worksheet 9.2 from *The Student EQ Edge: Student Workbook*
- Board or flip chart and markers
- Internet connection and the following YouTube clip, called "Sharing Secrets—Saints and Soldiers," http://www.youtube.com/watch?v=2XkLOT9J1vs&feature=fvst
- This clip is also available for free on hulu.com. The scene begins approximately 31 minutes into that particular video, which can be accessed at http://www.hulu.com/watch/32278/saints-and-soldiers

  Note: You can also rent the movie and show the clip that way. The clip begins with the soldiers sitting in the woods; one of them asks each to share a secret. If these clips are no longer available, use the scene from the movie *Notting Hill* in which the adults are sitting around the dinner table and each decides to reveal something very personal. This clip appears about 25–30 minutes into the movie.

- *The Student EQ Edge: Emotional Intelligence and Your Academic and Personal Success*

Facilitating the Activity

Directions
- Assign Worksheet 9.2 and the video clip.
- Watch the clip yourself prior to debriefing it; this clip can engender strong reactions from students who believe the soldiers were made to look foolish. One of the biggest obstacles to allowing ourselves to form meaningful relationships is the fear of being embarrassed or hurt.

Debriefing Questions
- What is the greater risk—a life without connection to others or allowing ourselves to get close and risk getting hurt?
- See the reflection questions at the end of the worksheet.

Worksheet 9.2: Sharing Secrets

Name:

Go to http://www.youtube.com/watch?v=2XkLOT9J1vs&feature=fvst and watch the YouTube clip called "Sharing Secrets—Saints and Soldiers." If this clip is not active, the movie *Saints and Soldiers* is also available on hulu.com; the assigned scene is about 31 minutes into the movie. If these sources are no longer available, use the scene from the movie *Notting Hill* in which all of the adults are sitting around the dinner table and decide to share something very personal (about 25–30 minutes into the movie). Next, answer the reflection questions. Your class leader should make it clear ahead of time whether you will have to turn in your responses to these questions.

Reflection Questions

1. What secret would you have told in that group? Or would you have refused to tell one?
2. As you were watching the clip, how did your feelings or thoughts about each person change? For example, were you turned off by the sharing, did it make you like the person more, or what other reaction did you have?
3. If you had been the soldier who asked the last guy what his secret was, how would you have responded (internally and externally) to his response?
4. What is your biggest concern about sharing a secret?
5. What is the best thing that's ever happened to you because you did share a secret?

Activity 9.3
Scaling the Intimacy Wall

EI Dimensions Targeted: Interpersonal Relationship, Reality Testing

Brief Description/Objective: Students will identify what they consider to be an appropriate level of personal sharing to engage in with a stranger, an acquaintance, or a close friend.

Planning the Activity

Time Expected
- Worksheet: 10–15 minutes
- Reflection Questions: 10 minutes
- In-Class Debrief: 10 minutes

Materials
- Worksheet 9.3 from *The Student EQ Edge: Student Workbook*
- Board or flip chart and markers
- *The Student EQ Edge: Emotional Intelligence and Your Academic and Personal Success*

Facilitating the Activity

Directions:
- Assign Worksheet 9.3.
- If you choose to conduct this activity in class, allow the students about 10 minutes to come up with their lists. Do not assign the reflection questions; instead, begin the debriefing questions.

Debriefing Questions:
- Why do you think it's easier for some people to reveal personal details to a total stranger than to a friend?
- See the reflection questions at the end of the worksheet.

Worksheet 9.3: Scaling the Intimacy Wall

Name:

Consider each area of the following table. Fill in what types of personal details (such as your joys, troubles, dreams, disappointments, interests, and activities) you would be comfortable telling someone based on the relevant quadrant. You can either fill in a word like "disappointments" or briefly describe your actual disappointments. Your class leader should tell you ahead of time whether this worksheet will be turned in or shared with anyone else.

	Know Person Well	Person Is an Acquaintance
Desire Close Relationship	What I would share about myself is . . .	What I would share about myself is . . .
Desire Less Close Relationship (But Not Distant)	What I would share about myself is . . .	What I would share about myself is . . .

Reflection Questions

1. Which quadrant did you have the most difficulty completing? Explain why that one was the most difficult.

2. In real life, which of the types of interpersonal relationships listed in the table do you struggle with the most in terms of revealing enough but not too much about yourself? Explain.

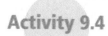

Activity 9.4

Beginning a Relationship

EI Dimensions Targeted: Interpersonal Relationship, Independence, Emotional Self-Awareness

Brief Description/Objective: Students will approach an acquaintance and begin a conversation as a way to practice interpersonal skills with those they don't know very well.

Planning the Activity

Time Expected
- Worksheet: 10 minutes
- Reflection Questions: 10 minutes
- In-Class Debrief: 5 minutes

Materials
- Worksheet 9.4 from *The Student EQ Edge: Student Workbook*
- Board or flip chart and markers
- *The Student EQ Edge: Emotional Intelligence and Your Academic and Personal Success*

Facilitating the Activity

Directions
- Assign Worksheet 9.4.
- Stress to the students they should complete this activity alone (otherwise, they are lacking independence!).

Debriefing Questions
- What are some ways that engaging in this activity more often could help you in the future?
- See the reflection questions at the end of the worksheet.

Worksheet 9.4: Beginning a Relationship

Name:

1. Pick out someone you barely know from your school, a team you're on, a group you belong to, or some other area of your life. The next time you see that person, approach him or her and begin a conversation. Who do you plan to approach? If you don't know his or her name, describe the person.

2. Write down at least three good opening comments that would help you get a conversation started. The first one may not work, but chances are one of the other two will.

3. Once you have had the conversation, write a brief summary here of what you talked about. Then answer the following questions:
   - How long did you talk?
   - Did the other person talk about the same amount as you did, or more or less?
   - Did you get to know the person better?
   - Do you plan on having another conversation or doing something with that person?

Reflection Questions

1. Explain whether this experience will make you more willing to have this type of conversation in the future.
2. What were your biggest concerns or fears before the conversation?
3. How did you feel after the conversation?

Activity 9.5
Getting Closer

EI Dimensions Targeted: Interpersonal Relationship

Brief Description/Objective: Students will approach someone he or she feels close to and tell the person something he or she does not already know.

Planning the Activity

Time Expected
- Worksheet: 5 minutes
- Reflection Questions: 10 minutes
- In-Class Debrief: 5 minutes

Materials
- Worksheet 9.5 from *The Student EQ Edge: Student Workbook*
- Board or flip chart and markers
- *The Student EQ Edge: Emotional Intelligence and Your Academic and Personal Success*

Facilitating the Activity

Directions
- Assign Worksheet 9.5.

Debriefing Questions
- Ask students whether they found it easier to approach an acquaintance and begin a conversation (Activity 9.4) or to share something more personal with someone they know well (Activity 9.5). Ask students representing each side to explain their answers. The goal is to help students understand that trust is fundamental to more personal sharing, and that fear of rejection often motivates us to avoid interaction with those we don't know well.
- See the reflection questions at the end of the worksheet.

Worksheet 9.5: Getting Closer

Name:

This worksheet is similar to Worksheet 9.4, except that now you are going to repeat the activity with someone you know fairly well but would like to get to know better. Think about "scaling the intimacy wall" and trying to let the other person learn something new about you.

1. Who do you plan to approach? What topic do you want to talk about?
2. Write down at least three good opening comments that would help you get a conversation started.
3. Once you have had the conversation, write a brief summary here of what you talked about. Then answer the following questions:
   - Did you get to know the person better?
   - Do you feel closer to the person as a result of the conversation?
   - Do you plan on having another conversation or doing something with that person?

Reflection Questions

1. Explain whether this experience will make you more willing to have this type of conversation in the future.
2. What were your biggest concerns or fears before the conversation?
3. How did you feel after the conversation?
4. If you have completed Worksheet 9.4, compare and contrast the conversation you had with someone you did not know well and the one you had with someone you already know well but would like to get to know better. Which type of conversation is easier for you? What does that tell you about yourself?

Activity 9.6

Self-Development Plan for Interpersonal Relationships

The directions and template for students to create a self-development plan appear in Appendix D of this *Facilitation and Activity Guide*. *The Student EQ Edge: Student Workbook* contains a template for developing interpersonal relationships in Chapter 9.

Activity 9.7

Case Study—Interpersonal Relationships

See Chapter 2 to assign a case study relevant to interpersonal relationships. Chapter 2 of *The Student EQ Edge: Student Workbook* contains all of the same case studies.

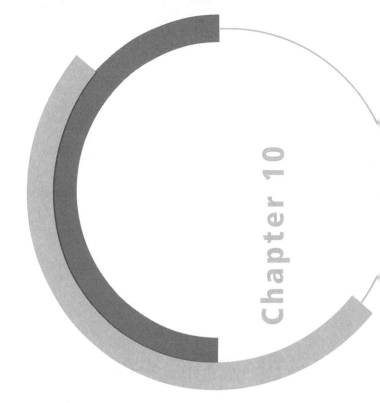

Chapter 10

Empathy

What is empathy? Empathy involves the ability to understand someone else's perspective; thus it's first and foremost a *cognitive skill*. Once we understand what someone else is thinking or feeling and why, then we are open to feeling the same emotion they feel, or perhaps a different one. Unless we understand someone's thoughts or feelings, it's difficult to feel anything ourselves. And it's even more difficult to help that person solve a mutual problem, or heal a relationship without empathy. Empathy is *not* sympathy (feeling sorry for someone), nor does it mean that you have to agree with someone's opinions (though you do have to understand them), and being willing to understand someone else definitely does not mean you lack courage. Empathy allows us to shift from an adversarial or unhelpful relationship into a collaborative relationship. We can feel a broader range of feelings once we cue into others' feelings and the reasons for them. Relationships become richer, conflicts are more easily resolved, and misunderstandings are averted if we possess empathy.

But can someone be too empathic? Someone who scores extremely high on empathy will need to also possess an appropriate amount of assertiveness. Otherwise, there's an imbalance: taking too much care of others and taking too little care of oneself. As a result, someone may get taken advantage of.

STUDENT LEARNING OUTCOMES

Students will:

- Gain an understanding of what empathy means and be able to distinguish it from sympathy
- Develop listening skills
- Understand their current empathy skills
- Learn how to ask questions to better understand someone else's perspective

SUGGESTED READINGS, MOVIES, AND TELEVISION SHOWS

- *The Student EQ Edge: Emotional Intelligence and Your Academic and Personal Success*, Chapter 10

Movies

- *Erin Brockovich*—Scene 21, "Ed and Erin at Jensen's"—Erin understands the perspective of small town people about big lawsuits and payouts to lawyers; Scene 29, meeting PG&E lawyers—Erin asks them to put a dollar value on a spine or uterus.
- *One Fine Day*—About two thirds of the way through the movie, one of the children wanders away to follow a stray cat; this makes the father very late for a meeting, but instead of yelling at her, he gently talks to her about her love of cats.
- *Patch Adams*—Scene 5, "Dr. Clown"—Patch cheers up the sick children; Scene 6, "Walcott's Warning"—Patch again tries to cheer up the patients and gets in trouble with the dean, who has no empathy for the sick.

Television Shows

- *The Office*—Episode 75, "Business Ethics"—During a required ethics seminar, many of the Dunder Mifflin employees show their lack of empathy and respect for one another.
- *Glee*—Episode 9, "Wheels"—The school won't pay for the specialized bus needed to take Arty to sectionals.

PLANNING YOUR CLASS

50–60 Minute Class

Assign Worksheets 10.1 and 10.4 for homework. Debrief these activities, making sure students understand what empathy is and how much they possess. Then pick either Activity 10.2 (question asking) or 10.3 (reflective listening) to conduct in class. It's usually easier to master open-ended questions than reflective listening, especially in a limited time frame.

3–4 Hour Class

Assign Worksheets 10.1 and 10.4 for homework. Debrief these activities, making sure students understand what empathy is and how much they possess. Then complete Activity 10.2 in class, helping students improve their wording for open-ended questions. To test their ability, spontaneously make several statements about issues on your campus or in your life and have students ask you open-ended questions to explore your perspective in more depth. Then do Activity 10.3 with students, making sure to review some examples in class to ensure that students are mastering the skill. Then ask for two volunteers—one to mention something that has created strong emotions and one to respond with reflective listening. Coach the student doing the reflective listening. Continue this role playing until students are better able to identify their own mistakes and give better responses. Then conduct a modified version of Activity 10.5 in class by having two students who disagree on an issue (for example, a policy at your school, or whether animals should be used in research) volunteer to discuss the issue in front of the class. Assign one student to do reflective listening. If that student gets stuck, have the class provide suggestions. If time allows, have students complete either a self-development plan or a case study (Activities 10.6 and 10.7).

Activity List

Activity #	Activity Name	Brief Description and Activity Notes
10.1	What Is Empathy?	Empathy is a misunderstood concept, so this activity gives students practice distinguishing statements that are empathic from those that are not.
10.2	The Art of Questions	Students learn to ask open-ended questions that will help them discern others' perspectives.
10.3	Reflective Listening	Students learn how to reflectively listen to others—summarizing content and reflecting on the person's emotions.
10.4	Empathy Assessment	Students self-assess the level of empathy they show in different behaviors.
10.5	Listening Even When It's Hard to Do!	Students hold a discussion with someone on an issue on which they disagree. Students will practice listening and reflecting the other person's perspective. Encourage them to pick an issue they can stay calm about!
10.6	Self-Development Plan for Empathy	Students create strategies for self-improvement related to their empathy skills.
10.7	Case Study—Empathy	Students analyze the behavior of a person who faces challenges related to empathy.

Activity 10.1

What Is Empathy?

EI Dimensions Targeted: Empathy, Interpersonal Relationship, Emotional Self-Awareness

Brief Description/Objective: Students will identify what types of responses are helpful (empathic) when they are upset.

Planning the Activity

Time Expected
- Worksheet: 10 minutes
- Reflection Questions: 10 minutes
- In-Class Debrief: 5–10 minutes

Materials
- Worksheet 10.1 from *The Student EQ Edge: Student Workbook*
- Board or flip chart and markers
- *The Student EQ Edge: Emotional Intelligence and Your Academic and Personal Success*

Facilitating the Activity

Directions
- Assign Worksheet 10.1
- This *Facilitation and Activity Guide* denotes which statements do *not* show empathy and which ones do. The *Student Workbook* does not include these answers.
- During the debrief, make sure you point out how more empathic responses tend to make us feel better and help us avoid conflict.

Debriefing Questions
- Take a poll for the class about which responses they decided were most helpful and least helpful and compare that to the responses they use the most with other people. Explore the likely discrepancies between what we want others to do for us and how we typically respond to them.
- See the reflection questions at the end of the worksheet.

Worksheet 10.1: What Is Empathy?

Name:

Imagine that you are really upset about something and begin telling a friend about it. In the space after each possible response from your friend, note whether this would *help* or *not help* you and give a brief reason why.

1. "I had the same thing happen to me once" (the friend then begins to tell you the story, which takes several minutes).   *NOT empathic*

2. "That sounds pretty bad. No wonder you're mad."   *Empathic*

3. "What else happened?"   *Empathic*

4. "There's no need to get so upset. You won't be able to decide what you want to do."   *NOT empathic*

5. "It sounds like . . ." (the friend then summarizes how he or she thinks you feel and why, such as "It sounds like you're pretty ticked off because Chris made fun of you in front of so many people").   *Empathic*

6. "Don't worry about it. If you act like you don't care, the other person won't know they upset you."   *NOT empathic*

7. "Wow, I can see why you're so upset."   *Empathic*

Reflection Questions

1. Which two of these responses would make you most likely to keep talking about the issue?
2. Which two responses would make you least likely to keep talking?
3. Which of the responses do you most often use? Explain why you use this one.

Activity 10.2
The Art of Questions

EI Dimensions Targeted: Empathy

Brief Description/Objective: Students will learn how to ask open-ended questions.

Planning the Activity

Time Expected
- Worksheet: 10 minutes
- Reflection Questions: 10 minutes
- In-Class Debrief: 15 minutes

Materials
- Worksheet 10.2 from *The Student EQ Edge: Student Workbook*
- Board or flip chart and markers
- *The Student EQ Edge: Emotional Intelligence and Your Academic and Personal Success*

Facilitating the Activity

Directions
- Assign Worksheet 10.2.
- Go over a few different question structures in class so that students will have some examples to refer to; for example, "What made you feel that way?" "How did that make you feel?"

Debriefing Questions
- How can learning to ask open-ended questions help you in a variety of situations?
- See the reflection questions at the end of the worksheet.

Worksheet 10.2: The Art of Questions

Name:

Open-ended questions keep other people talking, giving you a better chance to understand their thoughts, feelings, or opinions. These questions avoid judgment, do not lead the other person to a particular response, and cannot be answered with just one word. Pretend that someone has just made each of the following comments to you. Write an open-ended question you could ask to learn more about that person's perspective.

Example: "That math test was unfair."

Question: "Which questions or problems made you think it was unfair?"

1. "I can't stand it when she nags me so much."
   Question:

2. "He was a real jerk."
   Question:

3. "You made me mad when you didn't answer my text."
   Question:

4. "I don't think capital punishment is right under any circumstance."
   Question:

5. "I think your opinion about abortion is wrong."
   Question:

6. "I'm so excited."
   Question:

Reflection Questions

1. Which types of questions or comments were the hardest for you to respond to? Why do you think that is so?
2. How likely are you to use any of these responses in a real conversation? Explain your answer.

Activity 10.3
Reflective Listening

El Dimensions Targeted: Empathy

Brief Description/Objective: Students will learn how to engage in reflective listening.

Planning the Activity

Time Expected
- Worksheet: 10 minutes
- Reflection Questions: 10 minutes
- In-Class Debrief: 15–20 minutes

Materials
- Worksheet 10.3 from *The Student EQ Edge: Student Workbook*
- Board or flip chart and markers
- *The Student EQ Edge: Emotional Intelligence and Your Academic and Personal Success*

Facilitating the Activity

Directions
- Assign Worksheet 10.3.
- Go over the structure for reflective listening prior to assigning the worksheet. The two primary parts of reflective listening are (1) summarizing the essence of what you understood the person to say (not repeating it word for word!) and (2) identifying what emotion the person is experiencing, even if the person didn't specifically state an emotion.

Debriefing Questions
- How do you typically react when someone engages in reflective listening with you?
- See the reflection questions at the end of the worksheet, particularly question 2!

Worksheet 10.3: Reflective Listening

Name:

Reflective listening means you are able to accurately summarize the content and meaning of someone's thoughts or ideas, including any feelings that may have been expressed explicitly or implicitly. Don't just repeat what the person says (that tends to sound silly); instead, rephrase it so the person knows you really listened.

Example: "The coach didn't even give me a fair chance. I made one mistake and got pulled out of the game and never went back in. How's that fair when Kelly got to stay in after allowing that goal? I think the coach doesn't like me for some reason. I wonder if it's even worth it to play."

Reflective Listening Response: "You sound pretty frustrated with soccer, and you're steamed at the coach."

Now, write reflective listening responses to each of the following statements:

"I can't stand this class. The teacher demands so much work, he must think it's the only class we have. The material is so boring that I fall asleep every time I try to read the book."

Reflective listening response:

"I never have enough money. I never get to go out with friends and always have to work as many hours as I can. I'm sick of it."

Reflective listening response:

"I can't believe you teased me about my clothes in front of all those people. What were you thinking?"

Reflective listening response:

Reflection Questions

1. Read back over the scenarios. What do you think is the person's primary emotion in each scenario?
   a. Scenario #1
   b. Scenario #2
   c. Scenario #3
2. How do you typically react when you hear someone express those emotions?
3. What will be the hardest thing for you about doing reflective listening in real situations?

Activity 10.4

Empathy Assessment

EI Dimensions Targeted: Empathy, Reality Testing (comparing self-rating to other rating)

Brief Description/Objective: Students will take a survey to self-assess their empathy level.

Planning the Activity

Time Expected
- Worksheet: 5 minutes
- Reflection Questions: 10 minutes
- In-Class Debrief: 5 minutes

Materials
- Worksheet 10.4 from *The Student EQ Edge: Student Workbook*
- Board or flip chart and markers
- *The Student EQ Edge: Emotional Intelligence and Your Academic and Personal Success*

Facilitating the Activity

Directions
- Assign Worksheet 10.4.

Debriefing Questions
- Poll the class to see how many people rated themselves at least three points higher on either subscale (emotional or cognitive) than the other person who rated them. Discuss how our self-perceptions (and thus our self-ratings) are often inflated and hence the need to be open to feedback from others.
- See the reflection questions at the end of the worksheet.

Worksheet 10.4: Empathy Assessment

Name:

Respond to the following statements using the number scale.

1 = Strongly disagree	2 = Disagree	3 = Slightly disagree	4 = Slightly agree	5 = Agree	6 = Strongly agree

1. Seeing someone who is upset makes me upset.

1   2   3   4   5   6

2. I tend to cry during sad movies.

1   2   3   4   5   6

3. I think it's funny when others get teased and get upset about it.

1   2   3   4   5   6

4. I get upset when someone is mistreated.

1   2   3   4   5   6

5. When I see a homeless person on the side of the road asking for money, I get mad at the person for begging.

1   2   3   4   5   6

6. I like hearing about friends doing well in school even if I'm not doing as well as I want to.

1   2   3   4   5   6

7. When someone gets mad at me, I try to understand why that person is mad.

1   2   3   4   5   6

8. When a friend complains about something I think is trivial, I stop listening.

1   2   3   4   5   6

9. I have a hard time listening to someone else's opinion without arguing when the person's opinion differs from mine.

1   2   3   4   5   6

10. I can tell you the other person's main concerns even during the heat of an argument.

1   2   3   4   5   6

Scoring: For items 3, 5, 8, and 9, change your scores as follows: if you circled a 1, change it to 6; change a 2 to a 5, a 3 to a 4, a 4 to a 3, a 5 to a 2, and a 6 to a 1. Then add up your points for your first five items—this is your emotional empathy. Then add the scores for items 6–10. This is your cognitive empathy. The higher your score (maximum total = 30 for each section), the more empathic you think you are.

Now give these same 10 questions to the person you believe knows you the best and ask him or her to think about you when responding. (Do *not* tell the person your scores first.) Score the person's responses, following the same directions, and add up the total points for each section.

Empathy Assessment Completed by a Friend or Family Member

Student's Name:

Your relationship to the student:

Respond to the following statements using the number scale.

1 = Strongly disagree	2 = Disagree	3 = Slightly disagree	4 = Slightly agree	5 = Agree	6 = Strongly agree

1. Seeing someone who is upset makes this person upset.

1   2   3   4   5   6

2. This person tends to cry during sad movies.

1   2   3   4   5   6

3. This person thinks it's funny when others get teased and get upset about it.

1   2   3   4   5   6

4. This person gets upset when hearing about someone being mistreated.

1   2   3   4   5   6

5. When this person sees a homeless person on the side of the road asking for money, it makes him or her mad.

1   2   3   4   5   6

6. This person likes hearing about friends doing well in school even if he or she is not doing as well.

1   2   3   4   5   6

7. When someone gets mad at this person, he or she tries to understand why that person is mad.

1   2   3   4   5   6

8. When a friend complains about something this person thinks is trivial, he or she stops listening.

1   2   3   4   5   6

(continued)

1 = Strongly disagree	2 = Disagree	3 = Slightly disagree	4 = Slightly agree	5 = Agree	6 = Strongly agree

9. This person has a hard time listening to someone else's opinion without arguing when that opinion differs from his or hers.

1   2   3   4   5   6

10. This person can tell you the other person's main concerns even during the heat of an argument.

1   2   3   4   5   6

Reflection Questions

1. What is your reaction to how the other person scored you?
2. What did you learn about yourself by doing this exercise?

Activity 10.5

Listening Even When It's Hard to Do!

EI Dimensions Targeted: Empathy, Impulse Control

Brief Description/Objective: Students will practice listening and understanding someone else's opinion on a subject matter about which they disagree.

Planning the Activity

Time Expected
- Worksheet: 10–15 minutes
- Reflection Questions: 10 minutes
- In-Class Debrief: 10 minutes

Materials
- Worksheet 10.5 from *The Student EQ Edge: Student Workbook*
- Board or flip chart and markers
- *The Student EQ Edge: Emotional Intelligence and Your Academic and Personal Success*

Facilitating the Activity

Directions
- Assign Worksheet 10.5.
- Prepare students for the fact that it will be very hard to stay focused on listening and understanding the other person's perspective rather than trying to explain or argue the student's own perspective.

Debriefing Questions
- Raise the question of whether students believe it is more important to listen or more important to get their point across in a discussion with someone on a topic they disagree about. On the board, list the advantages and disadvantages of each approach.
- See the reflection questions at the end of the worksheet.

Worksheet 10.5: Listening Even When It's Hard to Do!

Name:

Think about a topic that you and a friend or family member have a strong disagreement about that you would be willing to discuss with that person. Ask that person to have a conversation with you about the topic and tell him or her that your job in this assignment is to practice empathy skills (reflective listening, asking good questions, understanding the other's perspective and emotions, and so on). Ask the person to stop you whenever you begin to argue your point rather than trying to understand his or her perspective. *Warning*: It may be hard for you not to argue your points!

Conversation topic:

Person I talked with:

Rate yourself on how well you listened and tried to understand the other person. Rate yourself as a 2 if you show some elements of 1 and 3; rate yourself as a 4 if your answer shows some elements of 3 and 5.

Not effective		**Somewhat effective**		**Very effective**
Interrupted, argued own points		Listened some, some questions but some arguing my own points		Listened, summarized his or her view, asked open-ended questions
1	2	3	4	5

Ask the person you talked with to rate you on the following scale about how well you listened to and tried to understand his or her perspective (your grade will not be affected by the rating!).

Not effective		**Somewhat effective**		**Very effective**
Interrupted, argued his or her points		Listened some, some questions but some arguing his or her points		Listened, asked questions to better understand me and my views
1	2	3	4	5

Reflection Questions

1. How hard was it for you to resist the urge to argue your perspective? What did you do to help yourself concentrate on the other person's views?
2. What *new information* did you learn about the other person or why he or she holds the expressed opinion?
3. What benefit came from listening to and trying to understand the other person?

Activity 10.6

Self-Development Plan for Empathy

The directions and template for students to create a self-development plan appear in Appendix D of this *Facilitation and Activity Guide*. *The Student EQ Edge: Student Workbook* contains a template for developing stronger empathy in Chapter 10.

Activity 10.7

Case Study—Empathy

See Chapter 2 to assign a case study relevant to empathy. Chapter 2 of *The Student EQ Edge: Student Workbook* contains all of the same case studies.

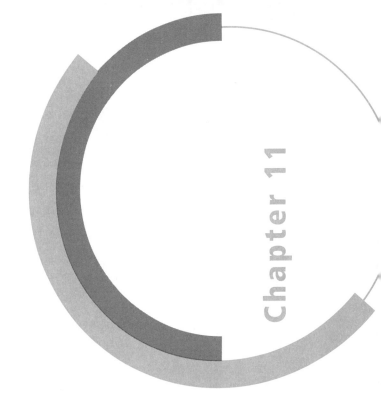

Chapter 11

Social Responsibility

What is social responsibility? This multifaceted skill involves being helpful to others, contributing to the greater good of the "group" (a partner, a team, an organization, your community), or being collaborative and cooperative with groups you interact with. Thinking only about one's own well-being is the antithesis of social responsibility. Being socially responsible does *not* mean that you engage in self-sacrifice or let others take advantage of you. Rather, it means that you are engaging in actions that benefit groups that you are a part of, thus also benefiting yourself. You may receive joy from what you did to benefit others; at a minimum, your social responsibility will likely make you a more valued partner or team member.

Social responsibility can be as simple as seeing a chore that needs to be done and doing it without being asked (for example, emptying a full trash can). Or it can involve engaging in volunteer work in the community. Socially responsible people are likely to be cooperative and contributing members of a group rather than the type of group member who does as little as possible and values his or her time above others' time.

But can we be too socially responsible? Think about individuals such as Mother Teresa. Would you say she was too socially responsible? Although our socially responsible behavior can have negative ramifications—less time or money for ourselves and those we care about—the joy and benefit can outweigh the costs. Those very high in social responsibility do need to be wary of others taking advantage of them and thus also need well-developed assertiveness skills.

STUDENT LEARNING OUTCOMES

Students will:

- Describe what social responsibility is within a smaller community (family, team, school, work group) and as part of the larger community (city, state, country, world)
- Identify companies or historical figures who have demonstrated social responsibility
- Identify ways they can become more socially responsible
- State the benefits to self and others when engaging in social responsibility

SUGGESTED READINGS, MOVIES, AND TELEVISION SHOWS

- *The Student EQ Edge: Emotional Intelligence and Your Academic and Personal Success*, Chapter 11

Movies

- *Erin Brockovich*—Scene 22, "Erin Interviews the Hinkley residents"—Erin contacts all the people in town to help them fight PG&E; Scene 23, "Erin Convinces Ed to Expand the Case"—as Erin realizes the gravity of what has occurred, she advocates strongly for the citizens of Hinkley.
- *One Fine Day*—Scene 3, "The Single Dad," through Scene 5, "Race for the Boat"—George Clooney's character is playing around instead of listening to important details, and as a result, his daughter and the other child in the carpool miss an important field trip.
- *Patch Adams*—Scene 11, "Gesundheit"—Patch opens a free clinic for the poor, and everyone pitches in to make the clinic work.

- *Remember the Titans*—From the opening scene in the gym to the game scene where a parent yells at the coach for taking his kid out of the game—An African-American coach takes over a racially divided team and tries to mold them into a cooperative unit. As the movie progresses, almost all of the players begin to put the team goals ahead of their self-interest or prejudice.

Television Shows

- *The Office*—Episode 28, "Casino Night"—The office hosts a charity casino night in the warehouse; employees discuss philanthropic endeavors; one employee admits to frequently stealing.
- *Modern Family*—Episode 57, "After the Fire"—After a neighbor's house is burned down, Clair organizes a neighborhood clothes and furnishings drive.
- *The Office*—Episode 75, "Business Ethics"—Lack of ethical practices and breaking of company policies are realized during an attempted ethics seminar.
- *The Andy Griffith Show*—This classic show from the '60s and '70s portrays a small-town sheriff who goes beyond the call of duty to help citizens of Mayberry. For example, he leaves a cell door unlocked for someone he has "arrested" because he wants that person to think about his actions and be free to leave when he's calmed down.

PLANNING YOUR CLASS

50–60 Minute Class

Assign Worksheets 11.1 and 11.2 for homework and debrief in class. During the debriefing, make sure to address questions about how much is "too much" to do for other people before we get taken advantage of. Bring in a discussion of assertiveness to help students understand the difference between cooperating, helping others, and contributing to some greater good versus being taken advantage of. Spend the rest of the class having students either develop their own social responsibility policy (Activity 11.4) or analyze a case study that involves social responsibility issues (Activity 11.7).

Assign Worksheets 11.1 and 11.2 for homework and debrief in class. During the debriefing, make sure to address questions about how much is "too much" to do for other people before we get taken advantage of. Bring in a discussion of assertiveness to help students understand the difference between cooperating, helping others, and contributing to some greater good versus being taken advantage of. Then show the first 20 minutes of the movie *One Fine Day*, in which George Clooney's character causes two children to miss a big field trip and another adult to have to take her child to work on a very stressful workday, all because he lacks social responsibility. Debrief the movie. If your class has internet access, do Activity 11.3 as a class, looking at the social responsibility policies of several major companies. Then give students about 20 minutes to do Activity 11.4, writing their own social responsibility policy (or Activity 11.6, writing a self-development plan for improving social responsibility). Conclude class by assigning a case study for students (Activity 11.7) to read and debrief as a group.

Note: An alternative 3–4 hour class could involve completing Activity 11.5 together as a class. If you choose to do this, assign Worksheets 11.1 and 11.2 for homework.

Activity List

Activity #	Activity Name	Brief Description and Activity Notes
11.1	Doing What's Right	Students think about times at home, at school, and with a friend or partner when they did and did not demonstrate social responsibility. This activity is based on a quote by Martin Luther King Jr. Talk about the relationship between social responsibility and "doing what's right."
11.2	Cooperation	Students watch a YouTube clip of *Sesame Street* characters singing a song about cooperation. We're never too old for the lessons taught on *Sesame Street*, but if you're worried students will think this activity is "too young," show them the opening 15–20 minutes of the movie *One Fine Day*.
11.3	A Company's Social Responsibility Policy	Students look up the social responsibility actions of a well-known company. If you prefer, give students a list of historical people such as Rosa Parks, Martin Luther King, Mother Teresa, and others and ask them to write a brief essay about how this person demonstrated social responsibility.
11.4	My Social Responsibility Policy	Students write their own social responsibility policy, something they are willing to put into action!
11.5	Take Action!	Students engage in four hours of activity that benefits another person or persons. If time permits, schedule a class community service project.
11.6	Self-Development Plan for Social Responsibility	Students create strategies for self-improvement related to their social responsibility skills.
11.7	Case Study— Social Responsibility	Students analyze the behavior of a person who faces challenges related to social responsibility.

Activity 11.1
Doing What's Right

EI Dimensions Targeted: Social Responsibility, Empathy

Brief Description/Objective: Students will identify times they have and have not engaged in socially responsible actions in their daily lives.

Planning the Activity

Time Expected
- Worksheet: 10 minutes
- Reflection Questions: 15 minutes
- In-Class Debrief: 10 minutes

Materials
- Worksheet 11.1 from *The Student EQ Edge: Student Workbook*
- Board or flip chart and markers
- *The Student EQ Edge: Emotional Intelligence and Your Academic and Personal Success*

Facilitating the Activity

Directions
- Assign Worksheet 11.1.

Debriefing Questions
- This activity begins with a quote by Dr. Martin Luther King, Jr. Conduct an agree-disagree activity with students about whether they agree with the quote. Most likely, some students will disagree with the quote, opening a fruitful discussion about "doing what's right."
- See the reflection questions at the end of the worksheet.

Worksheet 11.1: Doing What's Right

Name:

The time is always right to do what is right.—Dr. Martin Luther King, Jr.

Fill out the following chart. When coming up with examples for each column, think about these five areas of your life: (1) group projects at school; (2) helping around the house; (3) helping or not helping a parent, partner, or friend with a very big task that will not directly benefit you; (4) volunteering your time for a good cause; and (5) volunteering to take on a project that would help your work group, a club, or team.

I demonstrated social responsibility when:	I did NOT demonstrate social responsibility when:
At school:	At school:
At home:	At home:
With a friend, family member, or partner:	With a friend, family member, or partner:
By volunteering for a good cause:	Turning down an opportunity to volunteer:
By volunteering to take on a project that would help my work group, a club, or team:	Not volunteering to take on a project that would help my work group, a club, or team:

Reflection Questions

1. Which of these experiences do you feel the best about and why?
2. Which of these experiences do you feel the worst about and why?
3. If you think you need to become more socially responsible, what will motivate you to do so? If you don't think you need to become more socially responsible, do you think others close to you would agree with that self-assessment? Explain your answer.

Activity 11.2
Cooperation

EI Dimensions Targeted: Social Responsibility

Brief Description/Objective: Students will examine how cooperation is a part of social responsibility.

Planning the Activity

Time Expected
- Worksheet and YouTube video: 5 minutes
- Reflection Questions: 10 minutes
- In-Class Debrief: 15 minutes

Materials
- Worksheet 11.2 from *The Student EQ Edge: Student Workbook*
- Board or flip chart and markers
- *The Student EQ Edge: Emotional Intelligence and Your Academic and Personal Success*
- Internet connection, if you want to conduct the activity in class

Facilitating the Activity

Directions
- Assign Worksheet 11.2.
- Watch the YouTube clip "Sesame Street—Cooperation Makes It Happen" first by yourself; if you think your students will not respond well to this clip of Sesame Street characters, show the first 20 minutes of the movie *One Fine Day* in class as a substitute. If you use *One Fine Day*, change the reflection questions.

Debriefing Questions
- Conduct an agree-disagree activity based on the statement, "If I cooperate with others too much, they will just take advantage of me."
- See the reflection questions at the end of the worksheet.

Worksheet 11.2: Cooperation

Name:

Go to the following YouTube clip, which features the song "Cooperation Makes It Happen" by the *Sesame Street* gang. (You probably watched *Sesame Street* as a kid and you may even remember this song, so just enjoy yourself!) http://www.youtube.com/watch?v=5exvfbnFMUg

Reflection Questions

1. Most of the characters were smiling much of the time they were working together. Why do you think there's an established research link between helping others and our own level of personal happiness?
2. *Sesame Street* is known for teaching valuable lessons to children. Think back to your childhood. What other individuals or groups taught you about working to help others, cooperating, or other aspects of social responsibility? What points did they stress?
3. If you could get everyone in the world (or your country, your school, or within your family or any other group you wish to choose) to cooperate about one issue, what would that issue be and how would everyone benefit?

Activity 11.3
A Company's Social Responsibility Policy

EI Dimensions Targeted: Social Responsibility, Empathy

Brief Description/Objective: The student will identify a company whose social responsibility policy is in line with what the student values in terms of being good citizens of the world.

Planning the Activity

Time Expected
- Worksheet: 20 minutes
- Reflection Questions: 10 minutes
- In-Class Debrief: 10 minutes

Materials
- Worksheet 11.3 from *The Student EQ Edge: Student Workbook*
- Board or flip chart and markers
- *The Student EQ Edge: Emotional Intelligence and Your Academic and Personal Success*
- Internet connection, if you plan to do this activity in class

Facilitating the Activity

Directions
- Assign Worksheet 11.3.
- You may want to have researched several companies and their social responsibility policies ahead of time if you do this activity in class.

Debriefing Questions
- Is it socially irresponsible to buy products made in countries where workers are not paid fair wages?
- See the reflection questions at the end of the worksheet.

Worksheet 11.3: A Company's Social Responsibility Policy

Name:

Look up the social responsibility policy for a company such as Microsoft, McDonald's, The Body Shop, Ben and Jerry's ice cream, or Timberland.

Company Name:

Social Responsibility Policy: (if the policy is lengthy, write a one-paragraph summary)

Now pretend you are the president of a major organization. What are three things you would want your company to do to be more socially responsible?

Reflection Questions

1. Why did you pick the social responsibility areas you did for your company?
2. Some skeptics might believe the only reason some companies care about social responsibility is because it can help them increase sales. Suppose that assumption is true; would the company's behavior still be considered socially responsible? Explain.

Activity 11.4
My Social Responsibility Policy

EI Dimensions Targeted: Social Responsibility, Self-Actualization, Happiness

Brief Description/Objective: Students will write their own policy for social responsibility, identifying areas in their lives where they would like to contribute more to the well-being of others.

Planning the Activity

Time Expected
- Worksheet: 10 minutes
- Reflection Questions: 10 minutes
- In-Class Debrief: 10 minutes

Materials
- Worksheet 11.4 from *The Student EQ Edge: Student Workbook*
- Board or flip chart and markers
- *The Student EQ Edge: Emotional Intelligence and Your Academic and Personal Success*

Facilitating the Activity

Directions
- Assign Worksheet 11.4.

Debriefing Questions
- How did things change for you when you noticed that someone affected by your social responsibility policy would have to sign it? Were you more careful about what you promised? Did it make you nervous to make your commitment more public?
- See the reflection questions at the end of the worksheet.

Worksheet 11.4: My Social Responsibility Policy

Name:

Think about the area in which you are the least socially responsible from among the following areas: home/family; school; work; sports team, club, or organization.

Area chosen:

Write a social responsibility policy for yourself in this area. Make sure your policy addresses your current weaknesses in the area of social responsibility! When developing your policy, it might help to think about the following questions:

- *What* do I need to do more of or less of?
- *Who* would benefit from this and *how* would they benefit?
- *Why* did I pick this area?
- My social responsibility policy is:

Now share your policy with one person in the area you've chosen. It could be a parent, partner, teammate, coach, teacher, boss, or anyone else who is affected by your policy. Get them to sign your policy (or send an email indicating they have read it).

Signature of person reading your policy: _____

Reflection Questions

1. How much did you think about the challenges and costs of adhering to your policy when you wrote it? Why might this matter in your willingness to follow through?
2. What will motivate you to follow through with your policy?
3. How will others benefit from your policy?

Activity 11.5
Take Action!

EI Dimensions Targeted: Social Responsibility, Self-Actualization, Happiness

Brief Description/Objective: Students will engage in community service or some other socially responsible activity for four hours.

Planning the Activity

Time Expected
- Worksheet/Activity: 3–4 hours
- Reflection Questions: 15 minutes
- In-Class Debrief: 15 minutes

Materials
- Worksheet 11.5 from *The Student EQ Edge: Student Workbook*
- Board or flip chart and markers
- *The Student EQ Edge: Emotional Intelligence and Your Academic and Personal Success*
- If you have an office of community service on your campus, have them provide a list of agencies in need of volunteers, with their contact information

Facilitating the Activity

Directions
- Assign Worksheet 11.5.
- Decide whether you want the students to engage in a community service activity together as a class or do something alone. It would be appropriate for students to do something at home (for example, help a family member clean out a garage or paint a room) that they would not normally be asked to do.

Debriefing Questions
- Research shows a link between doing things for others and an increase in our happiness. Why do you think such a link exists?
- See the reflection questions at the end of the worksheet.

Worksheet 11.5: Take Action!

Name:

Spend at least four hours doing something for someone else. You can volunteer at a local soup kitchen or after-school program, help build a Habitat for Humanity House, ask family members to give you four hours' worth of work to do that you normally would not do, pick up trash along the street, or whatever else you can think of.

Describe your activity:

Reflection Questions

1. Why did you pick this activity?
2. How did you feel during and after the activity?
3. Would you be willing to do this activity again? Why or why not?

Activity 11.6

Self-Development Plan for Social Responsibility

The directions and template for students to create a self-development plan appear in Appendix D of this *Facilitation and Activity Guide*. *The Student EQ Edge: Student Workbook* contains a template for developing stronger social responsibility in Chapter 11.

Activity 11.7

Case Study—Social Responsibility

See Chapter 2 to assign a case study relevant to social responsibility. Chapter 2 of *The Student EQ Edge: Student Workbook* contains all of the same case studies.

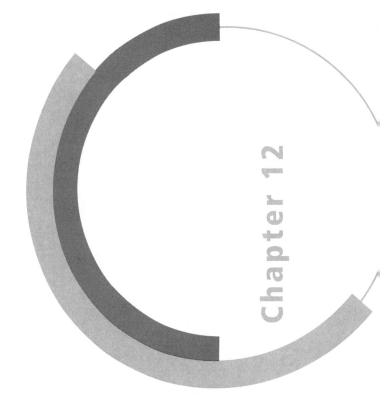

Reality Testing

What is reality testing? It involves the ability to notice the facts of a situation and then interpret those correctly. If effective empathy involves reading *people* accurately, then effective reality testing involves reading the *environment* (facts, situations) accurately. Sounds simple, right? What could be difficult about accurately assessing facts? A lot, especially when those facts or situations create emotions or interfere with something we want to do or want to avoid! How many of you have seen or heard about students who

- Severely underestimate how long it will take them to write a good paper?
- Go out the night before a big exam?
- Apply to schools that are prestigious or popular when they don't have a realistic chance of getting in?
- Get themselves in financial trouble because of overusing credit cards?
- Continue to drive a car for miles and miles even after a warning light comes on?
- Think they can work 40 hours a week, take a full load of classes, and maintain an acceptable GPA?

No doubt you could add many of your own examples! All of these actions involve the "ostrich" syndrome of sticking one's head in the proverbial sand. But there's also the "Chicken Little" variety

Chapter 12

179

of poor reality testing, which involves imagining dangers lurking around every corner and catastrophizing the ultimate results of the mildest setback—such as a B on the first test meaning you've lost any chance of going to med school.

Emotions can cause us to ignore the facts because those facts scare us, make us sad, or cause frustration. Or careful attention to the facts may mean we make different decisions, ones that will give us less immediate pleasure or happiness. It's easy to understand why students would want to believe that a term paper could be done well in just one day of work. That sounds much more appealing than expecting to have to work on the paper multiple hours each week over a month. So there are at least two emotions driving the decision to put off writing the term paper: anxiety (it can't be that hard) and happiness (I can spend my time doing more fun things).

Let's return to our bird friends—the ostrich and Chicken Little—for a moment and consider the following story. Both Kris and Shamica want to get into medical school, and both have the MCAT exam next month. Kris is a senior with a 3.0 average. She took the MCAT once and scored in the 5th percentile. She has not started studying yet for the test next month and isn't sure she'll have time to get to it. There are plenty of med schools out there, so if her scores aren't high enough for the best schools, she'll just apply to other med schools. Shamica has a 3.8 average, has shadowed three different types of doctors, and has volunteered at the local health clinic. She began studying for the MCAT a year ago, and the practice tests she's taken placed her in the 90th percentile or higher. She's convinced, though, that she's just made some lucky guesses. So she's turning down all social engagements and only studying for the MCAT and going to school.

Both students lack reality testing, but the consequences will be far different—one probably won't get into med school and the other will get in but will likely not have time to enjoy life.

Can someone be too high in reality testing? Very high reality testing is often accompanied by black-and-white thinking. Consider these two premedical students. Someone who scores very high in reality testing may know lots of facts about what it takes to get into each school and may have carefully chosen to apply to schools that offer an excellent chance of acceptance. But that same student may also *not* apply to her dream school simply because someone with her profile has only about a 20-percent chance of acceptance. If it's her dream school and there's any chance of acceptance, she should apply!

STUDENT LEARNING OUTCOMES

Students will:

- Identify their own style of reality testing and understand its impact on their decision making
- Describe how others have engaged in effective or ineffective reality testing and what consequences resulted
- Understand the consequences of poor reality testing in all aspects of life

SUGGESTED READINGS, MOVIES, AND TELEVISION SHOWS

- *The Student EQ Edge: Emotional Intelligence and Your Academic and Personal Success*, Chapter 12

Movies
- *Catch Me If You Can*—Scene 13, "Dr. Frank Connors"—Frank tries to become a medical doctor but fails to consider that the sight of blood makes him gag and that he must have medical knowledge to be successful with his charade. *Note*: This movie is based on a true story of criminal behavior; the person eventually gets caught and helps the FBI track other white-collar criminals.
- *Odd Girl Out*—Final 10 minutes—Back at school, Vanessa receives an apology from Stacey and tells Stacey she's so glad they're best friends again; she cannot recognize that Stacey still has not done anything nice for her and is still hanging out with the kids that bullied her.
- *What About Bob?*— Scene 1, opening credits—Neurotic Bob is shown avoiding all harmless actions (holding a hand railing) because they could hurt him; in Scene 14, "Death

Therapy"—Bob interprets Leo's tying him up and strapping dynamite to him as a therapeutic act rather than retribution.

Television Shows

- *Glee*—Episode 45, "Purple Piano Project"—A new student tries out for the New Directions. Unfortunately, her singing talent is in question.
- *The Office*—Episode 1, "The Pilot"—Michael Scott, regional manager, is unaware of how his subordinates feel about him and of what constitutes acceptable conversation in an office.

PLANNING YOUR CLASS

50–60 Minute Class

Assign Worksheets 12.2 and 12.3 for homework. Debrief 12.2 as suggested, helping the students to better understand their reality-testing skills. Next, debrief Activity 12.3. Steer the discussion toward the importance of reality testing (and other EI skills such as emotional self-awareness and assertiveness) and the cost of poor reality testing. End the class by having students work in small groups to come up with responses to Worksheet 12.5.

3–4 Hour Class

Assign Worksheets 12.2, 12.3, and 12.4 for homework. Debrief 12.2 as suggested, helping the students to better understand their reality-testing skills. You could further help the students by assigning Worksheet 12.1 immediately following the debrief of 12.2. Students should be more aware of their reality testing ability and thus would engage in better reflection about a big decision. Next, debrief Activity 12.3. Steer the discussion toward the importance of reality testing (and other EI skills such as emotional self-awareness and assertiveness) and the cost of poor reality testing. The costs of poor reality testing can be further illuminated by discussing the results of Worksheet 12.4. Next, have the class practice effective reality testing by having students work in small groups to come up with responses to Worksheet 12.5. End class by having students read the case study "A Costly Decision" (Activity 12.7). If time allows, ask students to begin working on their self-development plan (Worksheet 12.6).

Activity List

Activity #	Activity Name	Brief Description and Activity Notes
12.1	My Big Decision	Students examine an upcoming important decision and develop effective reality-testing skills to help them make a better decision. Remind students that a failure to take action can also be considered a decision (and evidence of poor reality testing).
12.2	The Mirrors Around You	Students compare their self-perceptions about their reality testing ability with the perceptions of someone who knows them well.
12.3	Failed Reality Testing	Students examine how the lack of effective reality testing led to two very bad decisions—the launch of the space shuttle *Challenger* and Kennedy's decision to invade the Bay of Pigs. (These examples are not meant to assign blame or make political statements; both incidents are widely written about in terms of bad decision-making processes.)
12.4	Decision-Making Interviews	Students gain insight into how others use reality-testing skills when faced with a difficult decision.
12.5	Reality-Testing Scenarios	Students practice developing reality-testing skills by responding to scenarios students may face.
12.6	Self-Development Plan for Reality Testing	Students develop a plan for improving reality-testing skills.
12.7	Case Study— Reality Testing	Students analyze the behavior of a person who faces challenges related to reality testing. The case study "A Costly Decision" is highly recommended.

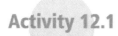

Activity 12.1
My Big Decision

EI Dimensions Targeted: Reality Testing, Emotional Self-Awareness

Brief Description/Objective: Students will examine a big decision they are facing soon and practice reality-testing skills.

Planning the Activity

Time Expected
- Worksheet: 15 minutes (much longer if they collect all of the facts they need to)
- Reflection Questions: 10 minutes
- In-Class Debrief: 5–10 minutes

Materials
- Worksheet 12.1 from *The Student EQ Edge: Student Workbook*
- Board or flip chart and markers
- *The Student EQ Edge: Emotional Intelligence and Your Academic and Personal Success*

Facilitating the Activity

Directions
- Assign Worksheet 12.1.
- Before debriefing the class as a whole, you can pair students and have them read each other's scenarios. (If you plan to do this, tell the students prior to the activity, as this may affect their choice of a decision.)

Debriefing Questions
- Ask whether anyone reached a final decision as a result of doing this activity. Ask whether the student is willing to share the decision and the information considered. Have the class help the student—again, with his or her permission—think of anything important the student may have omitted.
- Ask students their opinion about whether the process used in this activity is effective for making important decisions. If they believe it's not effective, explore their reasons. If they don't want to use it because it's time consuming or might make them think about things they'd rather ignore, challenge them.
- See the reflection questions at the end of the worksheet.

Worksheet 12.1: My Big Decision

Name:

1. Identify a big decision you will need to make in the next 6 to 12 months. Examples might include picking a college, deciding a major, determining whether to break up with a romantic partner, buying a car, moving to a new city to take a job, and so on. Describe this decision you are facing:

2. Now imagine your decision is like the funnel in the figure. At the beginning of the decision process, there's lots of information to consider and several, if not many, options. But as you answer the questions that follow, some decisions emerge as better options than others. Answer each question as thoroughly as possible.

Figure 12.1. The Information Funnel

- What information could I collect about this situation?
- What are the facts related to this situation?
- What are my opinions and assumptions about this situation?
- What would I like to do and why?
- Do the facts and information collected support what I would like to do? Explain.

Reflection Questions

1. If a friend were facing the same situation, what advice would you offer? Explain your answer.
2. What factors most influenced your decision? Are these factors more reality based (based on facts), fantasy based (based on what you'd like to see happen), or worry based (based on what you fear)?

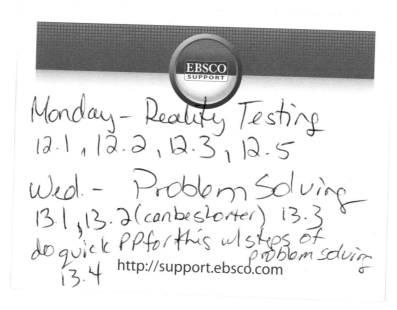

Activity 12.2

The Mirrors Around You

EI Dimensions Targeted: Reality Testing, Emotional Self-Awareness

Brief Description/Objective: Students will self-report their reality-testing ability and have someone close to them complete the same questions about the student.

Planning the Activity

Time Expected
- Worksheet: 5 minutes each for student and friend or family member
- Reflection Questions: 10 minutes
- In-Class Debrief: 10 minutes

Materials
- Worksheet 12.2 from *The Student EQ Edge: Student Workbook*
- Board or flip chart and markers
- *The Student EQ Edge: Emotional Intelligence and Your Academic and Personal Success*

Facilitating the Activity

Directions
- Assign Worksheet 12.2.
- Make sure students understand that there are several ways we can demonstrate poor reality testing. One way involves taking factual information and exaggerating its meaning (for example, every headache means a brain tumor) and the other type is to ignore or purposefully deny the importance of factual information (for example, believing that an abusive person will suddenly stop being abusive, or refusing to go to a doctor after six months of chronic headaches).

Debriefing Questions
- What are some advantages of living in a fantasy world? Of exaggerating the importance of some facts? (Note that these tendencies must provide some value to people or they would not keep making the same mistake over and over.)
- See the reflection questions at the end of the worksheet.

Worksheet 12.2: The Mirrors Around You

Name:

Answer the following questions about yourself, using the numerical scores provided.

1	2	3	4	5
Not at all like me	A little bit like me	Somewhat like me	A lot like me	Very much like me

_____1. I worry a lot about little things.

_____2. Others accuse me of exaggerating.

_____3. I imagine the worst.

_____4. I often realize that I've made too big of a deal about something.

_____5. I collect facts and information beyond what is needed to make a good decision.

_____6. I don't like to hear information that contradicts what I want to do.

_____7. I tend to ignore things I don't like to think about.

_____8. Others would describe me as unrealistic or idealistic.

_____9. I believe that my emotions should guide my decisions as much as facts should.

_____10. I'm often surprised at how a situation turns out.

Add your scores for items 1–5 and record that number here: _____

The higher your score for these questions (the range is 5–25), the more you tend to err toward being too focused on reality, too rigid in your perceptions, or too negative about possible outcomes.

Add your scores for items 6–10 and record that number here: _____

The higher your score for these questions (the range is 5–25), the more you tend to err toward being unaware of or uninterested in facts and reality.

Now ask your best friend or a family member to answer the same questions about you.

Student's name:

Your relationship to the student:

Answer these questions about the student, using the numerical scores provided.

1	2	3	4	5
Not at all like him/her	A little bit like him/her	Somewhat like him/her	A lot like him/her	Very much like him/her

_____1. This person worries a lot about little things.

_____2. Others think this person exaggerates.

_____3. This person imagines the worst.

_____4. This person often realizes that he/she made too big of a deal about something.

_____5. This person collects more facts and information than needed.

_____6. This person doesn't like to hear information that contradicts what he or she wants to do.

_____7. This person tends to ignore things he or she doesn't like to think about.

_____8. Others would describe this person as unrealistic or idealistic.

_____9. This person lets emotions guide decisions as much as facts do.

_____10. This person is often surprised at how a situation turns out.

Add your scores for items 1–5 and record that number here: _____

The higher the score for these questions (the range is 5–25), the more this person errs toward being too focused on reality, too rigid in perceptions, or too negative about possible outcomes.

Add your scores for items 6–10 and record that number here: _____

The higher the score for these questions (the range is 5–25), the more this person tends to err toward being unaware of or uninterested in facts and reality.

Reflection Questions

1. Compare and contrast how you see yourself with how the other person sees you.
2. Would you like to become more grounded in reality or more carefree in how you approach information and decisions? Explain your choice.

Activity 12.3
Failed Reality Testing

EI Dimensions Targeted: Reality Testing, Social Responsibility, Problem Solving

Brief Description/Objective: Students will examine one of two historical events in which poor reality testing led to a flawed decision.

Planning the Activity

Time Expected
- Worksheet: 40–60 minutes (includes reading the articles)
- Reflection Questions: 10 minutes
- In-Class Debrief: 15–20 minutes

Materials
- Worksheet 12.3 from *The Student EQ Edge: Student Workbook*
- Board or flip chart and markers
- *The Student EQ Edge: Emotional Intelligence and Your Academic and Personal Success*

Facilitating the Activity

Directions
- Assign Worksheet 12.3.
- Explain that the purpose of this activity is not to place blame or discuss politics; rather, the sole focus is to examine problems with reality testing and how that contributed to the decisions made.

Debriefing Questions
- Most bad decisions that we make don't have such serious consequences. When lives are lost, should people be held accountable for their decisions even if they did not break a law? (*Instructor's Note*: Conduct an agree-disagree activity to produce maximum discussion.)
- See the reflection questions at the end of the worksheet.

Worksheet 12.3: Failed Reality Testing

Name:

Choose one of the following two situations and conduct research about the decision made, what information should have been considered that wasn't, how emotions affected the decision-making process, and what consequences occurred because of the failure to test reality.

Situation 1. Launch of the Space Shuttle *Challenger* with school teacher Christa McAuliffe on board

http://www.heroism.org/class/1980/challenger.htm

http://ethics.tamu.edu/ethics/shuttle/shuttle1.htm

For even more information, check out Chapter 1 of *The Challenger Launch Decision: Risky Technology, Culture and Deviance at NASA* by Diane Vaughan, available through Google Books.

Situation 2. President Kennedy's decision to invade the Bay of Pigs

http://www.globalsecurity.org/intell/ops/bay-of-pigs.htm

http://www.probe.org/site/c.fdKEIMNsEoG/b.4221087/k.4551/JFK_and_Groupthink_Lessons_in_Decision_Making.htm

Answer the following questions about the situation you chose.

1. What information was available to the decision maker(s) that could have changed the decision?
2. Why did that information not influence the decision maker(s)? Was the information not shared, was the information ignored, or was there some other reason the information did not factor into the decision?
3. How did emotions play a role in the decision making?
4. What consequences occurred based on the decision?

Reflection Questions

1. Pretend you have to explain to a friend why emotional intelligence is often more important than IQ in determining success. Use the scenario you read to help you formulate your points.
2. Is there evidence in your scenario that people learned from their mistakes and improved their reality testing?

Activity 12.4
Decision-Making Interviews

EI Dimensions Targeted: Reality Testing, Emotional Self-Awareness

Brief Description/Objective: Students will interview someone they know well about a really big decision the person made and how effectively reality testing was used to help make the decision.

Planning the Activity

Time Expected
- Worksheet and Interview: 15–20 minutes
- Reflection Questions: 10 minutes
- In-Class Debrief: 10 minutes

Materials
- Worksheet 12.4 from *The Student EQ Edge: Student Workbook*
- Board or flip chart and markers
- *The Student EQ Edge: Emotional Intelligence and Your Academic and Personal Success*

Facilitating the Activity

Directions
- Assign Worksheet 12.4.
- You can alter this activity by having students examine the situation from Activity 12.3 (*Challenger* or Bay of Pigs) that they haven't already examined.

Debriefing Questions
- What were some of the consequences of poor reality testing?
- Facilitate an agree-disagree exercise based on the following premise: *Reality-testing skills should be taught as part of every school's curriculum.*
- See the reflection questions at the end of the worksheet.

Worksheet 12.4: Decision-Making Interviews

Name:

Ask someone you know well to describe a very difficult decision he or she made. In the space provided, create interview questions for the person that will help you understand whether the person used good reality-testing skills or not. Make sure the questions will help you probe the person's reality-testing skills as part of the decision making.

Reflection Questions

1. Summarize what you learned in the interview.
2. Did the person use effective reality-testing skills or not? Explain your answer.

Activity 12.5

Reality-Testing Scenarios

EI Dimensions Targeted: Reality Testing, Problem Solving, Emotional Self-Awareness

Brief Description/Objective: Students will hone their skills in reality testing by responding to several scenarios.

Planning the Activity

Time Expected
- Worksheet: 20 minutes
- Reflection Questions: 10 minutes
- In-Class Debrief: 10–20 minutes, depending on method chosen

Materials
- Worksheet 12.5 from *The Student EQ Edge: Student Workbook*
- Board or flip chart and markers
- *The Student EQ Edge: Emotional Intelligence and Your Academic and Personal Success*

Facilitating the Activity

Directions
- Assign Worksheet 12.5.
- If you prefer, break the class into small groups and assign one scenario to each group, then have these smaller groups report back to the larger group.

Debriefing Questions
- Which situation is likely to yield the least reality testing? Explain your answer.
- See the reflection questions at the end of the worksheet.

Worksheet 12.5: Reality-Testing Scenarios

Name:

Read the following scenarios and describe what effective reality testing would look like for a student in that situation. What information would the student seek? What facts would be considered? What questions should the student ask and whom should the student ask?

Scenario	Effective reality testing would include. . .
A student who is trying to get into a very prestigious college has signed up to take four Advanced Placement classes and two honors classes. She is also playing on a year-round soccer team and for her high school team. A week before school begins, she is approached by a teacher to become the editor of the school newspaper, which is published weekly.	
A Caucasian male university student is majoring in Arabic and international relations, preparing for a career working for the U.S. government in Arab-U.S. relations. His advisor mentions a summer study program in Iraq where the student could live in Baghdad with a sponsor family and interview locals about their feelings toward the United States.	
A college female is interested in pursuing a singing career. She learns about an opportunity to try out for a reality TV show that will feature musical talent. She is three months from graduation with a degree in accounting and has already been offered two well-paying jobs that would help her pay off some of her student loans. The singing competition would require her to drop out of school right now.	
A young professional has been passed over for a promotion. He's upset and makes an appointment with the boss to find out why.	

Reflection Questions

1. Pick one of the above scenarios and compare how you would have typically handled that situation to your response.
2. What are the short-term (and thus short-lived) benefits to *not* being effective at reality testing?

Activity 12.6

Self-Development Plan for Reality Testing

The directions and template for students to create a self-development plan appear in Appendix D of this facilitator's guide. *The Student EQ Edge: Student Workbook* contains a template for developing stronger reality testing in Chapter 12.

Activity 12.7

Case Study—Reality Testing

See Chapter 2 to assign a case study relevant to reality testing. Case study number 6 is highly recommended. Chapter 2 of *The Student EQ Edge: Student Workbook* contains all of the same case studies.

Chapter 13

Problem Solving

What is problem solving? This EI ability is unique in that there are prescribed methods for the *process of problem solving*. So, theoretically at least, all one has to do is follow those steps and effective problem solving will be assured. But it's not that simple. Because our emotions are often triggered when we face problems, we must learn how to identify and manage those emotions in order to be able to use an effective process. In other words, we may know what to do but be unable to do it because our emotions get in the way. This chapter focuses on how to identify emotions and create the best possible emotional approach for problem solving. If we want to be creative, we need to be in a "good" mood, which would include emotions like joy and excitement on the more intense end and satisfaction and anticipation on the less intense end. In contrast, to solve a problem that might involve paying attention to small details, such as editing this *Facilitation and Activity Guide*, a "bad" mood is more likely to help us. Why? Because when we are in a bad mood, we're more skeptical and more likely to find fault—including, it seems, being more attentive to and critical of our own work and solutions. Bad moods can range from mildly negative emotions (irritated, uneasy) to much more intense emotions (rage, fear), so we need to calibrate the intensity of the emotion if we want to be most effective.

Can someone be too high in problem solving? Again, there is not a simple yes or no answer. Effective (very high) problem-solving skills are always preferable because that indicates a person is tuning into how emotions affect reactions to the problem and how to use an effective process. But if excellent problem solving is not accompanied by reality testing and emotional self-awareness (being aware of how our fears and dreams are affecting us), then we may get stuck in an endless cycle of evaluation without action. Problem solving implies action!

STUDENT LEARNING OUTCOMES

Students will:

- Identify what emotions they experience during problem solving
- Learn the steps of effective problem solving
- Understand the relationship between emotions and decision making in the problem-solving process
- Solve an ongoing problem using emotional information and an effective problem-solving process

SUGGESTED READINGS, MOVIES, AND TELEVISION SHOWS

- *The Student EQ Edge: Emotional Intelligence and Your Academic and Personal Success,* Chapter 13

Movies
- *Catch Me If You Can*—Scene 10, "Barry Allen, Secret Service"—When an FBI agent comes to his hotel room, Frank controls his emotions and pretends to be a Secret Service agent who is also hunting for Frank.
- *Odd Girl Out*—Scene about 55 minutes into the movie, in which Stacey and Vanessa have been accused of cheating—Stacey lies, but Vanessa's strong emotions prevent her from confronting Stacey about the lie.
- *The Pursuit of Happyness*—Scene 23, "Safe Cave"—the son is bored, and they have no place to sleep that night; the father develops an imaginary scene in which they are chased by dinosaurs and they run into the "cave" (restroom) to take cover, where they sleep for the night.

- *What About Bob?*— Scene 10, "Sleepover"—The psychiatrist has been unable to solve the problem of getting Bob to leave, and as the psychiatrist steadily unravels, Bob becomes more a part of the family.

Television Shows

- *The Office*—Episode 27, "Conflict Management"—Michael tries to solve office issues using mediation and his own special approach.
- *Modern Family*—Episode 47, "See You Next Fall"—While trying to get to Alex's graduation, the family is stuck at home due to a faulty gate.

Note: Cast members on both TV shows continually (unwittingly) create and solve problems in almost every episode. In many cases their process is flawed, or their emotions cloud their thinking, or both. Watching what not to do can be just as productive (and funny, when it's fictional) as observing effective problem solving.

PLANNING YOUR CLASS

50-Minute Class

Assign Worksheets 13.1 and 13.2 to be completed outside of class. Debrief both in class to ensure that students understand the steps of problem solving and how emotions can affect problem solving. Then ask students to complete Worksheet 13.3 during class. To debrief these, ask students to pair off, share their scenarios, and help each other apply effective problem solving. If time allows, ask two or three students to share their scenarios with the class.

3–4 Hour Workshop

Assign Worksheets 13.1 and 13.2 to be completed outside of class. Debrief both in class to ensure that students understand the steps of problem solving and how emotions can affect problem solving. Then show a clip from *One Fine Day* and complete Worksheet 13.5 as a large group. Challenge the class to consider whether the same positive outcomes would have occurred if this had been a real-life scenario rather than a comedy. Then complete Worksheet 13.4 as a large group. Then have them complete Worksheet 13.3, emphasizing the need to understand how their emotions are affecting problem solving. Debrief this by having one or two students share their problems, the previous solutions, and the new solutions identified as a result of completing the worksheet. For the remainder of class, have students begin a self-development plan or work on a case study.

Activity List

Activity #	Activity Name	Brief Description and Activity Notes
13.1	What Is My Emotion?	Students analyze hypothetical scenarios and identify what emotion was probably driving the problem-solving process.
13.2	Failed Decisions Revisited	Students examine the problem-solving process and effectiveness of the engineers and NASA executives who made the decision to launch the Space Shuttle *Challenger*. If you prefer, you can use the Bay of Pigs invasion that was brought up in Chapter 12.
13.3	Solving Your Problems	Students identify an ongoing problem and which emotions have been hampering them in reaching a solution. Then they use the steps of problem solving to reach an acceptable solution. If you are planning to have students share their work with you or a classmate, let them know ahead of time.
13.4	But Can I Really Change My Emotion?	Students practice identifying ways to change their emotional state to better match what is needed in a given situation.
13.5	*One Fine Day*	Students watch a 20- to 25-minute clip from the movie *One Fine Day* and then analyze the problem-solving skills of the actors involved.
13.6	Self-Development Plan for Problem Solving	Students develop a plan for improving problem-solving skills.
13.7	Case Study—Problem Solving	Students analyze the behavior of a person who faces challenges related to problem solving.

Activity 13.1

What Is My Emotion?

EI Dimensions Targeted: Problem Solving, Emotional Self-Awareness

Brief Description/Objective: Students will analyze hypothetical scenarios and identify what emotion was probably driving the problem-solving process.

Planning the Activity

Time Expected
- Worksheet: 15 minutes
- Reflection Questions: 10–15 minutes
- In-Class Debrief: 10 minutes

Materials
- Worksheet 13.1 from *The Student EQ Edge: Student Workbook*
- Board or flip chart and markers
- *The Student EQ Edge: Emotional Intelligence and Your Academic and Personal Success*

Facilitating the Activity

Directions
- Assign Worksheet 13.1.
- You may want to give students a list of emotion words. This should lead to a more accurate identification of the emotion and its intensity.
- There are better and worse answers for the worksheet scenarios, as follows:

  Taking turns driving to see each other is more about differing commitment levels than driving turns. In this case, anger about not taking turns may be masking a different emotion: anxiety. Help students understand how understanding their emotions better could lead to a better solution.

  The allowance issue is probably not an issue of free time. Rather, it's about honoring commitments even when we'd rather not do so. We would all probably agree that doing chores may create unpleasant emotions (boredom, frustration), whereas communicating with friends provides more happiness and excitement. The key is to understand how emotions are playing a role in this issue.

Debriefing Questions
- Which will be more difficult for you: identifying the emotions involved or using an effective process for solving problems? How can you overcome this barrier?
- See the reflection questions at the end of the worksheet.

Worksheet 13.1: What Is My Emotion?

Name:

Identify which emotion is driving actions in the following situations and then come up with a way to change that emotion that would work for you if you were experiencing this situation.

- You and your dating partner attend universities 150 miles away from each other. You agree to take turns driving to see each other every other weekend. But when it's your partner's turn to drive, there's always a reason why *you* should drive that weekend instead. You spend lots of time texting back and forth, arguing about whose turn it is to drive.
    - What emotions would you be likely to experience if this was happening to you?
    - How would those emotions influence your problem-solving abilities?
    - Whose turn it is to drive is *not* the root problem in this scenario. What is the root problem?
    - What would your emotion be now that you've identified the root problem? How would that affect the way you are approaching this problem?
- Your parents give you spending money each month. In exchange, you are supposed to do some basic chores, such as walking the dog every day and cleaning your bathroom every week. That system works okay until school starts; then you're too busy to walk the dog daily. Your father points out, though, that you spend lots of time texting and playing computer games with friends. You tell your dad that everyone else in the family gets relaxation time and you should too. Your dad thinks you still have plenty of time to do your chores, keep up your grades, and relax. You dad tells you that he won't give you any more spending money until you do your chores.
    - What emotion are you likely to experience when your dad takes away your spending money?
    - Even if you did not say "angry" or "mad" (or something similar!) in response to the first question, pretend that you are mad. How would anger affect your ability to solve this disagreement with your dad?
    - What would you say if someone asked you what problem needs to be solved?
    - If your father was asked what problem needed to be solved, what would he say?

Reflection Questions

1. How would thinking about your emotions in these two scenarios help you problem solve more effectively?
2. Think about a situation in which you've had the same argument with the same person over and over. Explain that situation and identify at least one emotion you are experiencing that is interfering with your problem-solving ability. What could you do differently to solve the problem?

Activity 13.2

Failed Decisions Revisited

EI Dimensions Targeted: Problem Solving, Reality Testing, Empathy

Brief Description/Objective: Students will examine the problem-solving process and effectiveness of the engineers and NASA executives who made the decision to launch the *Challenger* space shuttle.

Planning the Activity

Time Expected
- Worksheet (including reading): 30–45 minutes
- Reflection Questions: None
- In-Class Debrief: 15 minutes

Materials
- Worksheet 13.2 from *The Student EQ Edge: Student Workbook*
- Board or flip chart and markers
- *The Student EQ Edge: Emotional Intelligence and Your Academic and Personal Success*

Facilitating the Activity

Directions
- Assign Worksheet 13.2.
- Be sure to stay focused on the problem-solving process and how emotions influenced that. The intent of this exercise is to build understanding, not to be critical.

Debriefing Question
- Take a recent issue facing your institution that students will be aware of (for example, tuition increases, creation of a new policy), about which emotions may be running high. Challenge students to identify their emotions and how emotions are influencing their ability to problem solve effectively.

Worksheet 13.2: Failed Decisions Revisited

Name:

Go back to Worksheet 12.3. Reread the information about the *Challenger* explosion and then answer the following questions.

- What emotions were driving the following people who were involved in the decision to launch the *Challenger*? If their emotions changed during the decision-making process, note that. Explain how their emotions affected their ability to problem solve.
  - The engineers who tested the O ring
  - The engineering supervisor
  - Upper management at NASA who made the final decision to launch
- What problem do you think each of the groups was trying to solve?
  - The engineers who tested the O ring
  - The engineering supervisor
  - Upper management at NASA who made the final decision to launch
- Think about the stages of problem solving:
  a. Sensing that a problem exists and being confident and motivated to handle it
  b. Accurately and clearly defining the problem (that is, the real issue) and then collecting information about it
  c. Generating multiple solutions through brainstorming
  d. Weighing the pros and cons of each possible solution
  e. Choosing the best solution and implementing it

  Write a two- to three-paragraph analysis of how the problem-solving process was applied when trying to decide whether to launch the *Challenger*. Note the points at which effective problem solving was and was not used. Identify which emotion or emotions drove the ill-fated decision to launch.

Activity 13.3
Solving Your Problems

EI Dimensions Targeted: Problem Solving, Reality Testing, Emotional Self-Awareness, Empathy

Brief Description/Objective: Students will identify an ongoing problem they have and identify which emotions have been hampering them; then they will use the steps involved in problem solving to reach an acceptable solution.

Planning the Activity

Time Expected
- Worksheet: 20 minutes
- Reflection Questions: 10 minutes
- In-Class Debrief: 10–30 minutes

Materials:
- Worksheet 13.3 from *The Student EQ Edge: Student Workbook*
- Board or flip chart and markers
- *The Student EQ Edge: Emotional Intelligence and Your Academic and Personal Success*

Facilitating the Activity

Directions
- Assign Worksheet 13.3.
- Make sure you let students know whether they will be sharing their scenarios with you or a classmate.

Debriefing Questions
- Have you tried to implement the solutions since doing this worksheet? Were you able to make progress in solving your problem?
- See the reflection questions at the end of the worksheet.

Worksheet 13.3: Solving Your Problems

Name:

Using the steps of problem solving noted in Worksheet 13.2, identify a problem you are having that you have been unable to solve. Then, in column 2, answer the question(s) about each problem-solving step. If you skipped a step or steps of the problem-solving process, leave that box empty. In column 3, identify the emotion you felt at each stage.

Steps of Problem Solving	Your Problem-Solving Steps	Emotion
1. Sensing that a problem exists and being motivated to fix it	What made you aware that a problem existed, and what did you do when you first became aware of it?	
2. Accurately defining the problem and collecting information about it	How did you define the problem? What information did you collect?	
3. Generating multiple solutions through brainstorming	What possible solutions did you generate?	
4. Evaluating solutions	Briefly explain your analysis of each idea you generated in step #3.	
5. Choosing the best solution, implementing it, and assessing whether it worked	What did you do to solve the problem? Did it work?	

Reflection Questions

1. Compare your answers to the steps for successful problem solving. Describe what is causing you the most difficulty.
2. How are your emotions affecting your problem-solving process? What emotion(s) might help you solve the problem more effectively?

Activity 13.4

But Can I Really Change My Emotion?

EI Dimensions Targeted: Emotional Self-Awareness, Problem Solving

Brief Description/Objective: Students will identify a likely or typical emotional response to a situation and then the emotion that might enhance problem solving in that situation. They will develop strategies to help them make use of the most productive emotion.

Planning the Activity

Time Expected
- Worksheet: 15 minutes
- Reflection Questions: 10 minutes
- In-Class Debrief: 10 minutes

Materials
- Worksheet 13.4 from *The Student EQ Edge: Student Workbook*
- Board or flip chart and markers
- *The Student EQ Edge: Emotional Intelligence and Your Academic and Personal Success*

Facilitating the Activity

Directions
- Assign Worksheet 13.4.
- Students may find this activity difficult to do on their own, so doing the worksheet with a partner may be helpful.

Debriefing Questions
- What was your reaction to the idea that you should and could change your emotion if you want to engage in optimal problem solving?
- Many people think emotions are something that happens to them, over which they have no control. What would you say to such a person?
- See the reflection questions at the end of the worksheet.

Worksheet 13.4: But Can I Really Change My Emotion?

Name:

Remember, when we need to be creative in our work or problem-solving, it's best to be in a "good" mood because it frees us to be creative; when we need a lot of focus and attention to detail, it's best to be in a "bad" mood because it helps us be more critical. Read the scenarios described in column 1 and then complete the table according to the following instructions:

- In the second column, identify the typical or most likely emotion you would experience in that situation.
- In the third column, identify which emotion or emotions would be helpful to you in that situation.
- In the fourth column, identify what you would do to change your emotion.

Issue	Likely emotion	Helpful emotion	Strategy for changing your emotion
Coming up with an idea for your biology class project			
Looking over your three-hour mathematics final exam for errors after you completed the last problem			
Working under a tight deadline to finish the layout for the student newspaper			
Resolving a heated argument with your best friend			
Determining how to arrange all your furniture in a very small room.			

Reflection Questions

1. What can you do to remind yourself to examine your emotions when you are facing a problem?
2. Choose one of these five scenarios and describe the likely outcome if you let your typical or likely emotion influence you.

Activity 13.5
One Fine Day

EI Dimensions Targeted: Problem Solving

Brief Description/Objective: Students will watch a movie clip from *One Fine Day* and analyze the problem-solving skills of the main characters.

Planning the Activity

Time Expected
- Worksheet and watching the movie: 15–35 minutes, depending on how much of the movie is shown
- Reflection Questions: 10 minutes
- In-Class Debrief: 10 minutes

Materials
- Worksheet 13.5 from *The Student EQ Edge: Student Workbook*
- Board or flip chart and markers
- *The Student EQ Edge: Emotional Intelligence and Your Academic and Personal Success*
- Copy of the movie *One Fine Day*

Facilitating the Activity

Directions
- Ask students to find Worksheet 13.5 and give them 15 to 20 minutes to complete it. Or break the students into small groups to discuss the questions.
- Cue the movie *One Fine Day* to Scene 7, "Sammy at the Office" and show through Scene 9, "Career Crisis." (If you want a shorter alternative, show Scene 5, "Race for the Boat.") In scenes 7–9, the two parents try to problem solve by taking their kids to work with them, creating more stress. Show enough of the movie so that students can determine whether the problem solving was effective and how emotions affected the problem solving.

Debriefing Questions
- What other EI characteristics did you see in the movie clip?
- See the reflection questions at the end of the worksheet.

Worksheet 13.5: *One Fine Day*

Name:

Cue the movie *One Fine Day* to Scene 7, "Sammy at the Office," and watch through Scene 9, "Career Crisis." Previously in the movie, the parents had "problem solved" by each taking their child with them to work that day. Scenes 7–9 show how that decision worked out.

Reflection Questions

1. Analyze the emotions of George Clooney's character and Michelle Pfeiffer's character when they were trying to determine how to take care of the kids that day. How did their emotions influence their decision-making process?
2. Think about what you learned about reality testing in Chapter 12. Analyze their reality-testing skills in this situation.
3. Based on your analysis and what you've learned about problem solving and reality testing, would you expect their decision to work? Explain.

Activity 13.6

Self-Development Plan for Problem Solving

The directions and template for students to create a self-development plan appear in Appendix D of this facilitator's guide. *The Student EQ Edge: Student Workbook* contains a template for developing stronger problem solving in Chapter 13.

Activity 13.7

Case Study—Problem Solving

See Chapter 2 to assign a case study relevant to problem solving. Case Study 7 is highly recommended. Chapter 2 of *The Student EQ Edge: Student Workbook* contains all of the same case studies.

Chapter 14

Impulse Control

What is impulse control? Impulse control issues plague many people. Like many troubling behaviors, impulse control problems leave a trail of destruction including broken relationships, crippling financial decisions, and unmet potential. It may seem, on the surface anyway, that some impulse control problems affect only the individual, but that's not the case. An overweight partner will have less energy and may be unwilling to participate in some social situations; an addiction affects all family members in one way or another; and uncontrolled impatience, frustration, or anger creates rocky relationships and greater conflict. Thus impulse control issues become relationship issues.

Our brains are hardwired to detect threats and react immediately (impulsively, if we don't think before we act). But this push to action must be mitigated by our more rational frontal lobe, which can weigh the pros and cons of firing off a confrontational email or screaming at a boss or coach. Unchecked, our brain will simply react impulsively, and sometimes this is the least effective choice.

A famous study conducted at Stanford University by Walter Mischel and colleagues (Mischel, Ebbesen, & Zeiss, 1972) tested young children's ability to resist the temptation to eat a marshmallow. If they could wait just a few minutes, they would get a second marshmallow. When followed up as teenagers, those subjects who had been unable to control their impulses and had eaten the one marshmallow were found to be not faring as well as those who had resisted. They were less socially competent and were not achieving at the same level. In fact, on average those who had given in to their impulses scored over 200 points lower on the Scholastic Aptitude Test (SAT) than their more controlled counterparts (Shoda, Mischel, & Peake, 1990)!

Our first reaction may be to dismiss the notion that impulse control alone could be the explanation. But a closer examination yields a different conclusion. Impatience, frustration, and the inability to delay gratification can affect most areas of one's life, including decision making (should I party or study?), relationships (what's the harm in expressing all my frustrations whenever I feel them?), or work (I don't have time to gather more facts, so let's just make a decision!).

Is it possible to be too high in impulse control? That's hard to imagine, especially when we think about impulse control as thinking before we act, being rational as opposed to impulsive, and patient as opposed to rash. But those highest in impulse control ideally would also be characterized by high emotional expression; otherwise, there could be lots of pent-up frustration and stifling of feelings in the name of "impulse control."

STUDENT LEARNING OUTCOMES

Students will:

- Identify their challenges related to impulse control
- Understand the consequences of impulse-control lapses
- Develop strategies for controlling their impulses

SUGGESTED READINGS, MOVIES, AND TELEVISION SHOWS

- *The Student EQ Edge: Emotional Intelligence and Your Academic and Personal Success*, Chapter 14

Movies

- *Catch Me If You Can*—Scene 15, "Calling a Truce" (fast-forward to where Frank and his father are having lunch)—When Frank meets his father for lunch, he promises not to forge any more checks; his father replies "You can't stop," and Frank begs his father to ask him to stop because he knows he cannot stop.
- *Odd Girl Out*—About 30 minutes into the movie—Vanessa tries to join her friends for lunch—they won't let her, and she throws down her tray and runs out of the cafeteria.
- *What About Bob?*— Scene 8, "The Diving Instructor," and Scene 9, "Heimlich Hero"—Leo, the psychiatrist, yells at neighbors, shows impatience with Bob, and makes rash decisions such as trying to send Bob out in a bad thunderstorm.
- Other movies: *A Few Good Men, Coach Carter, Georgia Rule, Runaway Bride, The Family Stone, To Kill a Mockingbird*

Television Shows

- *The Office*—Episode 85, "Frame Toby"—Michael and Jim act impulsively. Jim buys his parents' home without consulting Pam; Michael is having problems with Toby's return.
- *The Office*—Episode 137, "Classy Christmas" Part 1—Jim mocks Dwight.
- *The Office*—Episode 75, "Business Ethics"—Michael loses it when his subordinates do not want a follow-up seminar on ethics.
- Reality TV shows such as *Survivor, Scare Tactics, The Bachelor,* and *The Amazing Race* tend to reveal impulse control problems with impatience, frustration, and anger. Other reality shows focus on different issues, such as eating; watch, for example, *The Biggest Loser*. Watching the impact of poor impulse control can be quite eye-opening for students.
- Most sporting events will have a moment where an athlete or coach loses control over his or her emotions. Ask students to watch for such examples. One example you can show in class involves a football player driving another player's head into the ground and then stomping his arm. Go to http://www.youtube.com/watch?v=ZXDmCVSnn1U to see the clip.

Note: Students may become confused about the difference between healthy spontaneity and impulse control. Spontaneity involves being able to participate in an activity at the last minute, the ability to not always have to plan your day, and so on. Impulse control involves challenges with impatience, anger, or temptations. So while spontaneity can be very positive, impulse control issues usually do not yield positive outcomes.

PLANNING YOUR CLASS

50 Minute Class

Ask students to complete Worksheets 14.2 and 14.4 for homework. Debrief these activities together. Once you've covered a number of different consequences of poor impulse control—some less serious and others more serious—focus on what triggers impulse control problems in the students. Then show the YouTube clip in Activity 14.1. Again focus on the consequences of different levels of impulse control. Students between the ages of 13 and the early 20s have a strong sense of invincibility (for example, they think they will not get lung cancer if they smoke, they won't be the one to die in a car crash because of speeding), so making the consequences tangible can be helpful. Conclude class by acting out one or two of the scenarios found in Worksheet 14.5 (see the Activity 14.5 instructions).

3–4 Hour Class

Ask students to complete Worksheets 14.2 and 14.4 for homework. Debrief these activities together. Once you've covered a number of different consequences of poor impulse control—some less serious and others more serious—focus on what triggers impulse control problems in the students. Then show the YouTube clip in Activity 14.1. Again focus on the consequences of different levels of impulse control. Students between the ages of 13 and the early 20s have a strong sense of invincibility (for example, they think they will not get lung cancer if they smoke, they won't be the one to die in a car crash because of speeding), so making the consequences tangible can be helpful. Next, have them complete Worksheet 14.5 in class, working with a classmate if they prefer. Debrief this by allowing students to act out some of the scenarios. Then ask students to spend 15–20 minutes either working on a self-development plan (Activity 14.6) or reacting to a case study (Activity 14.7). If time allows, show them an episode (full or partial) of *Survivor* or *The Amazing Race* (see Activity 14.3) to further illustrate the consequences of poor impulse control.

Activity List

Activity #	Activity Name	Brief Description and Activity Notes
14.1	Marshmallow Cravings	Students view a YouTube clip simulation of a famous study in psychology that tested children's impulse control.
14.2	But I Want . . .	Students analyze an area in which they struggle with impulse control and what the consequences are.
14.3	*Survivor*	Students analyze a reality TV character's problems with impulse control.
14.4	No Regrets?	Students interview someone who exhibited poor impulse control and record the consequences.
14.5	Strategies for Success	Students develop strategies for coping with situations involving the need to control impulses.
14.6	Self-Development Plan for Impulse Control	Students develop a plan for improving impulse control.
14.7	Case Study—Impulse Control	Students analyze the behavior of a person who faces challenges related to impulse control.

Activity 14.1
Marshmallow Cravings

EI Dimensions Targeted: Impulse Control

Brief Description/Objectives: Students will learn about the long-term consequences of poor impulse control by watching a YouTube clip about a famous study with children.

Planning the Activity

Time Expected
- Worksheet and YouTube video:15 minutes
- Reflection Questions: 10 minutes
- In-Class Debrief: 10 minutes

Materials
- Worksheet 14.1 from *The Student EQ Edge: Student Workbook*
- Board or flip chart and markers
- *The Student EQ Edge: Emotional Intelligence and Your Academic and Personal Success*
- Internet connection and TV

Facilitating the Activity

Directions
- Show the YouTube clip to the class.
- Assign Worksheet 14.1.

Debriefing Questions
- Conduct an agree-disagree activity using the following statement: "Exhibiting good impulse control makes life no fun."
- See the reflection questions at the end of the worksheet.

Worksheet 14.1: Marshmallow Cravings

Name:

Go to http://www.youtube.com/watch?v=4y6R5boDqh4&feature=relmfu and watch the YouTube clip, "The Marshmallow Test." If this link is no longer active, search YouTube with the key phrase of "marshmallow study" and watch any clip related to this famous research.

Do you think having good impulse control as a child made a difference in these children's lives as a teenager? Justify your answer.

Children were followed into their teenage years and later as adults to determine the relationships among impulse control, academic and career success, social and emotional functioning, and coping skills. The following list contains results found during the teenage years (Shoda, Mischel, & Peake, 1990). Children who were able to delay gratification and wait to eat two marshmallows exhibited the following advantages as teenagers:

- More adept at making social connections
- Less stubborn and more decisive
- Superior coping mechanisms
- Better grades
- Higher SAT scores

Pick two of these advantages and explain how better impulse control in a preschool child could be associated with such advantages as a teenager.

Reflection Questions

1. Do you think you would have eaten the marshmallow right away or waited so that you could have two marshmallows? Explain.
2. Take a position on the following statement: "Always exerting impulse control takes the fun and spontaneity out of life."

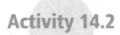

Activity 14.2

But I Want . . .

EI Dimensions Targeted: Impulse Control, Reality Testing

Brief Description/Objective: Students will analyze an area where they have trouble with impulse control.

Planning the Activity

Time Expected
- Worksheet: 10 minutes
- Reflection Questions: 10 minutes
- In-Class Debrief: 5–10 minutes

Materials
- Worksheet 14.2 from *The Student EQ Edge: Student Workbook*
- Board or flip chart and markers
- *The Student EQ Edge: Emotional Intelligence and Your Academic and Personal Success*

Facilitating the Activity

Directions
- Assign Worksheet 14.2.

Debriefing Questions
- Ask students to share stories about people they know (or have heard of) who had trouble controlling impulses and what consequences the person suffered as a result. (If students cannot think of any, begin the discussion with the drug overdoses that killed Elvis Presley, Michael Jackson, or another famous performer. Students may argue that these were addictions, not issues with impulse control. Explain that the addiction began as a failure to control impulses.)
- See the reflection questions at the end of the worksheet.

Worksheet 14.2: But I Want . . .

Name:

Pick an area in which you struggle with impulse control. Here are the likely categories: anger, impatience (for example, in traffic, waiting in line, waiting for something to happen), food, alcohol, cigarettes, drugs, partying before studying, computer use, TV watching, and anything else you can think of for which you find it hard not to react quickly or give in to temptation.

My impulse control challenge is:

When I don't control this impulse, the consequences usually are:

I find it harder to control this impulse when:

Here's what could motivate me to gain better control over this impulse:

Reflection Questions

1. What did you learn about yourself by doing this exercise?
2. How motivated are you to change your behavior related to this impulse?

Activity 14.3
Survivor

EI Dimensions Targeted: Impulse Control, Emotional Self-Awareness

Brief Description/Objective: Students will analyze the impulse control issues of a reality TV participant.

Planning the Activity

Time Expected
- Worksheet and TV Episode: 70 minutes
- Reflection Question: 10 minutes
- In-Class Debrief: 5–10 minutes

Materials
- Worksheet 14.3 from *The Student EQ Edge: Student Workbook*
- Board or flip chart and markers
- *The Student EQ Edge: Emotional Intelligence and Your Academic and Personal Success*

Facilitating the Activity

Directions
- Assign Worksheet 14.3.

Debriefing Questions
- If the person you observed saw himself or herself on television, what do you think the person's reaction would be?
- See the reflection question at the end of the worksheet.

Worksheet 14.3: *Survivor*

Name:

Watch an episode of the reality TV show *Survivor*. Pick a person on the show who has impulse control problems and answer the following questions. More than likely you will see issues with impatience or frustration or anger. If you cannot find an episode of *Survivor*, use the reality TV show *The Amazing Race*.

- What type of impulse control issue does this person have?
- How did the other people react to the lack of impulse control?
- Was the individual aware of the loss of control? If so, did he or she do anything to make amends? If not, how did the failure to acknowledge a problem affect the individual?

Reflection Question

If you were a contestant on *Survivor*, what issues or situations would be most likely to incite impulsive behaviors for you?

Activity 14.4
No Regrets?

EI Dimensions Targeted: Impulse Control

Brief Description/Objective: Students will interview someone about a time he or she struggled with impulse control and what the consequences were.

Planning the Activity

Time Expected
- Worksheet and Interview: 30 minutes
- Reflection Questions: 10 minutes
- In-Class Debrief: 15 minutes

Materials
- Worksheet 14.4 from *The Student EQ Edge: Student Workbook*
- Board or flip chart and markers
- *The Student EQ Edge: Emotional Intelligence and Your Academic and Personal Success*

Facilitating the Activity

Directions
- Assign Worksheet 14.4.
- Tell students to get informed consent prior to the interview by telling the person what the interview questions are about.

Debriefing Questions
- In round robin format, get students to name the biggest consequence of impulse control that the person chose to reveal. Write these on the board. Then lead a discussion about the possible costs of poor impulse control.
- See the reflection questions at the end of the worksheet.

Worksheet 14.4: No Regrets?

Name:

Interview someone who will be honest with you about a time he or she engaged in one of his or her most impulsive behaviors and what the consequences were.

Relationship to me of the person I interviewed:

Age the person was at the time of the impulsive episode:

Question 1. Describe one of the most impulsive actions you have taken in your life.

Question 2. What were the consequences of your impulsive behavior? (Ask follow-up questions about relationships, physical and mental health, job performance, and happiness if the person does not mention these areas.)

Question 3. How has your life changed because of that issue? *or* What do you differently now as a result of that experience?

Reflection Questions

1. What was your reaction to hearing this person's story? What impact do you think this will have on you?
2. What was the individual's response to recalling this event?

Activity 14.5
Strategies for Success

EI Dimensions Targeted: Impulse Control, Assertiveness, Emotional Self-Awareness

Brief Description/Objective: Students will develop strategies for controlling their impulses in a variety of settings.

Planning the Activity

Time Expected
- Worksheet: 10 minutes
- Reflection Question: 5 minutes
- In-Class Debrief: 15 minutes

Materials
- Worksheet 14.5 from *The Student EQ Edge: Student Workbook*
- Board or flip chart and markers
- *The Student EQ Edge: Emotional Intelligence and Your Academic and Personal Success*

Facilitating the Activity

Directions
- Assign Worksheet 14.5.

Debriefing Questions
- Take a couple of the scenarios that can be role played in class. Ask for two different volunteers: one to react impulsively and the other to control impulses but act assertively if that is desirable. Have students comment on what they observe.
- See the reflection question at the end of the worksheet.

Worksheet 14.5: Strategies for Success

Name:

Write down something constructive you could do in the following situations that would demonstrate impulse control.

* It's Saturday morning and you've just started working on a big project that's due Monday. A friend calls and asks you to do something you really enjoy that will take all Saturday afternoon.
* You're on a diet but are out with a group of friends and everyone else orders dessert.
* You're waiting in a long line at the movie theatre for a show that begins in five minutes. The person in front of you recognizes friends and invites them to cut in. They buy the last tickets for that show.
* Your cell phone plan is not due for renewal for three more months, but the newest iPhone just came out, and the features on it are much better than your current phone, which you've had for over a year. You go with a friend to look at the new iPhone. It's fantastic. She buys one.
* Someone walks into the room, picks up the TV remote, and changes the channel from the show you were watching.

Reflection Question

How likely are you to use the strategies you came up with? Explain your answer.

Activity 14.6

Self-Development Plan for Impulse Control

The directions and template for students to create a self-development plan appear in Appendix D of this facilitator's guide. *The Student EQ Edge: Student Workbook* contains a template for developing stronger impulse control in Chapter 14.

Activity 14.7

Case Study—Impulse Control

See Chapter 2 to assign a case study relevant to impulse control. Chapter 2 of *The Student EQ Edge: Student Workbook* contains all of the same case studies.

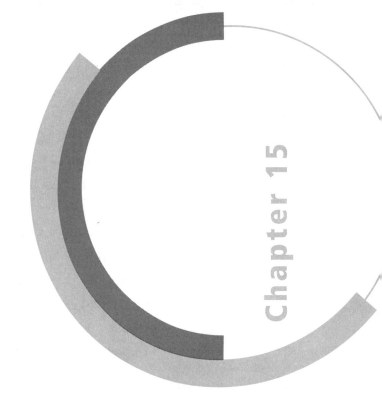

Chapter 15

Flexibility

What is flexibility? Flexibility is grouped with stress tolerance and optimism to form the stress management composite of emotional intelligence. Why is flexibility considered a form of stress management? Think about it this way—an individual who cannot adapt effectively to changes will be under constant siege and experience frequent stress. Being resistant to change does not stop change! Many life circumstances are either partially or totally beyond our control, yet the inflexible person tries his or her best to maintain control by refusing to adapt. So what happens to that person when significant changes occur? The inflexible person is likely to become more distressed, which is associated with cognitive disorganization and feelings of anxiety—both of which impede problem solving, further exacerbating stress.

Flexibility should not be confused with a lack of assertiveness or self-regard. People who demonstrate flexibility understand that some change is inevitable and that even when change is a choice, choosing to change can bring more benefits than choosing the status quo. If anything, their willingness to be flexible may be bolstered by strong self-regard—a belief in their ability to be successful in the changed situation. Nor does flexibility mean you sacrifice assertiveness. Acquiescing to others' needs or opinions is not the same as adapting to change. A lack of assertiveness leads us to experience unpleasant feelings, whereas demonstrating flexibility should bolster positive emotions. Finally, you should help students understand that true flexibility, spurred by adaptation, is quite different from compliance, which involves doing what others tell you to do.

What about the student who is too flexible, always changing decisions or going along with the crowd? High flexibility, like most other EI characteristics, needs to be balanced by other well-developed skills such as assertiveness (so you don't change just to please others) and reality testing (so you can effectively assess the impact of change or the cost of going along).

STUDENT LEARNING OUTCOMES

Students will:

- Understand how they react to changing situations
- Understand the inevitability of change and how flexibility helps to cope with change
- Practice being more flexible
- Identify change situations that create the most distress for them

SUGGESTED BOOKS, MOVIES, AND TELEVISION SHOWS

- *The Student EQ Edge: Emotional Intelligence and Your Academic and Personal Success*, Chapter 15

Movies
- *The Blind Side*—The entire movie shows the ability of Michael to adapt effectively to new situations and for his new family to adapt to having him as a family member. Scene 3, "White Walls," shows how Michael feels in his new school, yet he adapts and eventually succeeds.
- *The Pursuit of Happyness*—Scene 23, "Safe Cave"—Father and son deal with one challenging situation after another, getting kicked out of their apartment and sleeping in different places.

The safe cave scene shows both father and son adapting to the circumstances the first night they are homeless.

- *What About Bob?*—Throughout the movie Bob increasingly shows better flexibility as he adapts to each new circumstance while the psychiatrist does the opposite, becoming more rigid and more stuck. Chapter 11, "*Good Morning America*," shows their opposite reactions to Bob's appearing on *Good Morning America* with the psychiatrist.

PLANNING YOUR CLASS

50–60 Minute Class

Assign Worksheets 15.1 and 15.2 for homework. Debrief as described, making sure to address any confusion about flexibility and assertiveness. If you have shown or assigned the movie *What About Bob?* you can use the psychiatrist, Leo, as an example. He is consistently assertive, but not at all flexible. During class, have students (either individually or in small groups) complete Worksheet 15.5. As a class, create a list of positive self-talk statements that can help someone who needs to be more flexible. If time allows, assign either the self-development plan (Activity 15.6) or a case study (Activity 15.7).

3–4 Hour Class

Assign Worksheets 15.1, 15.2, and 15.3 prior to the class meeting. Debrief as described, making sure to address any confusion about flexibility and assertiveness. Show a portion of the movie *What About Bob?* using the psychiatrist, Leo, as an example of the cost of inflexibility. He is consistently assertive, but not at all flexible. Show 5–10 minutes of the scene in which Leo is being interviewed about his book to demonstrate the cost of inflexibility, which not only ruined his book debut but also hurt his relationships with family members. Next, have students complete Worksheet 15.5 individually or in small groups, focusing the debrief on the differences between the perceived short-term benefits of inflexibility compared with the long-term benefits of flexibility. Next, have students who believe they need to develop more flexibility work on a self-development plan (Activity 15.6) while others complete a case study (Activity 15.7) related to flexibility. Assign Worksheet 15.4 to complete for the next class period.

Activity List

Activity #	Activity Name	Brief Description and Activity Notes
15.1	Reflections About Change	Students identify times in their lives that required flexibility and then answer a series of reflection questions.
15.2	Flexibility Survey	Students complete a self-report survey about flexibility. Expand the activity by asking students to explain their choice.
15.3	The Price of Inflexibility	Students investigate changes at the societal level that require flexibility by either interviewing someone over 60 years of age or conducting internet research.
15.4	Stretching Yourself	Students pick a routine they engage in and then practice flexibility by changing this routine.
15.5	Flexibility Forecasting	Students respond to hypothetical situations they may face in young adulthood that require flexibility.
15.6	Self-Development Plan for Flexibility	Students develop a plan for improving flexibility.
15.7	Case Study—Flexibility	Students analyze the behavior of a person who faces challenges related to flexibility.

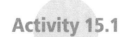

Activity 15.1
Reflections About Change

EI Dimensions Targeted: Flexibility, Emotional Self-Awareness, Stress Tolerance

Brief Description/Objective: Students will identify times in their lives that required flexibility and then answer a series of reflection questions.

Planning the Activity

Time Expected
- Worksheet: 15–20 minutes
- Reflection Questions: Included in the worksheet
- In-Class Debrief: 10 minutes

Materials
- Worksheet 15.1 from *The Student EQ Edge: Student Workbook*
- Board or flip chart and markers
- *The Student EQ Edge: Emotional Intelligence and Your Academic and Personal Success*

Facilitating the Activity

Directions
- Assign Worksheet 15.1.
- Remind students to choose events that required them to be flexible or make adaptations in their lives.

Debriefing Questions
- Ask a few students to volunteer their most difficult flexibility challenge. As a class, brainstorm ways someone could practice flexibility in that type of situation and how such flexibility would help make the situation better.
- See the reflection questions at the end of the worksheet.

Worksheet 15.1: Reflections About Change

Name:

List the three biggest changes in your life so far (for example, parental divorce, getting fired, leaving home to attend a university, sibling with special needs, a new coach, changing schools, moving to a new city):

1.

2.

3.

Pick the change that was most difficult for you to adapt to and answer each of the reflection questions. (Suggestion: Focus on how the situation required you to show flexibility more than on the emotions you felt, such as sadness or fear.)

Reflection Questions

1. How did the change affect you?
2. What did you do to help yourself adapt to the change?
3. Looking back, how successful were you in demonstrating flexibility or adapting to the change? Explain why you were or were not able to adapt successfully.

Activity 15.2

Flexibility Survey

EI Dimensions Targeted: Flexibility, Emotional Self-Awareness

Brief Description/Objective: Students will complete a self-report survey about flexibility.

Planning the Activity

Time Expected

- Worksheet: 5 minutes
- Reflection Questions: 10 minutes
- In-Class Debrief: 10 minutes

Materials

- Worksheet 15.2 from *The Student EQ Edge: Student Workbook*
- Board or flip chart and markers
- *The Student EQ Edge: Emotional Intelligence and Your Academic and Personal Success*

Facilitating the Activity

Directions

Assign Worksheet 15.2.

Debriefing Questions

- Ask the class to brainstorm the short-term (today, this week) costs and benefits of inflexibility. Then ask them to generate a list of long-term costs and benefits of inflexibility. If they understand flexibility well, they will have a harder time generating long-term benefits tied with inflexibility. Short-term inflexibility, however, can help some people temporarily manage the stress associated with change.
- See the reflection questions at the end of the worksheet.

Worksheet 15.2: Flexibility Survey

Name:

Answer each question below by circling the number for the response that most closely matches how you are, not how you would like to be.

Use the following scale:

Always or Almost Always	Usually	Sometimes	Occasionally	Rarely or Never
5	4	3	2	1

I get mad or nervous if a friend changes our plans at the last minute.

  5   4   3   2   1

I get upset if I have to change my plans for the day.

  5   4   3   2   1

When I eat out, I order the same items over and over.

  5   4   3   2   1

I like to make decisions and then stick to them.

  5   4   3   2   1

I get frustrated or upset when family members or roommates move furniture around.

  5   4   3   2   1

I avoid trying new things.

  5   4   3   2   1

I like to experience the same holiday rituals year after year.

  5   4   3   2   1

It bothers me if someone puts my clothes away and doesn't follow the system I use for organizing them.

  5   4   3   2   1

I have trouble shifting my attention from one priority to a different one.

  5   4   3   2   1

Scoring Instructions: Assign these points to your answers:

5 Always or almost always = –5 (negative 5)

4 Usually = –3 (negative 3)

3 Sometimes = 0

2 Occasionally = +3

1 Rarely or never = +5

Scores below 0 (negative numbers) indicate you probably have some challenges with flexibility. Those close to 0 indicate you are neither flexible nor inflexible, and those well above 0 indicate you are flexible.

Reflection Questions

1. Are you surprised by your score? Explain why or why not.
2. If you asked the person who knows you best to answer the same items about you, how do you think your score might change? Explain.

Activity 15.3
The Price of Inflexibility

EI Dimensions Targeted: Flexibility

Brief Description/Objective: Students will investigate changes at the societal level that require flexibility by either interviewing someone over 60 years of age or conducting internet research.

Planning the Activity

Time Expected
- Worksheet: 30–60 minutes
- Reflection Questions: 10 minutes
- In-Class Debrief: 10 minutes

Materials
- Worksheet 15.3 from *The Student EQ Edge: Student Workbook*
- Board or flip chart and markers
- *The Student EQ Edge: Emotional Intelligence and Your Academic and Personal Success*

Facilitating the Activity

Directions
- Assign Worksheet 15.3.
- You may need to brainstorm a list of societal changes that students can research or include in their interview of an older person. Some good examples are the use of computers and mobile devices, more women working outside the home, working greater distances from home, divorce, and blended families.

Debriefing Questions
- Take a poll to learn how many students liked and disliked being given a choice of how to complete this activity. Discuss the implications for flexibility.
- See the reflection questions at the end of the worksheet.

Worksheet 15.3: The Price of Inflexibility

Name:

There are two possible ways you can complete this activity: (1) interview someone who is at least 60 years of age, using the following questions, or (2) conduct internet research and find events since 1950 that created the need for some flexibility if a person wanted to remain productive and happy.

Option 1

Interview someone who is at least 60 years of age. Ask that person these questions:

1. What is the biggest change that happened during your lifetime that affected you as an individual? Explain how you adapted to the change.
2. What is the biggest change that happened during your lifetime that affected you as a professional? (If the person was a stay-at-home parent, ask the following: What is the biggest change that affected how you parent?). Explain your answer and the impact of the change on you.
3. What is the biggest change in our society that has affected you personally? Explain how you adapted to that change.
4. Name one more change in any area of your life that caused you to make adaptations. How did you adjust to that change?

Reflection Questions

1. Would you characterize the person you interviewed as flexible, lacking flexibility, or somewhere in the middle? How has this person benefited or been harmed by his or her flexibility or lack thereof?
2. What was your reaction to being given options for this assignment? What does that indicate about your flexibility?

Option 2

Conduct internet research and find at least three major changes that have happened since 1950 that created the need for some flexibility if a person wanted to remain productive and happy.

1. List the three major areas of change. Describe how each required flexibility.
2. Which of these changes has had the most impact on American society? What would happen to someone who is inflexible, especially related to this change?
3. Which of these changes do you think you would have struggled with the most, given what you know about yourself right now? Explain.
4. Which of these changes would you have adapted to most easily, given what you know about yourself right now? Explain.

Reflection Questions

1. What is your reaction to the amount of change that has occurred since 1950? Explain your answer.
2. What was your reaction to being given options for this assignment? What does that indicate about your flexibility?

Activity 15.4
Stretching Yourself

EI Dimensions Targeted: Flexibility, Emotional Self-Awareness

Brief Description/Objective: Students will pick a routine that is important to them and then change it, challenging their ability to be as flexible as possible.

Planning the Activity

Time Expected
- Worksheet: 10 minutes
- Reflection Question: 10 minutes
- In-Class Debrief: 15 minutes

Materials
- Worksheet 15.4 from *The Student EQ Edge: Student Workbook*
- Board or flip chart and markers
- *The Student EQ Edge: Emotional Intelligence and Your Academic and Personal Success*

Facilitating the Activity

Directions
Assign Worksheet 15.4.

Debriefing Questions
- What are the benefits of routines?
- How can we tell the difference between having a helpful routine and being inflexible?
- See the reflection question at the end of the worksheet.

Worksheet 15.4: Stretching Yourself

Name:

Pick a routine that is very important to you, such as how your clothes are ordered in your closet, a daily trip to the nearest Starbucks, or what you do after getting home each day. For five days, do *not* engage in this routine. Answer the following questions:

Day 1: The routine I will stop as of today is:

What were your emotional and behavioral reactions to changing this routine?

Days 2–4: Have you been able to maintain this change in your routine?

If so, explain how you are feeling on day 4 about the change.

If not, and you reinitiated the routine, what caused you to do that? Explain.

Day 5: What were the benefits of changing this routine? Were there any consequences of changing this routine *other than* some nervousness on your part? If so, explain.

Reflection Question

Was changing a cherished routine harder or easier than you expected? Explain.

Activity 15.5

Flexibility Forecasting

EI Dimensions Targeted: Flexibility, Assertiveness, Emotional Self-Awareness

Brief Description/Objective: Students will respond to hypothetical situations they may face in young adulthood that require flexibility.

Planning the Activity

Time Expected
- Worksheet: 15 minutes
- Reflection Questions: 10 minutes
- In-Class Debrief: 15 minutes

Materials
- Worksheet 15.5 from *The Student EQ Edge: Student Workbook*
- Board or flip chart and markers
- *The Student EQ Edge: Emotional Intelligence and Your Academic and Personal Success*

Facilitating the Activity

Directions
- Assign Worksheet 15.5.

Debriefing Questions
- How is flexibility different from lacking assertiveness? How can you tell the difference when you are in the middle of a tough situation?
- See the reflection questions at the end of the worksheet.

Worksheet 15.5: Flexibility Forecasting

Name:

There are many possible scenarios you could face as an adult that will require you to be flexible. For each scenario, write down your likely first reaction and then challenge yourself to see the benefits of flexibility.

Scenario 1. You have always spent the Thanksgiving holiday with your family. So has your fiancé. Your family homes are five hours apart, and both families have asked you to come for dinner on Thanksgiving Day.

My first reaction would be to . . .

One benefit to me of considering a different routine could be . . .

One thing I could say or do that would help me cope with this situation is . . .

Scenario 2. You are employed in your first job and have just gotten comfortable with your job responsibilities and your performance. Your boss approaches you about moving over to a different department where you will have to learn new skills. The pay and chances for promotion in the short term will be the same, but long term the move may have better opportunities. It's too soon to tell.

My first reaction would be . . .

One benefit to me of switching jobs could be . . .

One thing I could say (self-talk) or do to help me make this change is . . .

Scenario 3. You have been involved in a romantic relationship with someone for two years; you thought you would be together for the rest of your lives. Much of the excitement has evaporated from the relationship, but you know you both love each other. Unexpectedly, this person asks for some time away from you to think things over about the relationship.

My first reaction would be . . .

One benefit to me in this situation could be . . .

One thing I could say or do that would make this change easier would be . . .

Reflection Questions

1. Did you notice a common emotional or behavioral reaction in your initial responses to the changes? What does that tell you about your flexibility?
2. If these situations actually happened to you, would you be able to stop and think about the possible benefits of the change? Explain your answer.
3. What types of self-talk statements could you develop now that would help you cope with the need for change in the future?

Activity 15.6:
Self-Development Plan for Flexibility

The directions and template for students to create a self-development plan appear in Appendix D of this facilitator's guide. *The Student EQ Edge: Student Workbook* contains a template for developing stronger flexibility in Chapter 15.

Activity 15.7
Case Study—Flexibility

See Chapter 2 to assign a case study relevant to flexibility. Chapter 2 of *The Student EQ Edge: Student Workbook* contains all of the same case studies.

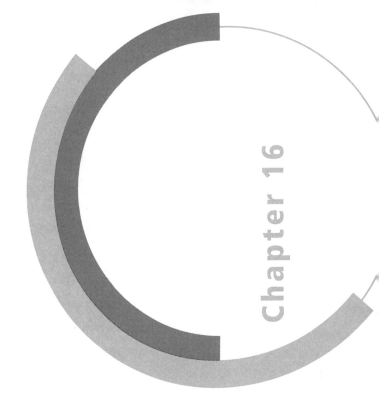

Chapter 16

Stress Tolerance

What is stress tolerance? Hans Selye, a famous stress researcher, commented that the only way to be free of stress was to die (Selye, 1976). Does that sound extreme to you? Unfortunately, he was correct. Stress refers to any demand made on us, so stress can be experienced in acts as simple as doing laundry or making a phone call. It's how we *perceive the stressor and its likely level of threat to us* that determines how stressful the action will be. Furthermore, if we have *resources to help us cope* with the stressor, then the stress is minimized. Think about doing laundry. If you're trying to leave for vacation and won't have access to a washer and dryer, and you've run out of time to do all the laundry and get it dry, then doing laundry can be very stressful to you. In contrast, if you're spending a relaxing day at home with no agenda, then doing a few loads of laundry—assuming you have a washer and dryer in your home—probably does not create enough stress to even notice. Also, stress can be exacerbated or minimized by whether we engage in irrational thoughts related to the stressor. Staying with the example of the laundry that needs to get done, if you imagine wearing a pair of jeans with a slight stain on them and conclude that other people would reject you because of that stain, then you are probably engaging in an irrational belief that will only serve to worsen the stress. Using the A-E model covered in Chapter 3 helps us to monitor how much our internal thought patterns are creating stress.

Stress tolerance is a key skill in managing our physiological, emotional, and behavioral reactions to events. Stress is associated with the release of cortisol, a hormone designed to activate our bodies to either "fight" or "flee" from the stressor. If our cortisol levels stay high over long periods of time, then the body begins to wear down and we can become physically ill because our immune system is suppressed. Cognitive changes, such as disorganization and forgetfulness, join the parade of negative outcomes associated with too much stress. And the cycle continues. Our goal should be learning to minimize our reactions to stressors by interpreting them realistically and then developing coping mechanisms that help release stress.

Is it possible to be too free of stress? Is it a good thing to be unfazed by most events that surround you? Again, the answer depends on whether you have well-developed EI skills in other areas. Someone who is highly tolerant of stress (remains calm, reacts rationally) may underreact to some situations if other EI areas are too low. Suppose, for example, that a student receives an email from a faculty member indicating he or she is failing the class and should drop it immediately so the student's GPA won't be negatively affected. The student who remains too calm (and perhaps is not skilled at reality testing) may wait several days or weeks to respond to such an email, and the time period for dropping a class could be closed before the student takes action.

A NOTE ABOUT THIS CHAPTER

This chapter will be organized differently from the others in the student workbook. Each activity builds on the next so, if possible, the activities should be completed in order.

STUDENT LEARNING OUTCOMES

Students will:

- Identify their biggest stressors (Activity 16.1)
- Understand why these issues produce stress (Activity 16.2)

- Practice using the A-E model to minimize daily and ongoing stress (Activity 16.3)
- Analyze their resources for coping with stress (Activity 16.4)
- Implement coping strategies for short-term or daily stressors (Activity 16.5)
- Create a long-term plan for dealing with stress (Activity 16.6)

SUGGESTED READINGS, MOVIES, AND TELEVISION SHOWS

- *The Student EQ Edge: Emotional Intelligence and Your Academic and Personal Success*, Chapter 16

Movies
- *Catch Me If You Can*—Scene 5, "Running Away"—The main character shows inappropriate coping with stress as he runs away from his family due to the pressure of choosing who to live with after his parent's divorce. Scene 18, "Out of Control" —The main character, Frank, is hysterical as the FBI closes in on him, showing the long-term effects of intensive stress.
- *The Pursuit of Happyness*—Scenes 24, "Four Spots Left," and Scene 25, "Climbing Mountains"—The main character deals with the stress of single parenthood, a demanding job, and homelessness.
- *What About Bob?*—Scene 5, "Next Stop: Winnipesaukee," and Chapter 6, "Meet the Family"—The psychiatrist begins to show signs of stress when Bob shows up at his vacation destination and then again when Bob shows up at his lake house.

Television Shows
- *The Office*—Episode 86, "Stress Relief" Part 1—Dwight, acting as a safety monitor, stages a stressful event for employees. At the end, Michael attempts to help the employees relieve stress.
- *Scare Tactics*—Unsuspecting individuals are lured into situations designed to evoke extreme fear. Watch any episode to see how individuals cope with these stressful situations.

● PLANNING YOUR CLASS

50–60 Minute Class

Assign Worksheets 16.1 and 16.2 for homework. Ask whether students have any questions about the difference between ongoing stressors and daily hassles, and if not, proceed to Activity 16.3. Ask for a class volunteer to choose one of his or her stressors and work through the A-E model. Then ask students to complete 16.3. As students finish Worksheet 16.3, have them pair with a classmate to check their understanding of the A-E model and how it relates to stress. If needed to enhance understanding, have two or three students share their A-E model with the class. Next, have students brainstorm as a large group about all of the different resources most of us have to cope with stressors (time, money, friends or family, learning or counseling centers on campus, free information from the Web, and so on). Next, have them brainstorm all the healthy ways we can release stress (for example, exercise, daily nap, or yoga). Assign Worksheets 16.4 and 16.5 for homework.

3–4 Hour Class

Assign Worksheets 16.1 and 16.2 for homework. Ask whether students have any questions about the difference between ongoing stressors and daily hassles, and if not, proceed to Activity 16.3. Ask for a class volunteer to choose one of his or her stressors and work through the A-E model. Then ask students to complete Worksheet 16.3. As students finish Worksheet 16.3, have them pair with a classmate to check their understanding of the A-E model and how it relates to stress. If needed to enhance understanding, have two or three students share their A-E model with the class. Next, show a segment from *What About Bob?* (5–15 minutes) in which the psychiatrist handles stress poorly. Analyze the mistakes he made because he did not handle stress well. Next, have students brainstorm as a large group about all of the different resources most of us have to cope with stressors (time, money, friends or family, learning or counseling centers on campus, free information from the Web, and so on). Next, have them brainstorm all the healthy ways we can release stress (for example, exercise, daily nap, or yoga). Assign Worksheets 16.4 and 16.5 to be completed during class (with a recommendation you collect these and review them). If time allows, have them analyze a case study related to stress (Activity 16.7) or watch an additional movie clip and analyze what the main character could have done differently to cope effectively with stress.

Activity List

Activity #	Activity Name	Brief Description and Activity Notes
16.1	Identifying Your Stressors	Students rank ongoing and daily hassle stressors to determine which stressors have the most impact on them.
16.2	Understanding Why You Get Stressed	Using the stressors identified in 16.1, students analyze why that issue threatens them.
16.3	Irrational Thinking and Stress	Students explore whether they are exacerbating the amount of stress they experience (using stressors identified in 16.1) by engaging in irrational thoughts.
16.4	Resources for Coping	Students identify resources for coping with the stressors identified in 16.1.
16.5	Stress Busters	Students identify and begin using one or two major coping strategies that help to relieve stress.
16.6	Self-Development Plan for Stress Tolerance	The student development plan for stress tolerance is different from the ones in other chapters!
16.7	Case Study— Stress Tolerance	Students analyze the behavior of a person who faces challenges related to stress tolerance.
Note: These activities build on one another and thus should be assigned sequentially for the best learning outcomes to occur.		

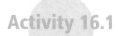

Activity 16.1
Identifying Your Stressors

EI Dimensions Targeted: Stress Tolerance, Emotional Self-Awareness

Brief Description/Objective: Students will rank ongoing and "daily hassle" types of stressors to determine what type of stressors they are most reactive to.

Planning the Activity

Time Expected
- Worksheet: 10–15 minutes
- Reflection Question: 10–15 minutes
- In-Class Debrief: 5–10 minutes

Materials
- Worksheet 16.1 from *The Student EQ Edge: Student Workbook*
- Board or flip chart and markers
- *The Student EQ Edge: Emotional Intelligence and Your Academic and Personal Success*

Facilitating the Activity

Directions
- Assign Worksheet 16.1.
- Review the difference between ongoing stressors and daily-hassle stressors to ensure student understanding.

Debriefing Questions
- Daily hassles can take a bigger toll on our emotional and physical health than ongoing stressors. Why do you think this is true?
- See the reflection question at the end of the worksheet.

Worksheet 16.1: Identifying Your Stressors

Name:

There are two categories of stressors. Ongoing stressors have been causing you stress for more than a couple of days and are likely to continue. Daily hassles come and go, but when they happen, they can be quite frustrating. It can be hard to predict daily hassles, but we have included a few that most of us experience. Follow the directions for each column.

Ongoing Stressors	Daily Hassles
Rank order your top three ongoing stressors, with #1 being the stressor that causes you the most distress, #2 the second most stressful situation, and #3 the third most stressful. Add ongoing stressors you face if they are not included in this list.	Identify the top five stressors for you, not in terms of their frequency but rather in terms of how much stress they cause for you when they do happen. Rank order the top five daily hassles for you, with the top stressor as #1, the next most stressful #2, and so on. Add any daily hassles you face that are not included in this list.
____ money problems ____ family problems ____ problems with a romantic partner ____ health issues for you ____ health issues of a family member ____ separation from someone you love ____ social issues (feeling left out, no one to hang out with, being bullied) ____ team or group turmoil ____ pressure to succeed academically ____ pressure to succeed athletically ____ work problems ____ other: ____ other:	____ losing important documents because of computer problems ____ being late to an important meeting or class ____ jammed printer ____ no money to buy a meal and no time to go to an ATM machine ____ fight with a good friend, parent, or sibling ____ being embarrassed by a teacher or coach ____ being stuck in traffic for 10 minutes or longer ____ no good food to eat in the refrigerator ____ lots of work to do and not much time ____ spilled food on your white shirt and nothing else to change into ____ other: ____ other:

Reflection Question

What did you learn about yourself as you ranked each type of stressor?

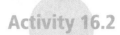

Activity 16.2

Understanding Why You Get Stressed

EI Dimensions Targeted: Stress Tolerance, Emotional Self-Awareness

Brief Description/Objective: Taking the stressors identified in 16.1, students will analyze why that issue threatens them.

Planning the Activity

Time Expected
- Worksheet: 10–15 minutes
- Reflection Question: 10 minutes
- In-Class Debrief: 10 minutes

Materials
- Worksheet 16.2 from *The Student EQ Edge: Student Workbook*
- Board or flip chart and markers
- *The Student EQ Edge: Emotional Intelligence and Your Academic and Personal Success*

Facilitating the Activity

Directions
- Assign Worksheet 16.2.
- Go over the directions at the beginning of the exercise to ensure that students understand what it means to evaluate the potential threat of a stressor.

Debriefing Question
Discuss the reflection question with the students, helping them to identify categories where they are more reactive and less reactive to events.

Worksheet 16.2: Understanding Why You Get Stressed

Name:

Stress researchers have found that the degree of stress we experience is related to how threatened we feel by a particular stressor. Not everyone responds to the same stressor in the same way. For example, some students get very stressed out for big tests, whereas others barely notice any stress. One athlete may get very nervous before a big game or match, whereas another may feel less nervous. If you have been counting on getting an academic scholarship to a prestigious university, the pressure to succeed academically is likely to cause you much more stress than if you plan to attend a local university with open admissions. Likewise, having lots of homework and not much time may be more stressful if a prestigious university is your primary goal. The perceived potential for a stressor to keep us from attaining our goals is one factor in determining how stressful that event will be to us. One key to dealing with stressors is to identify how threatened we feel by that stressor.

Refer back to Worksheet 16.1 and list your top three stressors from each category. Write down how or why you feel threatened by this stressor.

Top Three Ongoing Stressors and Why They Threaten Me (for example, they keep me from meeting a goal, create extra work)	Top Three Daily Hassles and Why They Threaten Me
1.	1.
2.	2.
3.	3.

Reflection Question

What patterns do you see in terms of the things that threaten you? (Most of us will feel more threatened around key areas for us—such as academics, sports, or relationships—no matter what the individual stressor is.)

Activity 16.3

Irrational Thinking and Stress

EI Dimensions Targeted: Stress Tolerance, Emotional Self-Awareness, Reality Testing

Brief Description/Objective: Students will explore whether they are exacerbating the amount of stress they experience (using stressors identified in 16.1) by engaging in irrational thoughts about the stressor.

Planning the Activity

Time Expected
- Worksheet: 15–20 minutes
- Reflection Questions: 10 minutes
- In-Class Debrief: 10 minutes

Materials
- Worksheet 16.3 from *The Student EQ Edge: Student Workbook*
- Board or flip chart and markers
- *The Student EQ Edge: Emotional Intelligence and Your Academic and Personal Success*

Facilitating the Activity

Directions
- Assign Worksheet 16.3.
- You will probably need to review the A-E model covered in Chapter 3.

Debriefing Question
Instead of a typical debrief, ask for a couple of students to share their A-E model to test for understanding of the model and how to use it.

Worksheet 16.3: Irrational Thinking and Stress

Name:

Refer to Chapter 3 for a more detailed review of the A-E model, which explains how our *beliefs* about certain events are more important in determining our reactions than the event itself. In sum, here's the model:

A—the *activating* event (something that happens, something that needs to get done, a thought)

B—your irrational *belief* about the event (beliefs that exaggerate the importance of the issue, beliefs that contradict the facts, beliefs that exaggerate possible consequences, and so on)

C—the behavioral and emotional *consequences* of your irrational belief

D—*disputing* the irrational belief with evidence

E— the *effects* of disputing your irrational belief and replacing it with a rational belief

Pick one ongoing stressor and one daily hassle and analyze each using the A-E model.

Ongoing Stressor

A—the activating event; think about the last event related to this ongoing stressor

B—the irrational belief; what are you assuming or believing that is *not* supported by the facts

C—the consequences of your irrational belief; include both emotional and behavioral consequences

D—dispute the irrational belief with facts; substitute other possible beliefs

E—the effects, behavioral and emotional, of your new belief

Daily Stressor

A—the activating event; this is likely to be the daily hassle itself

B—the irrational belief; what you are assuming or believing that is *not* supported by the facts

C—the consequences of your irrational belief; include emotional and behavioral consequences

D—dispute the irrational belief with facts; substitute other possible beliefs

E—the effects, behavioral and emotional, of your new belief

Reflection Questions

1. Pretend you have to explain the benefits of using the A-E model to a friend. What would you say?
2. How will applying the A-E model make an event less stressful?

Activity 16.4

Resources for Coping

EI Dimensions Targeted: Stress Tolerance, Interpersonal Relationships

Brief Description/Objective: Students will identify resources for coping with the stressors identified in 16.1.

Planning the Activity

Time Expected
- Worksheet: 10 minutes
- Reflection Questions: 5 minutes
- In-Class Debrief: 10 minutes

Materials
- Worksheet 16.4 from *The Student EQ Edge: Student Workbook*
- Board or flip chart and markers
- *The Student EQ Edge: Emotional Intelligence and Your Academic and Personal Success*

Facilitating the Activity

Directions
- Assign Worksheet 16.4.
- You may want to have students brainstorm a list of possible resources for coping before assigning the activity.

Debriefing Questions
- Ask students to give examples about how time, money, friends, professionals, and other things can be used as a resource. Remind students that very high independence is associated with a greater likelihood of *not* finishing college. Why is this true? Probably because the most independent students fail to use all of the resources available to help them and try to do everything on their own.
- See the reflection questions at the end of the worksheet.

Worksheet 16.4: Resources for Coping

Name:

Coping with stress involves resources. Those resources may include time, forms of social support (friends, family, and mentors), money, skill sets, daily routines to minimize stress, resources at your school, help from professionals, and others. Refer back to Worksheet 16.1 and list your top three stressors from each category in the chart. Write down all of the resources you have that can help you cope more effectively with the stress. For example, if a chronic health issue is an ongoing stressor for you, your resources might include exercise, a special diet, professionals who can prescribe medicine or other forms of treatment, friends and family members who support you as you cope, and even your own ability to research your illness and possible treatments. If you're having trouble thinking of resources that can help you cope, ask a friend—this would be an example of using social support when stressed!

Top Three Ongoing Stressors	Top Three Daily Hassles
1. Resources I could use:	1. Resources I could use:
2. Resources:	2. Resources:
3. Resources:	3. Resources:

Reflection Questions

1. What resources could you develop that you are *not* using effectively now?
2. What would you have to do to develop these resources?

Activity 16.5

Stress Busters

EI Dimensions Targeted: Stress Tolerance, Emotional Self-Awareness

Brief Description/Objective: Students will identify and begin using one or two major coping strategies that help to relieve stress.

Planning the Activity

Time Expected
- Worksheet: 10 minutes
- Reflection Questions: 10 minutes
- In-Class Debrief: 5 minutes

Materials
- Worksheet 16.5 from *The Student EQ Edge: Student Workbook*
- Board or flip chart and markers
- *The Student EQ Edge: Emotional Intelligence and Your Academic and Personal Success*

Facilitating the Activity

Directions
- Assign Worksheet 16.5.
- You may want to have the entire class brainstorm effective stress busters before assigning this activity.

Debriefing Question
See the reflection questions at the end of the worksheet. If students indicate that lack of time is an issue preventing them from stress busting, challenge them to keep a log for a few days of how they spend their free time.

Worksheet 16.5: Stress Busters

Name:

In this activity, you will develop a specific strategy for dealing with your top three ongoing stressors. Stress busters will relieve and relax you, ensuring that you cope better with your ongoing stressors. Stress busters will not eliminate the stressor itself, but they will enable you to be less reactive to it. First, identify an ongoing stressor that you need relief from.

My ongoing stressor:

Now list three specific things you will do to cope better with this stress. (*Note*: Specific strategies are ones that someone else could observe you doing, so avoid vague strategies such as "I'll get less upset" or "I'll avoid the situation." Also, stress busters do *not* remove the stressor; they just help you to better cope with it. Some examples of stress busters include exercise, yoga, meditation, hobbies, pets, a walk outside, and reading.

1.
2.
3.

Reflection Questions

1. Are you willing to commit to these strategies? Why or why not?
2. What might get in your way if you try to implement these strategies?

Activity 16.6

Self-Development Plan for Stress Tolerance

The directions and template for students to create a self-development plan for stress tolerance are slightly different than in other chapters. *The Student EQ Edge: Student Workbook* contains a template for developing stress tolerance in Worksheet 16.6.

Activity 16.7

Case Study—Stress Tolerance

See Chapter 2 to assign a case study relevant to stress tolerance. Chapter 2 of *The Student EQ Edge: Student Workbook* contains all of the same case studies.

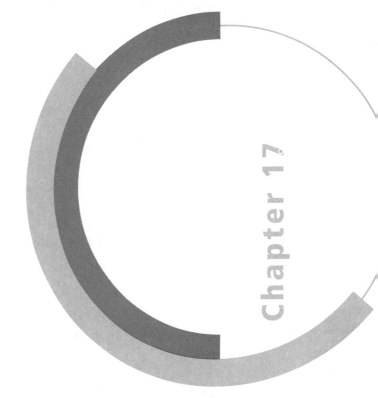

Chapter 17

Optimism

What is optimism? Simply put, optimism involves the ability to maintain a *positive attitude* or approach when faced with adversity and to *persist in overcoming challenges*. Those who express a positive attitude but without behavioral actions to match probably lack reality-testing skills because wonderful things don't usually happen to us solely because we hope or believe they will. But without a positive attitude and hope that we can succeed, facing challenges and adversity becomes too overwhelming. So a positive attitude is a necessary part of optimism but not the full story. Help students understand that being unrealistic, living in a dream world, or engaging in magical thinking are *not* forms of optimism because they don't require anything further from us. Remaining optimistic can be hard work, especially when the challenge seems to grow rather than fade.

It's hard to imagine someone who is too optimistic. In fact, the only time very high optimism could be problematic would be when someone is also unskilled at reality testing or problem solving. A low level of either of these factors, when combined with optimism, may create inertia. Rather than actively trying to solve the problem, a mind-set of "everything will work out" takes hold, but without accompanying behavior that demonstrates resilience.

STUDENT LEARNING OUTCOMES

Students will:

- Learn how to frame factual information or situations in a positive way
- Reflect on the costs and consequences of negativity
- Analyze their tendencies to be optimistic or pessimistic
- Develop skills in using positive self-talk
- Understand the benefit of optimism in facing a major challenge

SUGGESTED READINGS, MOVIES, AND TELEVISION SHOWS

- *The Student EQ Edge: Emotional Intelligence and Your Academic and Personal Success*, Chapter 17

Movies
- *Patch Adams*— Scene 11, "Gesundheit"—Patch shows his vision for a free medical clinic; Scene 15, "Patch's Appeal"—Patch makes an impassioned speech about caring, healing, and being a doctor no matter what happens.
- *The Pursuit of Happyness*—Scene 11, "Big Interview"—After being arrested for a failure to pay taxes, Chris has to run from the jail to an important job interview. With paint in his hair and only an undershirt on, Chris is asked what he would say if he was told someone hired a guy with no shirt, and he replies, "He must have some really nice pants."

Television Shows
- *The Amazing Race*—In this reality TV show, people team with a friend, partner, or family member to race across the globe against other teams. Every show presents obstacles the teams must overcome; thus every show also gives contestants the opportunity to display optimism or pessimism. Students can find their own episode to watch and list optimistic and pessimistic statements and behaviors.

- *Extreme Makeover: Home Edition*—This reality TV show features families who are struggling economically and live in a run-down and sometimes unsafe home. Because of their good works in the community or persistence in the face of serious obstacles, the family is picked to have a completely new home built for them at no cost. The show brims with optimism both in the stories of the families chosen and in the ability of the mostly volunteer crew to build a new house in just one week. Students can watch any episode and find multiple examples of optimism.

PLANNING YOUR CLASS

50–60 Minute Class

Have students complete Worksheets 17.1, 17.2, and 17.3 for homework. Debrief all of Activity 17.1 as a large group. For Activity 17.2, ask students to take turns providing the motivating alternative to the de-motivating statements. List these on the board. (If possible, provide the complete list to each student via email or a handout at the next class.) Watch the internet clip from Activity 17.5 as a class. Debrief by having the students answer the questions that appear at the end of this activity.

3–4 Hour Class

Have students complete Worksheets 17.1, 17.2, and 17.3 for homework. Debrief all of Activity 17.1 as a large group. For Activity 17.2, ask students to take turns providing the motivating alternative to the de-motivating statements. List these on the board. (If possible, provide the complete list to each student via email or a handout at the next class.) Watch the internet clip from Activity 17.5. Debrief by having the students answer the questions that appear at the end of Worksheet 17.5. If students need more practice with framing, assign small groups to work on the different scenarios in Activity 17.4 and then share their solutions with the class. Next, show an episode of *The Amazing Race*. Ask students to (1) write down all optimistic and pessimistic statements, (2) record what the person making the statement did next, and

(3) record what the partner on the show did in response to the optimism or pessimism. Debrief these results in class. Next, have students analyze a case study from Chapter 2 and, if time allows, create a self-development plan for enhancing their optimism (Worksheet 17.6). They should tie their self-development plan to the results obtained from the LOT-R assessment. Finally, wrap up class by asking students to complete this statement: "Optimism does not guarantee that only good things will happen, but it does guarantee . . ."

Activity List

Activity #	Activity Name	Brief Description and Activity Notes
17.1	Optimism Begins with Framing	Students take a factual situation that is accompanied by negative interpretations of the situation and change those to positive interpretations of the same factual situation. Provide a few examples to get them started.
17.2	De-motivators—Watch Your Self-Talk	Students practice converting negative self-talk into positive self-talk. Review the A-E model if needed.
17.3	Assessing Your Optimism	Students complete the Life Orientation Test—Revised (LOT-R; Scheier, Carver, & Bridges, 1994) to assess their relative levels of optimism and pessimism
17.4	Pep Talks and Persistence	Students respond to three scenarios by identifying a positive way to frame the event and what behaviors would demonstrate persistence.
17.5	Perseverance Defined	Students view an internet clip about a young man facing cancer at age 12 and how he displayed optimism. If the clip is no longer accessible, have them complete the activity based on a movie character, a famous person, or someone they know who has "persevered" through bad circumstances.
17.6	Self-Development Plan for Optimism	Students develop a plan for increasing their optimism.
17.7	Case Study—Optimism	Assign a case study from Chapter 2. The same case studies appear in *The Student EQ Edge: Student Workbook*.

Activity 17.1

Optimism Begins with Framing

EI Dimensions Targeted: Optimism, Reality Testing, Flexibility

Brief Description/Objective: Students will take a factual situation that is accompanied by negative interpretations of the situation and change those to positive interpretations.

Planning the Activity

Time Expected
- Worksheet: 10 minutes
- Reflection Questions: 10 minutes
- In-Class Debrief: 10 minutes

Materials
- Worksheet 17.1 from *The Student EQ Edge: Student Workbook*
- Board or flip chart and markers
- *The Student EQ Edge: Emotional Intelligence and Your Academic and Personal Success*

Facilitating the Activity

Directions
- Assign Worksheet 17.1.
- Students may experience challenges coming up with an optimistic interpretation or restatement. Provide an example or two, such as changing "I don't get many presents on my birthday" to "I have lots of different movies to watch because all my siblings have some of their own movies I can see."

Debriefing Questions
- Challenge students to differentiate between the facts (having 12 children in the family) and the different ways to react to that. Optimistic versus pessimistic framing is a *choice*.
- See the reflection questions at the end of the worksheet.

Worksheet 17.1: Optimism Begins with Framing

Name:

Suppose you come from a family with 12 children and that you are the seventh child born in the family. For each of the following scenarios, turn the pessimistic way of framing the situation into a more optimistic framing. In other words, think of the *advantages* of having 11 siblings!

I don't get much attention from my parents.

Reframe to . . .

I hardly ever get to buy new clothes.

Reframe to . . .

I don't get any privacy or time by myself.

Reframe to . . .

My family cannot afford to go on big vacations together.

Reframe to . . .

Reflection Questions

1. If you were from a 12-child family, it may be a *fact* that you would have to wear a lot of hand-me-down clothing. But that fact can be interpreted two ways: the pessimistic way (I don't get to buy new clothes) or the optimistic way (I have lots of choices of clothing and different styles). Try to think about *one fact* that you are currently framing either optimistically or pessimistically. Write the fact and your interpretation here.
2. How difficult was it for you to find an optimistic alternative for each statement? What does that tell you about yourself?

Activity 17.2

De-motivators—Watch Your Self-Talk

EI Dimensions Targeted: Optimism

Brief Description/Objective: Students will practice converting negative self-talk into positive self-talk.

Planning the Activity

Time Expected

- Worksheet: 10–15 minutes
- Reflection Questions: 10 minutes
- In-Class Debrief: 10 minutes

Materials

- Worksheet 17.2 from *The Student EQ Edge: Student Workbook*
- Board or flip chart and markers
- *The Student EQ Edge: Emotional Intelligence and Your Academic and Personal Success*

Facilitating the Activity

Directions

- Assign Worksheet 17.2.
- Bring a copy of the de-motivators to class with you. Students will take turns writing in a motivating statement for each one. Copy the motivating statements and give them to the class.

Debriefing Questions

- What are some of the short-term benefits or reasons someone would be pessimistic?
- See the reflection questions at the end of the worksheet.

Worksheet 17.2: De-motivators—Watch Your Self-Talk

Activity developed by Dawn Dillon

Name:

The following is a list of pessimistic sayings that can be considered de-motivators. These quotes are intended to parody inspirational sayings that most of us have heard. These were taken from the website http://www.despair.com (retrieved July 10, 2010). Take each statement and change it from a pessimistic or deflating statement to an optimistic one.

I expected times like this. But I never thought they'd be so bad, so long, and so frequent.

When the winds of change blow hard enough, the most trivial things can turn into deadly projectiles.

The secret to success is knowing who to blame for your failures.

Dreams are like rainbows. Only idiots chase them.

Not all pain is gain.

At some point hanging in there just makes you look like an even bigger loser.

Hope may not be warranted at this point.

If it can make your job easier, it can probably make it irrelevant.

No single raindrop believes it is responsible for the flood.

If at first you don't succeed, failure may be your style.

Less is more. Unless you're standing next to the one with more. Then less just looks pathetic.

Hard work always pays off over time, but laziness pays off now.

Pressure can turn a lump of coal into a flawless diamond or an average person into an absolute basket case.

If you never try anything new, you'll miss out on life's great disappointments.

How can the future be so hard to predict when all of my worst fears keep coming true?

Reflection Questions

1. What sayings do you use to motivate you?
2. What negative sayings have you heard that you believe are true? How could you challenge those sayings?

Activity 17.3

Assessing Your Optimism

EI Dimensions Targeted: Optimism

Brief Description/Objective: Students will complete the Life Orientation Test—Revised (LOT-R; Scheier, Carver, & Bridges, 1994) to assess their relative levels of optimism and pessimism.

Planning the Activity

Time Expected
- Worksheet and Survey: 5 minutes
- Reflection Questions: 10 minutes
- In-Class Debrief: 5 minutes

Materials
- Worksheet 17.3 from *The Student EQ Edge: Student Workbook*
- Board or flip chart and markers
- *The Student EQ Edge: Emotional Intelligence and Your Academic and Personal Success*

Facilitating the Activity

Directions
- Assign Worksheet 17.3.
- You may need to explain the scoring directions to ensure accuracy.

Debriefing Question
See the reflection questions at the end of the worksheet. Focus the discussion on how we acquire a tendency to be optimistic or pessimistic from our family.

Worksheet 17.3: Assessing Your Optimism

Name:

Directions for the Life Orientation Test–Revised

Scheier, Carver, and Bridges, 1994

Please be as honest and accurate as you can throughout. Try not to let your response to one statement influence your responses to other statements. There are no "correct" or "incorrect" answers. Answer according to your own feelings, rather than how you think "most people" would answer. Fill in the letter that best represents you in the blank space beside the item number.

A	B	C	D	E
I agree a lot.	I agree a little.	I neither agree nor disagree.	I *disagree* a little.	E = I *disagree* a lot.

_____1. In uncertain times, I usually expect the best.

_____2. It's easy for me to relax.

_____3. If something can go wrong for me, it will.

_____4. I'm always optimistic about my future.

_____5. I enjoy my friends a lot.

_____6. It's important for me to keep busy.

_____7. I hardly ever expect things to go my way.

_____8. I don't get upset too easily.

_____9. I rarely count on good things happening to me.

____10. Overall, I expect more good things to happen to me than bad.

Score your results as follows: Group 1: Add items 1, 4, and 10: A = 5, B = 4, C = 3, D = 2, E = 1

My total score for these items is:

Group 2: Add items 3, 7, and 9: A = 5, B = 4, C = 3, D = 2, E = 1

My total score for these items is:

Now, subtract your score for group 2 from your score for group 1. For example, if you scored 15 for group 1 and 10 for group 2, your score would equal +5; if you scored 10 for Group 1 and 15 for Group 2, your score would equal –5.

My overall score is:

Score Interpretations

A score of 0 means you are balanced in your tendency to be optimistic and pessimistic. A positive score, +1 to +12, indicates a trend toward optimism; the higher your score, the more optimistic you are. A negative score, ranging from –1 to –12, indicates more pessimism; the larger the negative number, the more pessimistic you are.

Reflection Questions

1. What is your reaction to your results? Explain.
2. What do you think were the most influential factors in your development of optimism or pessimism?

Activity 17.4

Pep Talks and Persistence

EI Dimensions Targeted: Optimism

Brief Description/Objective: Students will respond to three scenarios by identifying a positive way to frame the event and what behaviors would demonstrate persistence.

Planning the Activity

Time Expected
- Worksheet: 15 minutes (5 minutes if you assign different groups to do each scenario)
- Reflection Question: 10 minutes
- In-Class Debrief: 10 minutes

Materials
- Worksheet 17.4 from *The Student EQ Edge: Student Workbook*
- Board or flip chart and markers
- *The Student EQ Edge: Emotional Intelligence and Your Academic and Personal Success*

Facilitating the Activity

Directions
- Assign Worksheet 17.4.
- You can assign small groups to complete one full scenario and then have each small group share their responses with the class.

Debriefing Questions
- Persistence usually pays off, but not always. Conduct an agree-disagree activity in response to the following statement: "It makes sense to persist at something only if you know your efforts will pay off in the end."
- See the reflection question at the end of the worksheet.

Worksheet 17.4: Pep Talks and Persistence

Name:

Take each of the following three scenarios and describe an optimistic response in terms of framing, self-talk, and persistence.

Scenario 1

You have been a starting member of the soccer team for two years. You are a senior, and a sophomore super-star has taken your place in the starting line-up.

- How can you frame this development to help you stay motivated?
- What things can you tell yourself to help you become the best soccer player you can be?
- How will you know whether you are persisting or have given up?

Scenario 2

You hope to get into graduate school in your field. You take the Graduate Record Exam (GRE) and score 100 points below what you need to score in order to get into a good school.

- How can you frame this development to help you stay motivated?
- What self-talk can you engage in to help you remain positive?
- How will you know whether you are persisting or have given up?

Scenario 3

You are graduating from your university in a year when the economy is bad. As a result, only 50 percent of graduates are getting a job that requires a bachelor's degree, 40 percent are working at a job that does not require a degree, and 10 percent have not found a job at all.

- What things can you tell yourself to help you be motivated to improve your chances of getting a job that requires a college degree?
- Imagine that it is August after graduation in May and you still do not have a professional job.
  a. What would your self-talk be like if you were persisting?
  b. What behaviors would you be engaging in if you were persisting?

Reflection Question

Writing these worksheet responses is much easier than living them. Who do you admire that you could seek motivation from? Explain how or why this person motivates you to remain persistent.

Activity 17.5

Perseverance Defined

EI Dimensions Targeted: Optimism, Emotional Expression

Brief Description/Objective: Students will view an internet clip about a young man facing cancer at age 12 and how he displayed optimism.

Planning the Activity

Time Expected
- Worksheet and Internet clip: 20 minutes
- Reflection Question: 10 minutes
- In-Class Debrief: 10 minutes

Materials
- Worksheet 17.5 from *The Student EQ Edge: Student Workbook*
- Board or flip chart and markers
- *The Student EQ Edge: Emotional Intelligence and Your Academic and Personal Success*
- Internet connection and projection device if you plan to show the clip in class

Facilitating the Activity

Directions
- Assign Worksheet 17.5.
- If you want to enhance this activity, have students do research about how optimism is related to health; ask each student to summarize the findings from one scientific study.

Debriefing Questions
- Would you rather be around an optimistic person or a pessimistic one? Why? Assuming most of the class indicates they prefer optimism, challenge them to think about how others may respond to them when they exude pessimism.
- See the reflection question at the end of the worksheet.

Worksheet 17.5: Perseverance Defined

Name:

Optimism does not guarantee us positive outcomes or getting what we want. What it does guarantee is that our journey, no matter what we confront, will be filled with hope, positive attitudes, and persistence. To see an example of optimism, go to http://www.chordomafoundation.org/perseverance-pledge/. Scroll down to the first paragraph and click on the phrase "powerful speech." Watch the speech by Justin Straus, a bright and loving young man who died from a devastating form of cancer when he was just 13 years old. (Justin's speech is preceded by a speech by his father who also displays optimism related to the family challenge of Justin's battle with cancer. The entire clip lasts about 15 minutes.)

Listen to Justin's speech for signs of optimism. Even though treatments for his cancer robbed him of energy and made participating in sports difficult, Justin never gave up. The defining moment of Justin's optimism occurred shortly before his death. He was hospitalized, unable to swallow, speak, or do basic self-care. Physical therapy, designed to keep his muscles strong while he was bedridden, exhausted him. Yet one day, upon returning Justin to his hospital room from physical therapy, the therapists tried to transfer him from the wheelchair to his bed. Although exhausted and weak from the effort he had put forth in physical therapy, he wanted to sit in the chair rather than lie in the bed. He motioned to the white board (which he used to communicate because he could no longer talk) and scrawled (he was also losing fine motor skills) the word "perseverance." (His actual handwriting is viewable if you click the link mentioned in the preceding paragraph.) Justin died just days after he scrawled "perseverance," but he never gave up, and as a result, his story has inspired many people.

Reflection Question

Justin was diagnosed at age seven. Optimism did not prevent his death, but it did help him cope with the illness and possibly extended his life longer than predicted. Listen to the speech and list at least three behaviors Justin engaged in that showed he was

- Remaining positive and hopeful
- Persisting in his efforts to fight the cancer

Activity 17.6

Self-Development Plan for Optimism

The directions and template for students to create a self-development plan appear in Appendix D of this facilitator's guide. *The Student EQ Edge: Student Workbook* contains a template for developing stronger optimism in Chapter 17.

Activity 17.7

Case Study—Optimism

Choose a case study from Chapter 2 that relates to optimism and ask students to analyze the behavior of the main characters.

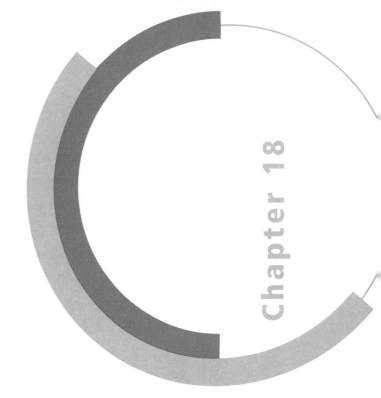

Chapter 18

Happiness

What is happiness? Happiness can be a challenging topic to discuss with students. When unhappiness becomes intense enough or long-lasting, depression may be a better description for what is happening than unhappiness. *The Student EQ Edge: Student Workbook* contains a paragraph describing symptoms of depression and encourages students to seek help if they believe that what they are feeling may be depression. In addition, there can be situational events in students' lives that are making them unhappy right now (for example, parental divorce, not getting into the college or graduate school of choice, financial burdens), but factors that cause situational unhappiness tend to resolve or pass with time. The primary goals of activities included in the *Student Workbook* are to help students better understand what is and is not associated with greater happiness and how to improve their current level of happiness. These activities are not designed to fight depression.

Feelings such as satisfaction, joy, and excitement are indications someone is experiencing happiness. Having fun, laughing frequently, being satisfied, and spreading positive emotional energy to others are tangible outward signs of happiness. Help students understand that strengthening other elements of their emotional intelligence—particularly self-regard, self-actualization, interpersonal relationships, and optimism— can improve their happiness levels.

Considering whether anyone could be too high in happiness seems almost absurd. And the answer is simply "no." Happiness results from the multiple effective areas of emotional intelligence just mentioned. If happiness bred complacency and someone stopped pursuing meaningful goals or quit investing in meaningful interpersonal relationships, then it's feasible that happiness could wane. It's far more likely, though, that the person would continue to practice the same EI skills and thus retain the level of happiness.

STUDENT LEARNING OUTCOMES

Students will:

- Distinguish among factors associated with (and not associated with) higher levels of happiness
- Assess their current and general levels of happiness
- Understand how their behaviors relate to their happiness levels
- Understand the four other emotional intelligence characteristics that are related to happiness
- Apply what they have learned about happiness to themselves and to a movie clip

SUGGESTED READINGS, MOVIES, AND TELEVISION SHOWS

- *The Student EQ Edge: Emotional Intelligence and Your Academic and Personal Success*, Chapter 18

Movies
- *Erin Brockovich*—Scene 42—Erin takes George along to show him what he's helped do to make good things happen for others; Donna is overjoyed by the news Erin shares.
- *Patch Adams*—Scene 6, "Walcott's Warning"—Patch makes patients happy and lets the dean know that laughter decreases cortisol, making people happier; Scene 16, "Board Decision"—The culmination of Patch's efforts to become a medical doctor.

- *The Pursuit of Happyness*—Scene 28, "Happyness"—The father is offered a full-time job, ending the struggles he and his son have faced; he races to get his son from day care and expresses joy as he hugs him tightly.

Television Shows
- *Extreme Makeover: Home Edition*—The TV show focuses on deserving families who are facing a major challenge and who need a new home. Despite the enormous challenges these families face, there is often joy or sources of satisfaction in their lives.
- *Modern Family*—Season 2, Episode 24, "The One That Got Away"—All Jay wants to do on his birthday is spend the day fishing. But at the end of the day, he realizes it's his relationships with others that make him happy.
- *The Office*—Episode 137, "Classy Christmas," Part 1—The office coworkers appear happy and content on the day of the party, but Michael changes the party to meet his own needs.

PLANNING YOUR CLASS

50–60 Minute Class

Assign Worksheets 18.1, 18.2, and 18.4 to complete for homework. Debrief Activity 18.2, stressing the importance of surrounding ourselves with people who exude positive emotion if we want to be happier ourselves. Before debriefing Activity 18.4, briefly summarize the factors that are and are not associated with happiness as summarized in the *Time* article referenced in Activity 18.3. Debrief Activity 18.4 to ensure student understanding of how each factor contributes to well-being and happiness. If time allows, watch some of the movie clips from Activity 18.5.

3–4 Hour Class

Assign Worksheets 18.1, 18.2, and 18.3 to complete for homework. Debrief Activity 18.2, stressing the importance of surrounding ourselves with people who exude positive emotion if we want to be happier ourselves. From their work on Activity 18.3, compile a list of factors that are and are not associated with greater happiness. Then introduce the idea that four areas of emotional intelligence—self-regard, self-actualization, interpersonal relations, and optimism—relate to happiness. Show the YouTube clips found in Activity 18.5 and have students complete the worksheet in class. After debriefing this, have students complete Activities 18.4 and 18.6. If students are willing, have each student share his or her one commitment with classmates.

Activity List

Activity #	Activity Name	Brief Description and Activity Notes
18.1	Taking Stock of Your Happiness Level	Students complete a survey related to their current happiness and their general well-being.
18.2	Laugh a Little, Laugh a Lot	Students watch YouTube clips of laughing infants and then reflect on the power of emotional contagion.
18.3	Does Money Buy Happiness?	Students conduct research about what factors are and are not associated with higher levels of happiness.
18.4	Well-Being Indicators	Students examine the four emotional intelligence areas that are associated with happiness and create strategies for how they can improve in each of these areas.
18.5	*The Pursuit of Happyness*	Students watch clips from the movie *The Pursuit of Happyness* and identify how self-regard, self-actualization, interpersonal relations, and optimism influenced the main character's happiness.
18.6	One Commitment—Self-Development Plan for Happiness	Students commit to engage in one behavior that will improve happiness.
18.7	Case Study—Happiness	Assign a case study from Chapter 2 related to happiness.

Activity 18.1

Taking Stock of Your Happiness Level

EI Dimensions Targeted: Happiness, Emotional Self-Awareness

Brief Description/Objective: Students will complete a survey related to their current happiness and their general well-being.

Planning the Activity

Time Expected
- Worksheet and Surveys: 5 minutes
- Reflection Questions: 10–15 minutes
- In-Class Debrief: 10 minutes

Materials
- Worksheet 18.1 from *The Student EQ Edge: Student Workbook*
- Board or flip chart and markers
- *The Student EQ Edge: Emotional Intelligence and Your Academic and Personal Success*

Facilitating the Activity

Directions
- Assign Worksheet 18.1.
- The surveys included in this activity are accessible via the Internet. The website is sponsored by Martin Seligman, a major author in the field of positive psychology and the University of Pennsylvania. Students will have to create an account to access the surveys, but their data is kept confidential.

Debriefing Questions
- What are some factors that can affect people's current level of happiness that tend to go away? What are factors that affect happiness that may not go away unless the person works to make changes?
- See the reflection questions at the end of the worksheet.

Worksheet 18.1: Taking Stock of Your Happiness Level

Name:

Martin Seligman and colleagues at the University of Pennsylvania have done a lot of research about happiness, optimism, and positive psychology (see, for example, Seligman, 1991, and Seligman & Maier, 1967). Go to http://www.authentichappiness.sas.upenn.edu/default.aspx and create an account (it's free!) by signing in with a username and password. You will be asked a few questions about yourself. Then complete the Fordyce Current Happiness survey and the General Happiness Questionnaire. Either print out your results or write down how you compare to others your age and on one of the other key comparisons (for example, your zip code).

Reflection Questions

1. Are your current happiness levels (Fordyce) and enduring happiness levels (General Happiness Questionnaire) about the same—that is, within 10 percent?
   a. If not, what is creating the difference?
   b. If the same, what elements of your life contribute to both your current and your enduring happiness?
2. What is your reaction to how you compared with others completing the same survey?

Activity 18.2

Laugh a Little, Laugh a Lot

EI Dimensions Targeted: Happiness

Brief Description/Objective: Students will watch YouTube clips of laughing infants and then reflect on the power of emotional contagion.

Planning the Activity

Time Expected
- Worksheet and YouTube videos: 5–10 minutes (Warning: Watching infants laugh can be addictive!)
- Reflection Questions: 15 minutes
- In-class debrief: 10 minutes

Materials
- Worksheet 18.2 from *The Student EQ Edge: Student Workbook*
- Board or flip chart and markers
- *The Student EQ Edge: Emotional Intelligence and Your Academic and Personal Success*
- Internet connection if you want to do this activity in class

Facilitating the Activity

Directions
- Assign Worksheet 18.2.
- This is a fun activity to do in class. Doing so allows you to further emphasize the impact of positive emotional contagion.

Debriefing Questions
- Place a line down the middle of a flip chart or board. On one side, place the phrase "person who promotes positive contagion" and, on the other side, "person who promotes negative contagion." Ask the students to generate possible consequences for the people who interact with the person promoting positive or negative contagion.
- See the reflection questions at the end of the worksheet.

Worksheet 18.2: Laugh a Little, Laugh a Lot

Name:

Access at least one of the following YouTube clips. (If these are not available, put the words "baby laughing" or "infant laughing" in the YouTube search box).

Baby Laughing Hysterically at Ripping Paper (original), http://www.youtube.com/watch?v=RP4a biHdQpc&feature=related

Laughing Quadruplets—The Next Day, http://www.youtube.com/watch?v=zZH0sNsaAz4&feature= related

Reflection Questions

1. Most of us will laugh as we watch these videos. What does that tell you about the power of positive emotions?

2. The term "emotional contagion" has been used to describe how our moods are affected by others' moods, both negatively and positively.

   a. Think of someone in your life who provides you with positive emotional contagion. Write his or her name or initials here:
   How does your mood and behavior usually change when you are around this person?

   b. Think of the most negative person you have to interact with regularly. Write his or her initials or something to help you remember who that person is here:
   How does this person affect your mood and behavior?

   c. In general, what do you think your level of positive emotional contagion is? Explain.

Activity 18.3

Does Money Buy Happiness?

EI Dimensions Targeted: Happiness

Brief Description/Objective: Students will conduct research about what factors are and are not associated with higher levels of happiness.

Planning the Activity

Time Expected
- Worksheet: 30 minutes to 2 hours
- Reflection Question: 5 minutes
- In-Class Debrief: 30 minutes

Materials
- Worksheet 18.3 from *The Student EQ Edge: Student Workbook*
- Board or flip chart and markers
- *The Student EQ Edge: Emotional Intelligence and Your Academic and Personal Success*
- Optional: If you want to provide an overview of research that summarizes factors that are and are not associated with greater happiness, have students access the 2005 *Time* magazine article "The New Science of Happiness," using the following link, http://www.time .com/time/magazine/article/0,9171,1015902,00.html

Facilitating the Activity

Directions
- Assign Worksheet 18.3.
- Read the instructions for Worksheet 18.3. Provide students with specific instructions about what types of sources you want them to use (for example, only scientific journals, books, internet sites) and how much information you want them to include in their research summary.

Debriefing Questions
- Have students summarize what they found about happiness and its relationship to money, health, marriage, job success, and so on. Ask students which findings are most surprising to them.
- Be sure to address the research related to use of social media such as Facebook. Most research shows that the more time people spend on these types of media, the less time they will spend interacting directly with other people, which is usually associated with an increase in loneliness.
- See the reflection question at the end of the worksheet.

Worksheet 18.3: Does Money Buy Happiness?

Name:

1. Most of us have heard the saying "Money can't buy happiness." Choose one of the following areas and do research about the relationship between this area and happiness (follow your instructor's guidelines for acceptable sources for your research).
   - Money (including wealth and poverty)
   - Religion
   - Married versus single
   - Health
   - Use of social media

2. Write a brief summary of what you found:

3. List your sources of information here (journal article title, book title, internet link, and so on):

Reflection Question

What finding surprised you the most? Explain why this surprised you.

Activity 18.4

Well-Being Indicators

EI Dimensions Targeted: Happiness, Self-Regard, Self-Actualization, Interpersonal Relationships, Optimism

Brief Description/Objective: Students will examine the four emotional intelligence areas that are associated with happiness and create strategies for how they can improve in each of these areas.

Planning the Activity

Time Expected
- Worksheet: 15 minutes
- In-Class Debrief: 15 minutes

Materials
- Worksheet 18.4 from *The Student EQ Edge: Student Workbook*
- Board or flip chart and markers
- *The Student EQ Edge: Emotional Intelligence and Your Academic and Personal Success*

Facilitating the Activity

Directions
- Assign Worksheet 18.4.
- You may need to provide an example or two, preferably about yourself, about what strategies someone could use to improve self-regard, self-actualization, interpersonal relations, and optimism.

Debriefing Questions
In either small groups or a large group, have students share some of the strategies they identified for improving in each area. Other students may be inspired by the ideas they hear.

Worksheet 18.4: Well-Being Indicators

Name:

Several EI factors are associated with a greater likelihood of being happy. Four have been addressed in previous chapters in this workbook: self-regard, self-actualization, interpersonal relationships, and optimism. Look back at the definitions of each of these characteristics in the previous chapters and then fill in the right-hand column of the following table.

Emotional Intelligence Area	Relationship to Happiness	One Strength; One Improvement
Self-Regard	The ability to accept and love ourselves as we are, even while striving to improve, enables us to feel positive about ourselves. Being too self-critical inhibits happiness.	1. Name one area of your life in which you have high self-regard: 2. Describe one area of your life (for example, academic confidence, body image, social interactions, athletic skills) in which your self-regard needs to improve and one strategy for how you could make improvements. Area: Improvement Strategy:
Self-Actualization	The ability to realize our potential begins with being involved in activities that we find meaningful and fulfilling. Self-actualized people are excited about their pursuits and try to do their best.	1. Name an area of your life in which you experience excitement, meaning, and fulfillment: 2. Describe one strategy for how you could improve your self-actualization in another area of your life:
Interpersonal Relationships	Social support is associated with a stronger sense of well-being. All of us need to feel connected to others in meaningful ways.	1. Name one friendship or relationship that gives your life meaning and happiness: 2. Describe one strategy that you could use to improve other interpersonal relationships in your life:
Optimism	All of us face obstacles and adversity. The ability to remain positive, to keep trying, and to believe we will eventually succeed is critical to feeling happy.	1. Name one time (or one area of your life) when (where) you felt optimistic: 2. Describe one strategy that you could use to improve your optimism:

Activity 18.5

The Pursuit of Happyness

EI Dimensions Targeted: Happiness, Self-Regard, Self-Actualization, Interpersonal Relationships, Optimism

Brief Description/Objective: Students will analyze different scenes from *The Pursuit of Happyness* and describe how Will Smith's character demonstrated self-regard, self-actualization, interpersonal relationships, and optimism despite facing major challenges such as single parenting and homelessness.

Planning the Activity

Time Expected
- Worksheet and YouTube videos: 20–25 minutes
- Reflection Questions: 10 minutes
- In-Class Debrief: 15 minutes

Materials
- Worksheet 18.5 from *The Student EQ Edge: Student Workbook*
- Board or flip chart and markers
- *The Student EQ Edge: Emotional Intelligence and Your Academic and Personal Success*
- Internet connection if you want to do this activity in class

Facilitating the Activity

Directions
- Assign Worksheet 18.5.
- Alternative ways to lead this activity are to either show *The Pursuit of Happyness* in class or ask students to watch the movie outside of class. In addition, major portions of the movie are viewable on YouTube.

Debriefing Questions
- Which clip did you find most inspiring? Explain your answer.
- See the reflection questions at the end of the worksheet.

Worksheet 18.5: *The Pursuit of Happyness*

Name:

Access the following YouTube clips from the movie *The Pursuit of Happyness,* starring Will Smith. Explain how each of the clips relates to one or more of the four indicators of well-being covered in Worksheet 18.4. The relevant dimensions are listed in parenthesis after the clip.

- Basketball Dreams, http://www.youtube.com/watch?v=NyNyNphyIYU&feature=related (self-regard, self-actualization)
- The Time Machine and Dinosaurs, http://www.youtube.com/watch?v=Joaqf393lt0 (interpersonal relationships, optimism)
- Cold Calls, http://www.youtube.com/watch?v=emzARZsJntw (optimism, self-actualization)
- Job Offer, http://www.youtube.com/watch?v=U8uWmzLydsl&feature=related (self-actualization, interpersonal relationships)

Reflection Questions

1. Self-regard: How does Will Smith's character teach his son about self-regard? How does he show his own self-regard?
2. Self-actualization: What goals is Will Smith's character pursuing? What things give his life meaning and fulfillment?
3. Interpersonal relationship: What evidence is there of a strong interpersonal relationship with his son? How does he create mutuality and connection with someone so much younger?
4. Optimism: How does Will Smith's character display optimism? At what points might someone else have given up?

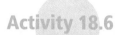

Activity 18.6

One Commitment—Self-Development Plan for Happiness

The directions and template for students to create a self-development plan for happiness are slightly different from those in other chapters. *The Student EQ Edge: Student Workbook* contains a template for developing stronger happiness in Worksheet 18.6.

Activity 18.7

Case Study—Happiness

Choose a case study from Chapter 2 that relates to happiness and ask students to analyze the behavior of the main characters.

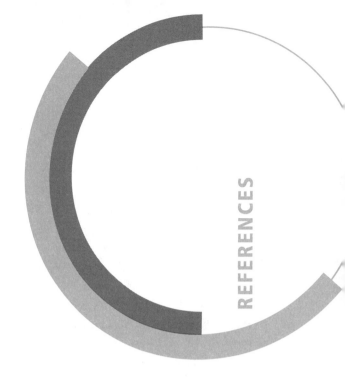

Mann, D., & Kanoy, K. (2010, February). *The EQ factor in student retention and success: From theory to practice.* Paper presented at the annual First Year Experience Conference, Denver, CO.

Mischel, W., Ebbesen, E., & Zeiss, A. (1972). Cognitive and attentional mechanisms in delay of gratification, *Journal of Personality and Social Psychology 21*(2), 204–218.

Pascarella, E. T., & Terenzini, P. T. (2005). *How college affects students.* San Francisco: Jossey-Bass.

Rotter, J. (1966). Generalized expectancies for internal versus external control of reinforcement. *Psychological Monographs, 80,* 609.

Scheier, M. F., Carver, C. S., & Bridges, M. W. (1994). Distinguishing optimism from neuroticism (and trait anxiety, self-mastery, and self-esteem): A re-evaluation of the Life Orientation Test. *Journal of Personality and Social Psychology, 67,* 1063–1078.

Schulman, P. (1995). Explanatory style and achievement in school and work. In G. Buchanan & M. Seligman (Eds.), *Explanatory style* (pp. 159–171). Hillsdale, NJ: Lawrence Erlbaum.

Schutte, N. S., & Malouff, J. M. (2002). Incorporating emotional skills content in a college transition course enhances retention. *Journal of the First-Year Experience, 14*(1), 7–21.

Seligman, M. (1991). *Learned optimism: How to change your mind and your life.* New York: Knopf.

Seligman, M. E. P., & Maier, S. F. (1967). Failure to escape traumatic shock. *Journal of Experimental Psychology, 74*(1), 1–9.

Selye, H. (1976). *The stress of life.* New York: McGraw-Hill.

Shoda, Y., Mischel, W., & Peake, P. (1990). Predicting adolescent cognitive and self-regulatory competencies from preschool delay of gratification: Identifying diagnostic conditions. *Developmental Psychology, 26*(6), 978–986.

Sparkman, L. (2009). Emotional intelligence as a non-traditional predictor of college-student retention and grades. *Dissertation Abstracts International: Section A. Humanities and Social Sciences, 69*(8), 3068.

Stein, S., & Book, H. (2011). *The EQ edge: Emotional intelligence and your success.* Ontario, ON: Wiley.

Stein, S., Book, H., & Kanoy, K. (2013). *The student EQ edge: Emotional intelligence and your academic and personal success.* San Francisco: Jossey-Bass.

YouTube Reference List

Baby Laughing Hysterically at Ripping Paper. (2011, January 24). [Video file]. Retrieved from http://www.youtube.com/wat ch?v=RP4abiHdQpc&feature=related

CBS News. (2010, April 21). The marshmallow test [Video file]. Retrieved from http://www.youtube.com/watch?v=4y6R5boD qh4&feature=relmfu

The Centre for Confidence and Well-being. (2008, April 24). Assertiveness scenarios: 10 examples [Video file]. Retrieved from http://www.youtube.com/watch?v=Ymm86c6DAF4

Fox Sports. (2011, November 24). Ndamukong Suh Stomp ejection from Thanksgiving day game [Video file]. Retrieved from http://www.youtube.com/watch?v=ZXDmCVSnn1U

Little, Ryan (Director). (2005, March 25). *Saints and Soldiers*: Sharing secrets [Video file]. Retrieved from http://www.youtube.com/watch?v=2XkLOT9J1vs&feature=fvst

Mathias, S. (2010, August 25). Laughing quadruplets—The next day [Video file]. Retrieved from http://www.youtube.com/wat ch?v=zZH0sNsaAz4&feature=related

Mucino, Gabriele (Director). (2006, December 15). *The Pursuit of Happyness*—Protect your dreams [Video file]. Retrieved from http://www.youtube.com/watch?v=NyNyNphyIYU&feature=related

Mucino, Gabriele (Director). (2006, December 15). *The Pursuit of Happyness*—Dinosaurs [Video file]. Retrieved from http://www.youtube.com/watch?v=JOaqf393It0

Mucino, Gabriele (Director). (2006, December 15). *The Pursuit of Happyness*—Cold calling [Video file]. Retrieved from http://www.youtube.com/watch?v=emzARZsJntw

Mucino, Gabriele (Director). (2006, December 15). *The Pursuit of Happyness*—Final scene [Video file]. Retrieved from http://www.youtube.com/watch?v=U8uWmzLydsI&feature=related

Public Broadcasting System. (2008, February 17). *Sesame Street*—"Cooperation makes it happen" [Video file]. Retrieved from http://www.youtube.com/watch?v=5exvfbnFMUg

WGN-TV Chicago. (2010, February 18). Helicopter parents: The lengths parents go to pamper and please their kids [Video file]. Retrieved from http://www.youtube.com/watch?v=ufEfeDP7vBA&feature=related

Model Syllabus

Note to the instructor: If you are not a certified user of the Emotional Quotient Inventory 2.0, you will need to become a certified user or have someone who is a certified user administer the assessment for you. (Go to https:ei.mhs.com for information about how to become a certified user of the Emotional Quotient Inventory 2.0 or to find a qualified professional.) There are free emotional intelligence assessments online, but these have not been evaluated for reliability or validity.

COURSE NUMBER AND NAME: XXX, EMOTIONAL INTELLIGENCE

Emotional intelligence (EI) will provide an important key to your college, career, and personal success. Throughout this course, you will examine studies that support this claim. Because EI is so important to workplace and life success, it's important to practice these skills! Here's how I expect you to demonstrate EI behaviors in class and the EI dimensions they reflect:

- Be willing to better understand yourself and why you react to certain situations as you do. (emotional self-awareness, self-regard, reality testing)
- Come to class every day and be fully prepared to participate. (self-actualization, social responsibility, stress tolerance, self-regard)

- Accept responsibility for your behavior. (emotional self-awareness, self-regard, problem solving, impulse control, stress tolerance, optimism)
- Work effectively with me and your classmates and resolve conflict—if it occurs—in a respectful and constructive way. (emotional self-awareness, assertiveness, emotional expression, social responsibility, interpersonal relationships, empathy, problem solving, stress tolerance, impulse control, and optimism)

Textbooks:

The Student EQ Edge: Emotional Intelligence and Your Academic and Personal Success by Steven J. Stein, Howard E. Book, and Korrel Kanoy

The Student EQ Edge: Student Workbook by Korrel Kanoy, Howard E. Book, and Steven J. Stein

Course Objectives

Knowledge: You will be able to describe components of emotional intelligence and identify them within behavior. Knowledge includes mastering information accurately, understanding that information, and applying critical thinking skills to further understand the material.

    Measurement: reading responses, EI assessment paper

Communication: You will be able to communicate effectively (orally and in writing) about emotional intelligence and demonstrate emotional intelligence through your communication with me and your classmates.

    Measurement: EI assessment paper, class participation

Application: You will practice skills for improving your EI.

    Measurement: exercises

● ASSIGNMENTS

Emotional Intelligence Assessment and Reflection
REQUIRED EI ASSESSMENT: EQ-i 2.0 Assessment
Part 1: Complete your EQ-i 2.0 assessment **by xxx date.**

Part 2: Write a reflection paper (three to four pages) about your EI scores based on your EQ-i results. The key to good reflection is self-awareness and a willingness to be honest about your thoughts and emotions. So consider this reflection paper a chance to talk to yourself about your scores. Include:

1. A copy of your EQ-i report.

2. A reaction to your scores: *Reflect* on what you learned about yourself by answering questions such as the following. You are not limited to these questions; rather, they are listed to help you get started.

    a. What are your emotional reactions? Pleased? Frustrated? Confused?

    b. Which areas did you score higher on than expected? Lower?

3. Take one or two of your higher scores and reflect about *why* these areas are strengths for you. Likewise, take one or two of your lower scores and reflect about *why* these are relative weaknesses for you. What experiences have shaped your EI strengths and weaknesses? For example, if you lack flexibility, where do you think you learned this behavior? Has rigidity benefited you at times and thus you continue the behavior?

READING RESPONSES

You will write a response (one or two paragraphs) for each assigned reading marked with an RR on the schedule. In one to three sentences, give a summary of the content and then comment on what you learned, challenge an opinion stated by the authors, or reflect on how some scientific data affects your opinion. I will randomly collect two of each student's reading responses during the semester and grade them.

PARTICIPATION/EXERCISES

You will be asked to complete EI exercises both inside and outside of class. I will randomly collect these exercises for grading. Grading will be based on the thoroughness and professionalism of your work, depth of reflection, demonstrated knowledge of EI in your responses, and effective communication of ideas.

Proposed Class Schedule

Week	Topic	Reading	Exercises
Week 1	Introduction to EI; ABCDE approach	All readings come from *The Student EQ Edge: Emotional Intelligence and Your Academic and Personal Success* Chapters 1 and 2	Instructor's Note: Consult *The Student EQ Edge: Facilitation and Activity Guide* for sample class plans for a 50–60 minute class or a 3–4 hour class.
Week 2	Emotional Self-Awareness	Chapter 3	
Week 3	Self-Regard	Chapter 4	
Week 4	Self-Actualization	Chapter 5	
Week 5	Emotional Expression	Chapter 6	
Week 6	Independence and Assertiveness	Chapters 7 and 8	
Week 7	Interpersonal Relationships	Chapter 9	
Week 8	Empathy	Chapter 10	
Week 9	Social Responsibility	Chapter 11	
Week 10	Reality Testing	Chapter 12	
Week 11	Problem Solving and Impulse Control	Chapters 13 and 14	
Week 12	Flexibility	Chapter 15	
Week 13	Stress Tolerance and Optimism	Chapters 16 and 17	
Week 14	Happiness	Chapter 18	
Week 15/16	Emotional Intelligence and Your Success	Chapters 19–23	Pick two research studies from these chapters that are most interesting to you and write a half-page summary of each. Explain why that study was helpful to you.

Sample Grading Rubric for EI Reflection Questions

EI Reflection—Grading Rubric	Assessment	Comments
Knowledge • Demonstrates knowledge of EI in use of concepts and facts • Shows accurate knowledge of scales and their definitions	1 2 3 4 1 2 3 4	
Reflection • Gives specific examples from his/her behavior related to EI characteristics • Identifies *specific EI behaviors* that need to be improved • Identifies *specific EI behaviors* that are well developed or were used effectively in a situation • Describes how emotional intelligence (or lack thereof) influenced a situation • Recognizes possible barriers to change	1 2 3 4 1 2 3 4 1 2 3 4 1 2 3 4 1 2 3 4 1 2 3 4	
Grade or Total Points Earned		

4 = Mastery: The student's performance or behavior show excellence in all facets. The student consistently demonstrates knowledge or reflection that indicates that the student is ready to succeed at a higher level of challenge.

3 = Proficiency: The student's performance, although excellent in places, has minor flaws or instances of inconsistency *or* the student consistently demonstrates an effective level of knowledge and reflection but omits a required element or necessary depth.

2 = Passable: The student's work contains at least one major flaw or is inconsistent and lacking in depth. Although the level of knowledge or reflection may earn a passing grade, there are errors in knowledge, a lack of ability to connect the student's behavior to emotional intelligence characteristics, or a lack of depth and specific examples when applying emotional intelligence concepts to the student's behavior.

1 = Unacceptable: The student's performance is seriously flawed. The student's work includes factual errors, a misapplication of EI concepts, and/or very limited and perfunctory reflection.

Movie Selections for Teaching Emotional Intelligence

A Note to Instructors: Most of the movies shown in this appendix will have instances of EI in addition to the ones marked in the table. You may want to ask students to identify scenes that they believe display other EI characteristics. A variety of movies (rated from G to R), is provided so that you can select movies appropriate for your student population. And you can always create an assignment for students to find movies that demonstrate different EI concepts.

Movie	Brief Description	Emotional Self-Awareness	Self-Regard	Self-Actualization	Emotional Expression	Independence	Assertiveness	Interpersonal Relationships	Empathy	Social Responsibility	Reality Testing	Problem Solving	Impulse Control	Flexibility	Stress Tolerance	Optimism	Happiness
12 Angry Men (not rated, drama)	A lone member of a jury slowly convinces the others of the defendant's innocence.					X	X		X		X				X		
All the President's Men (R, based on a true story, drama)	Two *Washington Post* reporters break the Watergate story, leading to Nixon's resignation.					X	X			X					X		
Avatar (PG-13, drama)	A marine is sent to carry out a mission to destroy a world he comes to love.	X	X	X	X	X	X	X	X	X							
Billy Elliot (PG-13, drama)	A young Irish boy discovers a love of dance despite objections from his family.	X	X	X		X										X	X
The Blind Side (PG-13, based on a true story)	A poor African-American boy is adopted by a family who helps him reach his potential.	X			X	X	X	X	X	X							
Born Free (PG, based on a true story, drama)	A lion cub is adopted by a family but has to be taught to live in the wild as she matures.	X				X			X	X		X					

Title	Description												
Catch Me If You Can (PG-13, based on a true story)	A young man commits financial crimes and escapes capture because of his intelligence.								x	x	x	x	x
Coach Carter (PG-13, based on a true story)	A successful businessman takes over an unruly group of high school basketball players who resist his discipline.	x	x	x				x	x				
Cool Runnings (PG, drama, based on a true story)	A group of Jamaicans decide to enter the Olympics to compete in the bobsled event.	x	x	x			x	x	x	x	x	x	x
The Devil Wears Prada (PG-13, comedy)	A critical boss terrorizes her staff until one employee stands up to her.				x	x						x	
Erin Brockovich (PG-13, drama, based on a true story)	A feisty single mother leads the effort to help residents of a small town fight a company that is poisoning their water.				x	x	x	x	x				
ET (PG, drama)	An extraterrestrial is adopted by children who help him hide from authorities eager to study him.	x		x	x	x	x	x	x				x
The Family Stone (PG-13, comedy, drama)	A close-knit family rejects their son's fiancé, leaving him confused and her devastated.		x	x	x	x	x			x	x		x
A Few Good Men (R, drama)	A lawyer defends two marines accused of murder who were given the order by a commanding officer.	x	x		x	x		x			x		

(continued)

Movie	Brief Description	Emotional Self-Awareness	Self-Regard	Self-Actualization	Emotional Expression	Independence	Assertiveness	Interpersonal Relationships	Empathy	Social Responsibility	Reality Testing	Problem Solving	Impulse Control	Flexibility	Stress Tolerance	Optimism	Happiness
Field of Dreams (PG, drama)	A man dreams of building a baseball field for baseball players accused of fixing games.	X		X												X	
Forrest Gump (PG-13, drama)	A mildly retarded young man lives a full life, yearning for a relationship with a childhood friend.				X	X		X								X	X
Georgia Rule (R, drama)	A rebellious teenager is sent to spend the summer with her strict grandmother.	X	X		X	X	X	X	X		X		X	X			X
The Hunger Games (PG-13, drama)	A young woman challenges an oppressive government and risks her life and others'.	X	X		X	X	X			X	X	X	X	X	X		
My Big Fat Greek Wedding (PG, drama)	A woman needs to assert herself with her large and loving Greek family who interfere with her wedding plans.	X	X		X	X	X					X			X		X
My Sister's Keeper (PG-13, drama)	A young girl—who was conceived to provide a bone-marrow match for her sick sister—refuses any further medical procedures that would help her sister.	X	X		X	X	X					X					

Movie	Description	1	2	3	4	5	6	7	8	9	10	11	12	13
Notting Hill (PG-13)	A famous actress connects with a bookstore owner but lets her fame interfere with the relationship.	X				X		X		X				X
The Odd Couple (comedy)	Two very different friends manage to share an apartment despite their differences.				X	X						X		
Odd Girl Out (PG-13, drama)	A teen girl is bullied by her friends because of her success and popularity.	X	X	X	X	X	X	X	X	X	X	X	X	X
One Fine Day (PG, comedy)	Two busy single parents share child-care responsibility when they both have big days scheduled at work.	X	X	X		X	X	X			X	X		
Patch Adams (PG-13, based on a true story, comedy)	An irreverent middle-aged man attends med school, rocking the health care establishment with his unconventional ways of helping the sick.	X	X		X	X	X	X	X	X	X		X	X
Pay It Forward (PG-13, drama)	A young boy teaches others to "pay back" kindness by "paying it forward" to someone in need.					X		X		X			X	X
The Pursuit of Happyness (PG-13, based on a true story, drama)	A single parent, homeless father struggles to care for his son while he works to land a job with a major corporation.	X	X		X	X		X		X	X	X	X	X

(continued)

Movie	Brief Description	Emotional Self-Awareness	Self-Regard	Self-Actualization	Emotional Expression	Independence	Assertiveness	Interpersonal Relationships	Empathy	Social Responsibility	Reality Testing	Problem Solving	Impulse Control	Flexibility	Stress Tolerance	Optimism	Happiness
Remember the Titans (PG, based on a true story, drama)	A coach takes over a racially divided football team and teaches them to work together and care for each other.		x				x			x		x	x				
The Rookie (G, based on a true story, drama)	A high school baseball coach takes on the challenge from his team to try out for a pro team; he makes it to the big leagues, only to question his decision.	x	x	x					x								x
Runaway Bride (PG-13, comedy)	A woman scared of marriage keeps running away from her wedding ceremonies.	x							x		x		x		x		
Schindler's List (R, based on a true story, drama)	A German factory owner helps Jews evade the Nazi death camps.					x		x	x	x							

School Ties (PG-13, drama)	A working-class Jewish high school senior tries to hide his religion while living amid conservative classmates at an elite private school; they accuse him of cheating to get him expelled.					x		x			x					
Sister Act (PG, comedy)	A nightclub singer takes up residence in a convent to escape the mob and has to adapt her behavior to her new life.	x			x			x	x	x	x	x				
To Kill a Mockingbird (drama, not rated)	A white lawyer defends an obviously innocent black man falsely accused of rape in the 1930s south.					x	x	x				x				
What About Bob? (PG, comedy)	A clingy patient follows his psychiatrist on a vacation and makes friends with his family, sending the psychiatrist to the brink of his own collapse.	x	x		x	x		x			x	x	x	x	x	
What Women Want (PG-13, comedy)	A chauvinist male is passed over for promotion and has to report to a female boss; suddenly he can hear everything women are thinking, giving him a new outlook.				x	x				x						
You've Got Mail (PG, comedy)	A bookstore owner unknowingly connects online to the large book chain owner about to shut down her business.	x	x		x			x								x

Self-Development Plan for Improving Emotional Intelligence

Note: This sample shows *interpersonal relationships* as the target EI skill to develop; the same format can be used for all 16 scales. *The Student EQ Edge: Student Workbook* includes a self-development plan worksheet in each chapter that targets the EI scale in question.

PART 1. DEVELOPING A PLAN

1. Describe at least one way you will personally benefit if you increase your skill in developing interpersonal relationships.

2. Choose two of the strategies listed in Appendix A of *The Student EQ Edge: Student Workbook* for improving interpersonal relationships and write them below. Or, come up with your own strategies. Identify a date you will begin using this strategy.

Date to begin:

Strategy 1:

Date to begin:

Strategy 2:

Part 2. Outcomes of Your Plan

Complete this part two weeks after you have implemented your strategies.

1. Describe what happened when you began using the above strategies. (If you never tried the strategies or gave up quickly, explain why you weren't motivated to try them.)
2. Do you think you will continue to use these strategies? Explain why or why not.

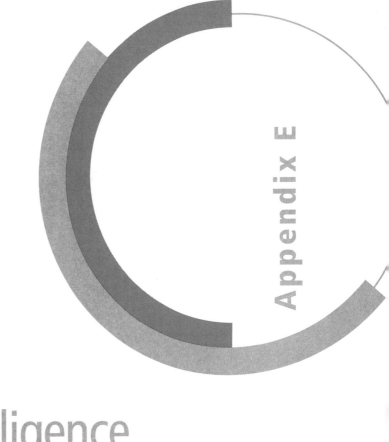

Resources for Teaching Emotional Intelligence

The following websites provide helpful information about emotional intelligence:

- www.ei.mhs.com

  This website will help you gain information about how to be certified to administer the EQi 2.0, the emotional intelligence model and assessment referred to throughout *The Student EQ Edge: Emotional Intelligence and Your Academic and Personal Success*. In addition, the resources section for EI provides research summaries and other helpful information.

- www.developmentalassociates.com

  This website details how emotional intelligence can be used on university, college, and high school campuses in at least three different ways: student learning, faculty and staff professional development, and selecting faculty and staff with an EI profile predictive of success in the job.

- www.casel.org

  The Collaborative for Academic Social and Emotional Learning provides you with curriculum resources and research results related to teaching emotional intelligence in kindergarten through high school.